Rita Hayworth

Rita Hayworth

The Time, the Place and the Woman

JOHN KOBAL

W·W·NORTON & COMPANY·INC·

New York

Printed in the United States of America.

First American Edition 1978

Library of Congress Cataloging in Publication Data
Kobal, John.
    Rita Hayworth: the time, the place, and the woman.
    Includes index.
    1. Hayworth, Rita, 1919–   2. Moving-picture
actors and actresses—United States—Biography.
PN2287.H38K6   1978   791.43′028′0924 [B]   77–18124
ISBN 0–393–07526–5

2 3 4 5 6 7 8 9 0

This book is dedicated to the
memory of Vernon and Eduardo
Cansino and Jack Cole

CONTENTS

Acknowledgements		9
Sources of Reference		11
Chapter I	'SHE'S BACK!'	13
Chapter II	THE IMAGE MAKERS	55
Chapter III	ENTER COHN!	83
Chapter IV	THE TIME, THE PLACE AND THE GIRL	125
Chapter V	MOTHER'S NIGHT IN A TURKISH BATH	189
Chapter VI	THEY ALL MARRIED GILDA	229
Chapter VII	'BACK AGAIN!'	266
Chapter VIII	TILL NOW	288
Epilogue	A MEETING	317
Index		331

ACKNOWLEDGEMENTS

For their various courtesies and generous co-operation the author and editors would like to acknowledge the following individuals who gave so generously of time, information and confidence. Their contributions made this book possible and my quest one of great pleasure:

Max Arno (agent)
Fred Astaire (co-star)
Joan Blondell (actress)
Lee Bowman (co-star)
Sammy Cahn (lyricist)
Nicholas Cann (painter)
Eduardo Cansino (brother)
Elisa Cansino (aunt)
Manuel Cansino (family historian)
Patricia Cansino (step-mother)
Vernon and Susan Cansino (brother and sister-in-law)
Bob Coburn (stills photographer)
Mrs Harry Cohn
Jack Cole (choreographer)
Alan Dwan (director)
Douglas Fairbanks Jr (actor)
Jose Ferrer (co-star)
Doris Fisher (composer)
Glenn Ford (co-star)
Henry Hathaway (director)
Howard Hawks (director)
Mrs Jean Haworth (in-law)
Edith Head (designer)
Tab Hunter (co-star)
Fred Karger (arranger, conductor)
Fritz Lang (director)
Jesse Lasky Jr (screenwriter)
Jean Louis (designer)
Rouben Mamoulian (director)
George Marshall (director)
Vinicius de Moraes (Brazilian composer)

Antonia Morales (friend)
Hermes Pan (choreographer)
Robert Parrish (director)
Victor Saville (director)
Arthur Schwartz (composer and producer)
Vincent Sherman (director)
Pinky Tomlin (co-star)
Dorothy Hawkes Valdespino (family friend)
Raoul Walsh (director)
Ruth Waterbury (Hollywood columnist)
Emrys Williams (Aly Khan's bodyguard)

Special thanks also

to Jose Miguel Rodriguez (in Spain), Cyril Fraden and Frank
Martin (in London), Michael Vollbracht (in New York), Alex-
andra de Lazareff (in Italy), all of whose paintings of the lady I
wish I could have used on the cover; to Hy Smith at United
Artists—always a good friend; to Walter Plunkett; to Joel Coler,
Jack Yaeger and Barbara de Lord of Twentieth Century Fox, for
all their valued help with data; to Pru Reading and Maureen
Clerkin for endlessly retyping the same pages; to David Meeker and
Philip Chamberlin for making it possible for me to see rare films;
Bill Douglas, Leo Madigan, Carlos Clarens, John Wykert,
Nicholas Cann and John Russell Taylor for invaluable advice
and guidance when doubt was uppermost.

To these people I owe many, many thanks.
I feel very lucky in knowing them.

The film stills in this book are from the Kobal Collection; the
rare family photos were acquired through the courtesy of the
Cansino family and Dorothy Valdespino.

Grateful acknowledgement is given to the following companies
for permission to use stills from their films: Columbia Pictures,
Grand National, M.G.M., N.B.C., Republic, R.K.O., Twentieth
Century Fox, United Artists, Warner Brothers.

And last, but never least, to all those people who gave aid and
succour along the way, I thank you.

SOURCES OF REFERENCE

Film Daily Yearbook 1935–1960 inc., Wid's Films and Folk, Inc.
Modern Screen, June 1952
Photoplay, October 1952, February 1943, August 1943, April 1949
Screen Stars, February 1946

Aly, Leonard Slater, W. H. Allen, 1966
Bodyguard, Emrys Williams, Golden Pegasus Books Ltd, 1960
Focus on Film, No. 10, Summer 1972
Gene Kelly, Clive Hirschhorn, W. H. Allen, 1974
King Cohn, Bob Thomas, Putnam 1967
Mamoulian, Tom Milne, Cinema One Ser: No 13, 1970
Memo from David O. Selznick, Rudy Behlmer, Avon 1973
Steps in Time, Fred Astaire, Harper 1959
West of the Rockies, Daniel Fuchs, Knopf 1971

'California Carmen', *Time*, 38:90, 10 Nov. 1941
'Carmen Hayworth', *Newsweek*, 32:78, 23 Aug. 1948
'Cult of the Love Goddess in America', W. Sargeant, *Life* 23:80,
10 Nov. 1947
'Oui oui', *Time*, 53:27, 6 June 1949

Rita's first day in front of the Hollywood cameras after a three-year recess was spent doing a torrid dance for Columbia's *Affair in Trinidad,* 1951, in which she stars with Glenn Ford. (Lippman/Columbia)

CHAPTER I

'SHE'S BACK!'

Take what you want from life—and pay for it.

Spanish proverb

It was April 1951 and Rita was back!

On the morning of Monday, April 2nd, the luxurious French liner *De Grasse* docked in New York harbour. Among its passengers was the Princess Aly Khan, her daughters Yasmin and Rebecca and their French nurse Susanne. Although her studio was unaware that Rita had returned to America, eighty newsmen and a sizeable crowd of gawkers had apparently received a psychic forecast. The next day the papers were full of it, from a modest paragraph in the *New York Times* (no picture), shruggingly headlined 'Actress denies rift. Wants to eat hotdog', to the *New York Herald Tribune*'s readership-conscious, two-column front-page report (plus photograph) showing Rita smilingly beautiful in a luxurious fur coat speaking before microphones on deck:

'Miss Hayworth had been to the hairdressers at 9.30 that morning on board the *De Grasse* and appeared before eighty newsmen looking stunning. Her hair had been described abroad as "a sumac bush waving its scarlet leaves in the afternoon sun". A docker working on the steerage deck asked, "Who's the big noise?" On being told it was Rita Hayworth he asked, "Where's the Aly?" He was told that Rita had arrived alone. "Huh!" he said. Dressed in a gabardine suit piped with leather, a turtle neck sweater and low-heeled alligator shoes, Miss Hayworth answered questions quietly and wistfully and hardly spoke above a whisper. "Will Aly join you?" "Oh yes, he may come over, I don't know exactly when. He hasn't finished his tour of the Middle East yet." She denied rumours of a separation in a quiet murmur, saying that she was glad to be back in America and planned to stay for two months or more, although she had no plans to return to Hollywood. She said that the first thing she planned to do was to eat an American hotdog. She refused to pose with her daughter for the press because Yasmin had been upset by the photographers and was crying in her cabin.'

The rest of New York's papers went to town on her, and their speculations on the moves of the reigning Love Goddess of the movies were far from discreet. But their conclusions were their own, for Rita said nothing to help them.

Rita's reserved nature, under the public spotlight on her personal life, lent a commanding dignity to her bearing when confronted by reporters' questions. This aspect of her personality went largely unappreciated by the press since it failed to tally with the tabloid image of the tempestuous siren triumphantly fostered by her films and the studio's publicity. Like a Garbo, despite the curiosity that hounds stars like her, Rita tried to protect her privacy with silence. Though, in the end, the reporters wrote what they wanted, the photos accompanying the articles made one doubtful of what was said. The camera loved her enough to tell her side.

Three years had elapsed since Rita's last film but in those years much had happened in the world, to which Hollywood had not been immune. One decade had ended and another begun. In the career span of an established star a new decade was often as traumatic an event then as the coming of sound had been. In 1948 Rita had been one of the highest paid actresses in the world. Her name on a film was a guarantee of profit. Her only serious rivals in the glamour sweepstakes had been M.G.M.'s Lana Turner and Betty Grable at Twentieth Century Fox. Ava Gardner, though gathering momentum, was still on the sidelines and nobody had even heard of Marilyn Monroe! Rita was the undisputed Love Goddess of the 'forties. But what about the 'fifties? Admittedly, she had never been out of the headlines but in those years away from the screen things had changed. Grable was tailing off, marking time till her contract ended, and Turner was slipping. Meanwhile there had been *Pandora and the Flying Dutchman* (1951) and Frank Sinatra, confirming Ava, both on screen and in private, as a potential replacement for Hayworth in the public's romantic fantasies. And Monroe's ascent to the top after *Asphalt Jungle* (1950) was nothing short of meteoric.

A matter of more immediate and far-reaching concern to stars, moguls and accountants were the crippling inroads on the box-office made by television. When Rita left, the little black tube was in its nickelodeon stage. By 1951, TV quiz shows, TV westerns, TV dramas, TV variety programmes, and TV stars like Milton Berle, Lucille Ball and George Gobel were providing a cheap and effective alternative to film that was shaking Hollywood and would eventually overshadow it. While these events were changing the face of the industry, Rita had been on the Riviera. Not that she would have worried about it had she given it any thought. Her mind didn't run that way. But these changing conditions would worry Columbia Pictures' powerful president Harry Cohn to whom Rita was solidly under contract and to whom the years she was away were only wasted money. Now, without any advance warning, Rita was back and, although she had previously stated that she wanted to make no more films, preferring to concentrate on being a wife and mother, there was speculation that Rita might be back to work.

Emotionally and professionally she stood at the crossroads. Her choice was the most difficult and its safe to assume that work was not uppermost in her mind.

Once again Rita was alone, only this time, though a princess, she was apparently broke as well. Her phone never stopped ringing—agents, lawyers, the studio, a lot of reporters, a few friends—but no decision about her future was forthcoming from the lady in question. While Hollywood wondered and rumour flew around town and across oceans, Rita sat in her suite at the Plaza overlooking Central Park, wondering, waiting, penniless.

As an investment Rita Hayworth was a glamorous concoction worth millions. But in her private manner there was no flamboyance and she had never been very good at mixing socially with people. Most of her friends, as with so many women stars, were people she worked with at the studio—her make-up men, hairdressers, dress designers, people who knew her from work, had few illusions and took her as they saw her. But when it came to giving advice their jobs dictated that their first loyalty was to the studio that paid their salary. Like agents, they would invariably try to convince the star that her best interest lay in complying with the studio. Whenever it came to a confrontation, this lack of true friends, concerned enough for her to put her interests ahead of their own, or the studio's, was exposed. It left stars in her position even more alone, prey to self-doubt, a feeling of guilt worked on by so-called friends and paid advisers about holding

Rita and daughters Yasmin (18 months) and Rebecca (6 years) facing a press conference in the Beverly Hills Hotel, July 1951, telling the press 'that nothing Aly Khan can say or do will make me change my mind about divorcing him.' (Associated Press)

up production, potential law-suits, ruined careers. Invariably it put them even more on the defensive.

Her mother was dead, she had no sister, and except for her Aunt Frances, her mother's sister, Rita had few close women friends or relatives with whom she could relax and unburden herself. But fortunately another relative, Jean Haworth (her husband Vinton Haworth, the radio and stage actor, was Rita's uncle), was in New York when Rita docked and telephoned her on the ship. During the weeks in New York, when Rita was trying to keep out of the public eye and avoid having to comment on speculations in the press that the marriage was over, Jean would come to play with the children and take the serious little seven-year-old Rebecca for walks in Central Park.

With Yasmin asleep next door and Rebecca out, there was time for Rita to catch up with news about herself in the press if she wished to. Stories about her and others about Aly kept gossip columns and front pages on the boil: what she had done; why she had done it; what she was going to do next; the new men in her life; the other women in Aly's. Rumours were printed as fact; her life and that of her children and family were put over a cooker, brought to a boil, then lanced, and the process with which she was so familiar but to which she could never harden herself would be

repeated—for days, weeks, months on end. Unless you've been
placed in that position, it is hard to understand the incapacitating
effect which a steady flow of rumours and gossip of this nature
ultimately have on someone like Rita. Who on reading the gossip
would believe or care that a woman thought to have everything
the world holds dear could feel mocked and conspicuous;
desperately wanted to shrink back; found that every meeting and
occasion was an everlasting ordeal? Aly's remarks to the press
when they tracked him down in Cairo, while typical of the man,
weren't the sort of thing to bring cheer and comfort to a wife who
had left him largely because she felt neglected and hoped, thus, to
jolt him into awareness about their crumbling marriage. In the
U.P.I. report, Aly nonchalantly explained that there was
absolutely nothing strange about his wife going to the United
States while he was staying in Europe. He ridiculed reports of a
separation, adding that it was impossible for him to leave Europe
to follow her when the racing season was opening—'Everyone
knows how devoted I am to racing'—but that he might well go to
the United States later. Photos of Aly showed him on dates with
beautiful women. Rita had made her dramatic move, hoping
perhaps that Aly would rush after her and reassure her.

More weeks went by. Rita had stayed and waited at the Plaza
long enough. Aly was still in Europe with his horses, and
meanwhile there was no one to turn to for ready money. Only as
an actress could she earn enough to live on. Every studio would
have been overjoyed to bid for her services, but there was a snag:
she was still under contract to Columbia Pictures and that meant
under contract to Harry Cohn—founder and ruler. The pressures
to come to a decision were piled on top of all her other problems.
Cohn's high-pressured efforts to get her on the screen without
delay were intense; though he was notorious for his lack of regard
for actors, he was too shrewd a film-maker to let Rita escape.

Their professional relationship had deteriorated long ago. Rita
was not afraid of him, but she didn't like him. She resented his
attitude to the people who worked for him; she knew that he spied
on her while she was working, and she found the vulgarity of his
speech and manner repulsive. But at this moment she needed
money, needed work and had no choice. Besides, Rita's frame of
mind virtually precluded any other choice. Work was the only
real life she had known since childhood. It didn't take much brain
power to realise that after all the running and fighting, the
marriages and the divorces, in the end you went where the money

told you to go. If you're broke you get a job at something you're good at. If you're a carpenter you carpent, if you're a filing clerk you file. If you're Rita Hayworth, Movie Star, you pick up your vanity case, get your hair done and go back to being Rita Hayworth, Movie Star. Her agents made the move in re-activating her career. They informed Columbia that the property known as Rita Hayworth was ready to resume work. This meant that she was back on the payroll, and her weekly salary of $3,500, which had been suspended during her absence, was automatically re-activated. Everybody was excited about another Hayworth picture. The clamour from his eastern office and from the studio's stockholders only added to his own convictions. His minions were set to work to find a suitable script for her come-back and the publicity department was sent banging drums to prepare the world.

THE LITTLE PRINCESS

Rita's private life was of her own making but from the cradle onwards her professional life had never been in doubt. Both her parents were in show business and met while working in a lavish musical revue starring the legendary Broadway producer Flo Ziegfeld's first wife, the enchanting French music hall star, Anna Held. Eduardo Cansino was a headliner in the show, Volga Haworth was in the chorus. Her stage career, though not her ambitions, ended with the birth of their first child—Rita. Toasting the birth in high good spirits one of Volga's Follies friends looked at the pretty, quiet baby girl looking out of her crib and exclaimed, 'She's a princess. She's gonna be a real little princess.' To her proud parents, especially her stage-struck mother, little Margarita Carmen Dolores Cansino was always their little princess. Probably most mothers feel that way about their daughters and many exuberant promises are said around a baby's crib with no further thought given to them, but the master plan Rita's parents had for a professional career for their daughter took germ back there. In time they saw their daughter become a star, but Volga died before the prophecy had come true. Rita never said whether or not she knew. But her brothers remembered Volga endlessly talking about 'her little princess'.

The Cansinos were an old and respected Spanish family. They had been famed as dancers for two generations before Rita was born and they were proud of it. Rita inherited that pride.

Cansino

The family crest. (Manuel Cansino Collection)

The history of the Cansino family has been traced back fifteen
generations to pre-Inquisition times in Spain. At that time the
family, who were Sephardic Jews, were regarded as very influential, highly educated and wealthy. They were vassals to the
King of Spain. Prior to the Inquisition they held important
positions in Seville and Carmona. It was a recognition of their
standing and contribution to their community that at the height of
the Inquisition, when Jews were expelled from Spain, the Cansino
family was welcomed in Oran and Mers-El-Kabir, then Spanish
colonies. While in Oran, members of the family were appointed
by the Kings of Spain to be royal interpreters. For a period of 107
years they held the titles of Spanish Ambassadors to the King of
Morocco. They lived in Oran until the Governor of Oran expelled
all Jews in 1668. Members of the family scattered across Europe
and the New World.

Rita's branch of the family probably descends from Isaac
Cansino who was born in Seville around 1430–1440. At the time
of the Inquisition, when to remain in Spain one had to renounce
one's religion or face torture and death, he became a Marrano
Jew,* changing his biblical name to Pedro Fernandez. He was
town councillor in Seville and took part in the conspiracy of the
Marrano Jews against the Inquisition. Like most of the Cansinos
he, too, was the scion of a large family which, by 1720, had shed
nearly all traces and memories of their Jewish connections. The
family history after this becomes more difficult to trace till the
arrival on the scene of Don Antonio Cansino—Rita's grandfather.

*A Marrano Jew was one who changed his faith in public and attended Catholic
services, but privately still kept to the faith of his fathers.

Rita's Spanish forbears had included statesmen, grandees of
Spain, lawyers, merchants and financiers; the famous twentieth-
century Spanish historian and supreme literary stylist Rafael
Cansino Assens was another, but 'Padre', as everyone in the
family called him, was the first 'dancing' Cansino.

Antonio, the only son of a second marriage, was born in 1865 in
a small village near Seville. As far as his daughter Elisa
remembers, her father's family had been ranchers and horse
breeders for several generations. Antonio was a year old when his
father died and his older half-brother and sister took over running
the ranch. The youngster's passion for dancing manifested itself
early. It was clear to his doting family that Antonio would never
make a happy rancher. While still a child, he learned to play the
guitar and bandurria. But music, though important, was not his first
love. Dancing was. There was at this time no school that taught
this native art. He learned from wandering around the tavernas
and gathering places of Seville where he could watch his
favourites—picking up dance steps as he went. As soon as he was
old enough to earn money, he took on odd jobs to pay for his
dancing lessons with a local teacher who trained the fiercely
dedicated youngster in the traditions of the fashionable classical
Italian ballet. At fourteen, Antonio was good enough to turn
professional, specialising in a blend of Spanish classical dancing
with its Iberian influence, and the gypsy-based Flamenco steps.
Much later he wove the strands—the traditional Spanish with the
classical Italian—to found a school of Spanish dance as we know it
today. His interest in music continued apace—more significant
than his occasional compositions however, were his transpositions
of Flamenco guitar music for piano and orchestra which he used
for his concerts, and which subsequently found their way into
many another dance troupe's repertoire.

Antonio's wife had also been a professional dancer, touring with
him until the first of their eleven children was born. Their first, a
boy, died in infancy; the next three were daughters, Gracia,
Carmellia and Elisa, who partnered their father on a triumphant
tour of South America. During that engagement Antonio
introduced and established the Bolero, a dance that quickly swept
the world. But a tragedy struck that eventually ended his career as
a performer.

A disease picked up by the girls on the trip resulted in the death
of the two elder ones, both talented dancers. The loss of his adored
daughters upset Antonio so deeply that he retired from pro-

fessional dancing and the gruelling travelling and long separation
from his family that this had entailed. From now on he
concentrated his energy on his dance school, which he had opened
in Madrid in 1905 with resounding success at the Calle
Encemienda No. 10. The building remains—still a dancing
school.

Elisa, who lives today in Cadiz, near the place of her birth, was
the fourth child and the last girl. Eduardo (March 2nd, 1895),
was followed by six brothers, Angel, Francisco (Paco), Jose,
Antonio, Joaquim (who died in childhood) and Rafael. All the
children, lovingly but strictly raised, were compelled to attend
dance classes. In accordance with Spanish tradition, the discipline
of the children in the home was left to their mother. When it came
to work, Padre's word was the law. He taught his children
separately from the other students, spurring them on with special
rewards of sweets or pennies to become more competitive.

'He never had to force us to dance all day for these prizes,' Elisa
remembered. 'We liked to dance and had a really good time
competing. Dancing was the only life we knew—living in a studio,
seeing dancing all the time. We did not attend a regular school
much because he liked having us home with him and Madre, but
Padre brought tutors in to teach us.'

Their father's fame as a dancer and as a teacher was such that
he was invited to perform at a Royal Gala given by King Alfonso
of Spain in honour of the visiting King of England. Spanish
dancing had become respectable and Antonio had played a large
part in this. Now it had also become fashionable. Sevillianas were
all the rage. Cansino's school was filled with society people
wanting to learn their own native steps, the same sort who, in
America, were to go mad over his children.

Not fate but convenience made Eduardo become Elisa's
dancing partner. As the oldest boy, he was nearest his sister in age
and height. Initially, however, he had rebelled against his father's
wishes. With the dream of becoming a bullfighter—that of most
Spanish boys—he'd run away from home, but Padre saw to it that
he was quickly brought to heel, and his friends in the police
arrested the young runaway. A night in jail and a talk with his
father made Eduardo see the light. Thereafter his devotion to
dancing as a career became absolute.

The new team, billed as the 'Dancing Cansinos' toured most of
the Spanish cities. As their reputation spread, they began to
receive more and more bookings on the Continent. It was 1913.

Eduardo and Elisa had been together now for four years when
their engagement at Madrid's smart Trianon Theatre brought
them into contact with their fate—Mrs Stuyvesant-Fish. She was
an American heiress—socially prominent, influential, a patron of
the arts and fashionable leader of New York's high society.

Mrs Stuyvesant-Fish had money and loved to spend it. She was
very American. In the United States, the early years of the new
century was a bonanza period, alternatively known as The Age of
Optimism, The Age of Confidence and The Age of Innocence.
The 'good life' was taken for granted as part of an American's
national heritage: some ten million Americans bought cars.
Actually everything was far from rosy, but few would have
thought so, for the future was a bright beacon that promised light
even in the darkest corners of that large new world.

The tempo of life in New York was accelerating, especially in
the social strata of the very rich, their spirits more and more
buoyant, led by Mrs Stuyvesant-Fish. She had done a great deal
to break down the previous austerity of New York society and
democratise it. Even in that reckless, rich world of the '400', of
Diamond Jim and Diamond Lil, her gaiety, wit and energy were
profligate. She took society by the hand and set it dancing,
knocking the staid ceremonials into a cocked hat. She first
introduced society to the fifty-minute dinner, replaced string
orchestras with jazz bands and with her good humour, coupled
with a shrewd sense of what could be done, converted potential
social gaffes into personal triumphs.

In 1913 on one of her European holidays, keeping an eye
forever open for talent that would amuse her New York and
Newport friends, she spotted the Cansinos and knew there was
nothing like them back home. She spoke no Spanish and they
spoke no English but they managed to communicate in French,
with her son acting as intermediary. Her naturally personal charm
and warmth overcame any doubts the young Spaniards had at the
long journey and lengthy separation from their family. Looking
after them as if they were her children, Mrs Fish brought them
back, launching them in America with considerable fanfare.

Expecting a success, even she was surprised by the sensation
they made. Quickly their fame outgrew the social circuit to exceed
anything they could have achieved in their homeland. 'At first we
did not intend to stay in New York,' Elisa wrote, 'but after living
and dancing there—we liked it so well we decided to try and see if

Eduardo and Elisa Cansino, *circa* 1919. (Vernon Cansino Collection)

we could become successful. Spanish dancing was still unknown at this time which made it difficult for us at first. No one really understood this type of dancing, neither did the musicians understand our music, so they were unable to give proper feeling to it. We realised that if we wanted to consolidate our success we had to hire our own orchestra leader. Another problem was the costumes. We wore typical traditional Spanish dancing costumes, but since no one in New York had seen them before, people found them funny. In the end we modified them to look more like evening dress with Spanish accents.'

They were a triumph in elegant cosmopolitan Newport society and became the darlings of the social circuit. The timing of their American debut couldn't have been better. Ballroom dancing, led by the extraordinarily graceful and attractive husband and wife team Vernon and Irene Castle, was all the rage. The Castles set the pace to which young Americans skipped and swirled. When they incorporated a Spanish dance in their act everybody followed. The first of the 'Super-stars', the Castles' influence was overwhelming. And not just as dancers. What they wore, what they ate, where they ate—all made headlines. When Irene bobbed her hair, there wasn't a woman in the land who didn't do the same. There were Castle hats, Castle shoes, Castle skirts.

Rita's mother around the time she left home for Ziegfield and the Follies. (Vernon Cansino Collection)

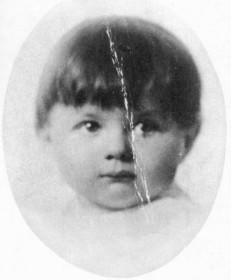

Rita—a baby photo—1919. (Vernon Cansino Collection)

Restaurants, where society would gather for dinner or tea, were named after them: Castles by the Sea in Long Beach; Castles in the Air in New York. They influenced scores of dancers who came in their wake, including another brother/sister act—Fred and Adele Astaire.*

Soon Eduardo and Elisa were making $1,500 a week. With the promise of all the work they could wish for, there was no thought of going back home, and with Spain caught up in World War I,

---

*By 1915 when Fred and Adele were booked to dance on the Orpheum Circuit, then not only the most prestigious but one of the best because of the treatment they gave their artists and the superior chain of theatres they controlled across the country, the Cansinos were headliners on the same bill. Recalled Astaire: '... [when] I met Eduardo and Elisa Cansino ... they were headliners with their magnificent [Spanish] dancing act. Adele and I were a small act on the bill. I watched Eduardo at almost every show. He was a marvellous dancer and he and his sister were exciting performers....'

they decided to set about bringing over the whole family to this land of milk and honey.

Their youngest brother Antonio was the last to leave Spain, joining them in 1920. By then Eduardo had married a beautiful showgirl from the Ziegfeld Follies, whom he met in 1917 when they both appeared in the same show. If it wasn't love at first sight, it was close enough.*

Rita's mother, Volga Haworth, who had appeared in the Follies with Marion Davies, was an inflammable Irish-American beauty who had run away from home when she was sixteen because of her obsession with the theatre. Throughout her life Volga left a strong impression on most of the people she met—though not always because of her beauty. But her high-strung, emotional temperament that would, when roused, become frequently shrill and hysterical in later years, served then to add spice to her out-going personality in attractive contrast to Eduardo's more reserved nature. As half of 'The Dancing Cansinos' Eduardo was a glamorous headliner when he met Volga. While not conventionally handsome, he was a commanding figure on stage, his aspect enhanced by his lithe, dark Spanish looks. Nor was Volga unaware that his star was on the ascendant for his success was such that he turned down an audition for the much-sought-after Follies because Ziegfeld would not match money he was already earning. That anyone could turn down a chance to work in the Follies only increased Eduardo's attraction for the young, stage-struck beauty. They married soon after they met.

Eduardo, with his feelings for the family shaped by strong Spanish Catholic traditions, was quite a contrast to the men Volga had known. For him she gave up the thing she had wanted since childhood, and for which she had defied family and run away from home. Her career. It was understood that once children were born she would have to give up her own ambitions, and devote herself to Eduardo and the home. Undoubtedly her husband and children took first place but she always remained a frustrated actress, which would become especially apparent after a few drinks. Her moods were mercurial, but her love for her husband, and his for her, remained steadfast. In a business where people change partners like musical chairs, theirs was a marriage that held to her death.

*Antonio also married a Follies' beauty, Catherine Stoneburn, who was known as 'The Golden Girl' of Ziegfeld's Follies.

Volga sublimated her desire for a career into wishing for one for her daughter, but when with friends recalling the old days, she would proudly bring out a worn, much fingered piece of folded paper, a treasured memento of her past: it was the telegram Ziegfeld sent after her marriage pleading with her to return to the Follies.

Volga's family was as old and as proud as Eduardo's. Her father, a very autocratic man, ruled his family stiffly like the Clarence Day character in *Life With Father*, and could shriek louder than anyone. He was self-made and never let anyone forget it, nor the fact that his people, who were originally from a small town called Haworth in Yorkshire, arrived in America soon after the *Mayflower* pilgrims. He had worked his way up from small beginnings to become the owner of the second largest printing business in Washington, which handled a lot of the Government's stocks and bonds. He was the one to add the 'y' to the name because, as he said, people used to think he didn't know how to spell his own name. As long as anyone remembered, Volga wanted to go on the stage. It was an ambition of which her father disapproved vehemently, even though he came from a long line of famous actors dating back to Shakespeare's time. A cousin of his (Joe Haworth) was Madame Mojeska's leading man and had toured with Booth, the one who shot Lincoln. There was limelight and greasepaint on her mother's side as well, for the O'Haras were Irish theatrical people. When her uncle was playing in Washington, Volga, aided by her mother, sneaked out of the house to see him. Later, when she decided to run away and get into showbusiness, her mother helped her, but they didn't dare let her dad know. Recalled her sister-in-law, Jean, 'Though he loved his family very dearly he just didn't like the theatre, and what he said went—or else! When he found out that Volga had run off it took years for him to forgive her.

'She must have been quite good because she'd toured in several plays before she got a job as a chorus girl in the Follies of 1916. To be a chorine you didn't have to be able to do all the dance patterns you need to know today. If you kicked pretty good, were able to do a few simple time steps and if you were pretty as well, you were a cinch. Though she takes after neither of her parents in looks, Rita is a lot like Volga when she loses her temper, but like Eduardo till she does.

'Volga wasn't very well for a long time before she died and the ravages of ill health took their toll on her. But when I first knew her she had a very delicate beauty. She was around five foot six inches, very slender, slim, delicate contours and an outgoing personality. I always found her very theatrical; she was very quick to take offence at the least likely things. You simply never knew where you were with her. One day she'd throw things at you for no reason, and the next she'd be crying on your shoulder and asking your advice about the kids. She'd always be talking about "Rita this ... Rita that...." In that respect she was a lot like my sister Lela with her daughter, Ginger.* Lela was a great talker too. Maybe that's why Rita, like Ginger, is such a very quiet person in private; though Ginger has more get up and go to her.'

Rita's youngest brother, Vernon, added that his mother took after her father, and that she had a strong influence on Rita. 'Rita's heritage is very proud, straight-laced, almost Victorian English on our mother's side. For instance, our grandfather would not speak to my mother for four years for having married a Spaniard. I mean, you just didn't marry Spaniards if you came from a fine American-English family. On the other side, the Spanish are not only a very proud race, they are also arrogant. I don't think it's any great virtue, but it *can* be virtuous. It creates an independence. For instance, my Aunt Elisa and my dad brought all their brothers over to America and set them up, but not one of them would ever admit that they owed them anything. Not that the brothers didn't appreciate what they'd done, but it just wasn't the way they were made.'

The newly-weds soon needed all the babysitters their families had to offer. Margarita was born on October 17th, 1918; a year and a half later came her brother Eduardo Jnr, whom the family nicknamed 'Sonny' because of his outgoing disposition. Three years later, Vernon rounded off the family. Meanwhile Eduardo's parents, homesick for their own country, had returned to Spain, content to have seen all their children prospering in the new world. Eduardo's mother had babysat with her granddaughter in New York when Eduardo and Volga were on the road. To support his family Eduardo had had to work more than ever, though this meant long months on the road, and Volga had travelled with him, covering for his lack of English and looking after his business. After the birth of their first son, Eduardo—then appearing in a show at the 125th Street Theatre—decided the time had come to stop living in theatrical boarding houses and to provide a permanent home for his family while he was on the

*Ginger Rogers and Rita Hayworth are related by marriage.

Eduardo Jr., Vernon and Rita Cansino posing against the wall of their New York home, 1923. (Vernon Cansino Collection)

Volga, Eduardo and their children outside the New York home, 1926. (Vernon Cansino Collection)

road. After a short period in an apartment in Brooklyn they moved to a more spacious residence in Jackson Heights, Queens, a prosperous middle-class suburb of New York. This would become Margarita's home for the first nine years. It was there that her Uncle Vinton, having also run away from home, as stage-struck and determined as his sister, spent much of his time between theatrical jobs in New York, paying for his keep by babysitting for the family. Margarita and her brothers attended school in the local Jackson Heights PS 79. Family snapshots of the little girl dating from these years convey a compelling intensity, and the beauty that would emerge a few years later is already evident in the dark-haired, chubby-cheeked little girl of six.

Since her brothers showed neither aptitude nor any interest in a

Rita at age 5½ in Atlantic City, N.J., August 1924. (Vernon Cansino Collection)

dancing career they were allowed to go their own way, but Rita was given no option. 'They had me dancing almost as soon as I could walk,' Rita has often said. From the age of four, she had to attend daily classes at a Spanish dance studio run by her Uncle Angel in Carnegie Hall. All through her formative years she would traipse out to her dance class after school was over. Even from afar, on his tours, her father controlled her life the same way as his father had controlled his. Like a well-brought-up Spanish daughter, she did as she was told, silently, uncomplainingly.

In later years Rita remembered her childhood with a tang of bitterness, though now she looks back at it quite philosophically: 'I suppose being a little girl it was assumed that I would be more likely to want to dance than my brothers. I learned a certain kind of discipline. I just don't think it's very good to have to learn it so young. I was so disciplined that I felt like the Charlie Chaplin character in *Modern Times*, when he works in the factory. Sometimes when my father was dancing in

New York, my mother would take us to see him and Aunt Elisa.
She was such a beautiful dancer. I guess I would have wanted to
be like her if somebody had asked me, but, honey, I didn't have
the choice. But I was never in their act then. I remember one
time, I was just a little kid, they were giving a recital at Carnegie
Hall and I was backstage with my mother, and I heard all this
applause, and you know how little kids are, I got so excited, I ran
on stage and took a bow. They didn't expect that; my father was
very angry with me after, but that was the first time I was on the
stage and it wasn't part of any act.'

Since she never voiced any objection to having to dance it came
as something of a surprise to her family when they heard her speak
of it in interviews, and they took her complaints with a large dose
of salts. 'Later, I heard Rita express a kind of self-pity,' Vernon
once told me, 'which is pretty hard for the rest of the family to
take because she made such a tremendous success at it. It was just
a mood that she'd get into and then she'd start to act up a bit,
which is fine because she's an actress.

'You've got to remember she's a *Latin*. The Cansinos were
Spanish in every way, besides being very successful people in their
work. I think most successful people have more pride and develop
more arrogance than the average person does. They don't admit
defeat even if you hit them on the head with it. Today, if you talk
to a Spaniard, they still say that the greatest man that ever lived
was Philip II and the hell with the Armada. Rita's the same. She
wouldn't tell you she was despondent about something, even as a
little kid. And later on she'd never, for instance, say anything
against her husbands. Now this takes a strong character; most
women won't do that. Sure she was shy, but she's the kind of
person who attracts people—they would come to her, she never
had to go to them. I don't know if that's all that good for you, but
it's a rare talent. It's the same with Yasmin, or my Aunt Elisa.
She's eighty now, but she can walk into a room and you get that
same feeling that this was someone who had accomplished
something and could look you straight in the eye and say "I did
it". And you know damn well she did, no "buts" about it. If her
name wasn't Rita Hayworth, it wouldn't make any difference; her
bearing, the way she holds herself, they'd still look.

'Of course it took Hollywood know-how to show her off to the
best advantage but her beauty and grace were natural attributes.
So was her intensity. That's what is most distinctive about her.
Even as a young girl Rita was so intense that she commanded you

through it. When she looked at you, boy she could turn it on. She could make you freeze in five seconds. She could even make our mother cry when she withdrew like that and became very proud and distant. Mom would say, "Why are you doing that to me? Why are you angry?" Rita wouldn't say a thing. Just this silence. Then of course she has the emotional temperament of an artist. Of course this is just a kid brother talking but I think that is what makes Rita unique. She was beautiful, attractive to look at but, what was more, beneath it there was this quality of intensity you couldn't run away from. She always gave you the feeling that something was going to happen—you didn't know what but it was there. I know her as well as anybody but I don't think any of us knows what makes her tick. I don't think Rita does either. But if any word could describe her it's intensity. she didn't have to practise or learn it, it was just a quality she always had, and I think she always will have.'

Before her brothers were born, her parents took Margarita along on their tours, Elisa and Volga babysitting in turn. She was an easy baby. Never any trouble. She lay for hours in the dressing rooms, quietly awake looking out and being looked at and cossetted by the other artists. With the birth of her brother it became impractical to take both children along. Eduardo Jnr was looked after by his Spanish grandmother. Once Vernon was born little Margarita's early touring life was over. The children were left in the care of relatives in New York or with Volga's parents in Washington D.C. For, with the birth of his grandchildren, Volga's father had come round completely, and the large house in Washington became almost a second home to the youngsters. On those rare occasions whenever their father's play dates brought him to towns near New York like Atlantic City, the children would come join their parents for holidays every part of which remained memorable for being so few and far between and happy.

Eduardo's bookings took them all over America, Canada, and on a triumphant tour of Europe in the summer of 1924. The summer was usually a dull spot in the Vaudeville calendar, when most of the acts were laid off until the autumn season, and only the largest star names found work at the prestigious Palace in New York. Eduardo and Elisa had now been away from Spain for more than ten years, they missed their old home and they wanted to see how their parents were getting on, living in the house they had bought for them in Madrid. So when a marvellously opportune offer came for a two-week engagement at London's famed Palladium theatre they

Volga and Eduardo in a joke photo they sent to friends and relatives in the U.S. when they were stopping over in Paris, in 1924, to visit his mother. (Eduardo Cansino Collection)

accepted. It enabled them to go to Europe for a free holiday and to see their mother and father. Plans to meet them in Paris were laid as soon as the booking had been assured. They could not have foreseen their success and the disappointment this would bring. After their opening-night triumph, a member of the Royal Household came backstage to invite Eduardo and Elisa to dance at a private party being given by friends for the Prince of Wales' birthday. It was an enormous compliment and placed them in a dilemma. In the end, and with much regret, since it was too late to inform their parents and change their plans for their reunion, they turned down the royal invitation.

For a long time Eduardo had looked for a way of keeping his family together when he was on the road by bringing the children into the act. It wasn't uncommon for showbiz parents to successfully incorporate their children in their acts—like Eddie Foy & the Seven Little Foys. Later, when a forgotten child had become an unforgettable star, unlikely people suddenly remembered seeing a girl they thought had been Rita on stage with her father's group. Actually there was never anything beyond an item in the *Vaudeville News* of July 31st, 1925, printed below a photograph of the three children taken in Atlantic City while on a holiday with their parents. The caption stated that they were being groomed for a stage career. If Eduardo ever harboured such a dream, it didn't long survive what Vernon called 'his sons' four left feet'. The item adds up to a free plug for the elder Cansino, nevertheless the caption is prophetic: 'Future generations will in all probability hear from the originals of the above photo.'

Rita's shyness and completely unaffected attitude to her own career dates from her childhood. For, while her father was concentrating on his work and her mother spent most of her time looking after him and attending to his business affairs, Margarita learned quickly to keep out of the way. A quiet, cuddly moppet with round cheeks and dark bangs, she looked like an adorable Raggedy Ann doll in her early photos, an appearance that must have been even more striking as she stood on the sidelines, watching the different acts come from the back-stage darkness to perform in the lights; or when she was found spending long hours by herself plastering her little face with make-up in her parents' dressing room. Always more gregarious, her brothers would be out playing baseball with other children, growing up like most American boys.

Eduardo's career was still thriving, but it was becoming apparent that by having brought over his brothers, who were also earning their living as dancers, he had, in effect, flooded the market with rival Cansinos. All of them had their own troupes and could be had for less than their famous brother. When, in 1929, Eduardo opened his dancing school, they all followed suit. Two of them taught in New York, another in Florida, while Elisa was a successful guest teacher in different studios throughout the United States and had her own school in San Francisco. Another brother, Jose, went so far as to open his dancing school in Los Angeles, not far from Eduardo's. Eduardo was far too easy-going and charming to object, even though Jose seemed to think that his was a swanker establishment than Eduardo's. But there was grumbling in the Haworth family about the way Eduardo let himself be used.

Like his father, Eduardo, while very disciplined in his work was a rotten businessman. It was Volga who always had to bail him out and run the business, whether on his tours or with the school. When she complained or sighed for her lost career she certainly had cause. She took care of the books, wrote the ads, booked the kids and did the paperwork as well as looked after the home. 'Eduardo', as his sister-in-law succinctly pointed out, 'was the artist. He had no idea about business.' But even with competition from within his own family and the new dance teams that came in his wake, Eduardo and Elisa remained a 'class' attraction on the circuits. Joan remembered the sensational act: 'He and Elisa were two of the most fantastic dancers I've ever seen so it wasn't surprising that theirs was one of the highest paid acts. They really

Eduardo and Elisa Cansino in the foreground with soprano Anna Case in
La Fiesta, one of the Vitaphone Prologues first shown to introduce Sound to
the public in 1926. (Warner Brothers)

knew their business, changing with the times, modernising their
costumes and steps—it may not have been pure Spanish, the
whips and all that, but it was great show business. It was one of
the fastest acts on the Orpheum circuit, always movement and
change, never a dull moment. That was the time that Nijinsky was
in America and the dance critics used to write about Nijinsky and
Eduardo in the same breath, not least because Eduardo could do
four *jetées*.'

Had things stayed as they were he might never have uprooted
his family from New York. But then came 1926. During one of his
periodic stays in New York, Eduardo and Elisa received a call
from the Warner Brothers' Vitagraph Studios in Brooklyn to
appear in a revolutionary film shortly to be made with sound. The
producers wanted a cavalcade of dance that could be contained in
ten minutes. This would form part of an extravagant musical
prologue including Efrem Zimbalist, Harold Bauer, Marion
Talley and Mischa Elman, the Metropolitan Opera Company
and chorus with Giovanni Martinelli and Anna Case in excerpts
from *I Pagliacci* and *La Fiesta* and the New York Philharmonic
Orchestra with 107 musicians! This, the 'Vitaphone Prelude'
would be followed by a feature film, *Don Juan*, starring John
Barrymore, accompanied by orchestral music and certain sound
effects. It was heralded as the first public demonstration of the
new miracle.

Like all movie miracles it was not the first of its kind, and was
due to economic rather than artistic causes, for the Warner
Brothers were facing financial ruin in uneven competition with the
other major studios. The only way they saw of saving themselves

was to come out with something that would secure their position through indirectly facing others with economic ruin. Perhaps they didn't see it quite like that but the coming of sound to movies was the beginning of the end for Vaudeville, and meant that the Dancing Cansinos had to start looking around for work from another source. Elisa, who was married and with a son, wanted to retire to spend more time with her family and return to Spain to live. Eduardo, without a female partner to replace Elisa and not wanting to find and train a new girl, had to think seriously about a new direction for his career. Here was a perfect opportunity to bow out while they were still at the top.

He was one of the first to realise that where there was sound, there would be music and dancing and his services, if he got there quickly, would come in handy. Dorothy Valdespino, who joined his school in 1929 as his rehearsal pianist and stayed a friend until his death, told me that: 'He could see the finish and wanted to get established in something else before it really was too late, so he decided to split the act and move to California. "Because that's where the movies are," he said. "I think I have a better chance there to dance or do choreography."'

The following year, any lingering doubts about the planned move were securely squashed by the astonishing success of Al Jolson in *The Jazz Singer*. The Cansino family packed their trunks and moved to a large comfortable house Eduardo had found on Stern Drive, a block or two from Pico Boulevard in a nice down-town area of Hollywood.

Back in 1913, when the Cansinos had first arrived in New York, Hollywood was barely a dot on the map, just an under-developed suburb of the city of Los Angeles. Admittedly, even then Americans were already in the thrall of the movies but not many had yet begun to trace the source to Los Angeles, still best known for its wide open spaces, broad, car-free streets and a strong line in citrus fruit. True, the star system was soon flourishing; Mary Pickford and Charlie Chaplin were fast becoming household names and D. W. Griffith had already made films that transformed a pastime into an art, but few there then could have foreseen the mushrooming of an immense fantasy empire.

By 1927, the transformation was complete, a partial art had become big business—to be precise, the fourth largest industry in America. Movies were not merely a pastime—they were a way of

life. By 1920 more than thirty-five million Americans were going
to the movies at least once a week. Movie stars were the gods and
goddesses whose influence went far beyond what anyone could
have foreseen. In an age of celebrities, they were the most
glamorous of all. Top personalities like Swanson, Gish, Valentino,
Clara Bow were now receiving about thirty-two million fan letters
a year. To their adoring public who grew up with the movies it
didn't seem like hard work being a movie star. It seemed more like
fun, like all you had to be was young and ambitious, have lots of
faith in yourself and you, too, could go to Hollywood and the
studio gates would fly open and fame, fortune, and happiness
would be yours. Magazines which helped promote the illusion in
their photo-gravure sections and dream-spreading articles didn't
actively encourage such a foolhardy attitude. On the contrary,
they tried their best to discourage newcomers by sporadically
printing, in heavy type, sermons warning young hopefuls of the
trials and tribulations—not to mention the hard work and little
hope Hollywood offered. And the hard work needn't even be in
movies. While you might get as far as the casting couch there
wasn't any guarantee that you'd get further than the canteen as a
result. But as an Eastern sage said: 'If they are dumb enough to go
to Hollywood, they're probably dumb enough to get into
pictures.'

Like every business, the studios needed men and women who
were skilled in their profession. Eduardo Cansino, famous as a
dancer, now became famous teaching others, and choreographing
many of the musicals then being churned out by Fox, Metro and
the Warner Brothers studios. There was more work than he could
handle and his dance studio* was prosperous.

His first studio was a big ballroom with barres and mirrors
around the high-ceilinged walls, as well as dressing rooms, showers
and an office. While Eduardo did teach a straight classical ballet
class; he specialised in Spanish. He had the showman's sense to
also teach all the latest Latin dance crazes—the Beguine, the
Samba and the Rumba. Anyone who wanted to learn could come,
not just professionals, though with the Talkie Revolution and the
wave of musicals in its wake there were a great many of those.

*The studio was originally located on the second floor of a building on the corner of
Sunset Boulevard and Vine Street, a couple of blocks up the street from the budding
Columbia Studios. As his business flourished, he moved to larger premises: first, over the
old Police and Fire Station on Cahuenga Avenue in 1930, then, in 1931, he took a whole
building with another dance teacher, Paul Draper. There they settled and there they
would stay.

Besides, if a company or a star was going to make a movie or appear in a stage show that needed a lift, they went to Eduardo. His school was the forerunner of institutions like the Arthur Murray and the Fred Astaire chain of dance studios that sprang up over the country to teach non-professionals the pleasures of being socially accomplished dancers. But to his family, this move to a permanent home in California had a far greater personal significance.

Vernon: 'It was the first time we were all together as a family. Dad had a very successful business choreographing over at Warner Brothers. He directed the dance numbers for films where they needed Spanish flavours—like *Song of the Flame*, *Noah's Ark*, *Golden Dawn* and *Under a Texas Moon*. Over at M.G.M. he did the dances for Ramon Novarro and Renee Adoree in her last picture, *Call of the Flesh*. And he had Irene Dunne there to teach her a dance for a movie she never made over at R.K.O. Old friends from Vaudeville, like James Cagney, would often drop by to see Eduardo and practise their steps. Besides the regular classes (which Rita attended) he had a lot of private students. 'Cause a lot of these gals in pictures didn't just have to know how to act, but how to sing and dance as well. Margo was taking lessons from him—she's a fantastic dancer—and Armida; and Betty Grable was another who was in his school. So was Grace Poggi, a sensational Rumba dancer. She had a very flamboyant act in the Foreign Club, Café de Lux in Tijuana, which my Dad staged, like the one she did in Eddie Cantor's *Kid from Spain*.

'Our mother was the dominating force in our home. But as far as Rita was concerned, when she went into that studio to take lessons, my father was the man of the family. He could bark at, say Margo, who was in the same class, and Margo would take it because she could go home, curse him on the street, and come back the next day saying, "Oh maestro, you're marvellous." But Rita couldn't do that—she could never get away from the guy, he was her teacher and he was her father. This made for a strained relationship.'

Dorothy: 'Eduardo wasn't any stricter with Rita than with any of the others in the class. He was just a strict teacher because he gave the best he knew. He never gave compliments—not ever to any of his students, even when they did something well. It wasn't his nature, but they understood that. They really liked him very much. You could tell from their friendly and relaxed way towards him when class was over. When work was over Eduardo was real easy-going.

Volga Cansino in 1927. (Eduardo Cansino Collection)

'To Aunt Elisa, To be as wonderful a dancer as you are is my heart's desire. Dearest Love, Margarita.' 1931. (Eduardo Cansino Collection)

He was actually a rather quiet, very unassuming man, never one to boast about his past, when you consider he had captivated the dancing world with his work. Rita's like him in that respect. Neither of them are comfortable with flattery.

'Being so shy, of course she didn't mix well. In the classes you'd see the other girls standing in groups, talk, talk, talk, twenty to the dozen, really getting to know each other well. Not Rita. Everybody noticed that she didn't talk; that she kept her thoughts to herself. She might have been intimidated too by the fact that her mother did all the talking in the family. Volga was quite tall—that's where Rita gets her height from—taller than Eduardo and thin like a pole. And a very emotional woman—you'd never know what could make her blow up at you or why. Because she was so intense she could appear quite menacing at times. Eduardo didn't seem to mind. He took her outbursts calmly, he'd just shrug his shoulders philosophically, say "well ...". That would be all. Volga's the one who made up her mind about how everything should be run, the family, the business.

'It was her dream as much as Eduardo's that Rita become a

dancer. Of course, Eduardo could teach her every day. In the back of their minds there was always the idea that if she grew up to be beautiful, they would groom her for movies. Sometimes, when I was around they talked about how they would like to see her as a star in pictures. It was never about the boys but then neither Sonny nor Vernon were that ambitious. Rita was just eleven when I first met her, and whenever there was a class for her age group, Eduardo put her in it. She had to do it. It wasn't easy to know if she enjoyed it, but when she got into that thirteen-year-old stage, you could see that she was really beginning to get interested in herself from the way she posed in front of the mirror, trying to get the exact style. You can see her pleasure and pride in the photos of her.'

Antonia Morales, one of the few close female friends in Rita's life, first met her when she was also a student at the school, and gave her impression: 'She doesn't really like to be with strangers. She doesn't feel comfortable. Though you always felt that she saw and heard, and remembered everything. But she was never one to go overboard about anything. Her attitude was always to do what she had to do quietly; to work. But she was still a little girl, she needed assurance; she needed a pat on the back. She and her mother appeared to me to be very close. When Rita talks about her family, she speaks a great deal about her mother, and her mother adored her. Volga really concentrated her ambitions on Rita, for Rita to have that great career that she never had. Sometimes when I came to the house, or at the class while Rita would be dancing, Volga would point and say, more to herself than anybody else, "Isn't she just beautiful."'

If her parents doted on Rita, the boys weren't left out. Vernon had his recollections of those times: 'After she came of age they'd take her out to get her hair done at an expensive place because she was going for an interview or that kind of thing but it would be unfair to say that they neglected either my brother or me in any way. She got a car when she was eighteen—but that's no big deal and besides, she was already a professional who'd earned money and helped the family. She and Dad were drawing quite a salary. We weren't neglected—it was a family. Why shouldn't the family adore her—she was the only girl, beautiful and talented. What parent wouldn't be proud if their girl went out on the football field waving the baton and everybody went mad about her and came knocking on your door.'

Although Rita was allowed what must have seemed luxuries in

the time of the Depression, the money was being used as an investment for the future. Eduardo was concerned that nothing should interfere with his plans for his daughter and therefore kept her on a very short rein. His attitude towards her was always strict. Vernon had his explanation for that.

'I've had time to think this out, I wasn't as successful as Rita and I didn't have her kind of pressures and, too, Dad didn't have to worry as much about us boys. What could happen to us? But Rita was a girl, men looked at her and Dad saw that. Like all those Latins, they chaperone their daughters. Here he was, in a strange country, and even though he was in show business—that's a different crowd—he never really understood the American mentality. Besides, American men are much more aggressive. I'm just giving you reasons why Rita would think Dad was too strict with her. I think that might account for her ambivalent feelings about dancing. The problem didn't come from not wanting to dance but because she was dancing with a famous dancer, who was not only older and, at least in the beginning, better, but who was also her father. What chance did she have? It wasn't a normal team relationship. There's no romance or glamour in that, and yet here she was in what was a romantic and glamorous profession. Then too, when you've got a growing daughter who looks more mature than she is, in towns like Tijuana and Agua Caliente where you had gambling boisterous crowds, and bordellos almost door to door, you watch them like a hawk. So he kept his thumb on her—he obviously felt he had to. God, she was a minor. Of course she became annoyed and she drew further away from Dad, especially later on. How many teenage girls do you know that don't think their parents are holding them back?'

Vernon was the baby of the family and his relationship with his famous sister was easy and loving. Through the years, until his death in March 1974, though they might not see each other for long periods at a time, he and Rita spoke often on the phone and remained close. She might grumble at having to babysit her kid brothers while their parents were busy at the studio, but it would only be to herself, as she took Sonny and Vernon along to the latest movies near their home. Or, during school holidays, they might spend the afternoon gulping pancakes at the house of their father's pianist. Afterwards, while the boys would play in the garden, throwing rocks at some other kids, Margarita would spend her time reading quietly in the living room.

The Cansino household was generally a hive of activity recalled

Vernon. 'We had every Vaudeville act in the world drop in as far back as I can remember. This was a real "You can't take it with you" family. All my Dad's old chums when they needed a bed would come and visit. We even had trained seals in the living room. The seals had to go in the bathroom to keep them wet—we didn't have a pool. We didn't have a bath either for a couple of weeks. We had one woman drop in, I don't know where she came from, it seems that she and her husband were travelling the States from Hawaii. She just dropped in and stayed for eight months. You couldn't throw people out in those days. That was the camaraderie of theatrical people. My father was very much an extrovert in that sort of situation. I remember Angel, and Carmina and Suzi—this is one of my uncles and his family—they drove in from New York sometime in 1937 with half a gallon of wine, a half a gallon of gasoline and Angel with half a dollar in his pocket. He drove up to the house and said, "I've made it!" and stayed for two years. There was always something going on.'

And still business prospered. Eduardo expanded his premises. When Dorothy joined him he had been the only teacher at his studio. About a year later he moved into a bigger studio, and took on Paul Draper, who taught tap, as a partner.

The only thing wrong with the move was the timing. Events outside the family circle were soon to change their way of life as they were to change that of most other Americans. The stock market crashed in October 1929. The United States, and most of the world, plunged into the worst economic débâcle in western memory. Like many people in show business, Eduardo lost his nest egg—$10,000 invested in a building society. Things were looking grim for everyone. Yet it would have been hard to see that the nation was down in the dumps from the movies they made. Hollywood's aim was to avoid the obvious by creating a world of escapism, cheap enough for even the poorest migrant worker. At the outset of the Depression, humorist Will Rogers could still joke, 'We are the first nation in the history of the world to go to the poor house in an automobile,' but by 1931 between thirteen and fifteen million were unemployed and the unemployed had thirty million mouths to feed. Wages had dropped by sixty percent for those who had jobs and it was still getting worse. For a great many Americans the Depression had pups on their doorsteps.

Having lost his money was bad enough. Now Eduardo's career suffered a double blow. One of the first things to go when money is tight is any luxury item and that meant pianos and dancing

Rita receiving a pair of castanets to celebrate her first professional stage appearance with her cousin Gabriel holding the box and her uncle Jose on her right. The rest are students from the school to dress up the picture. (Vernon Cansino Collection)

lessons. On top of that, after that first great boom in the movie industry, musicals had gone bust as well. Eduardo, who had earlier turned down lucrative studio contracts to concentrate on his school, now barely managed to keep it solvent. The new school had been a big investment. The bill for its upkeep kept coming in even as his students were dropping out.

By the end of 1932, with the school running at a loss, he was seriously contemplating re-activating the old act. He needed a partner. Elisa, who had re-married, had grown contentedly stout and happily divided much of her time between teaching in San Francisco, and Spain, where at last she settled. As luck, spurred by necessity, would have it an inevitable solution had already presented itself a year earlier. In the spring of 1931, Elisa's eighteen-year-old son, making his way as a dancer, had obtained a spot in the prologue Eduardo had been hired to stage at the Los Angeles Carthay Circle Theatre, to accompany the first-run feature film, Universal's classic tear-jerker, *Back Street*. Rehearsals were going well, until, on the day before the performance, Gabriel's partner broke her ankle. There was a panic. Without a partner he'd lose the job; he needed someone who could step in at the last minute. It wasn't Ruby Keeler, but his thirteen-year-old cousin Margarita.

It would be fun to write now that she went out there a kid—but that she came back, a Star. Regretfully, life isn't always exactly as shown in the movies. Yet, it was a beginning, in more ways than one.

Dorothy: 'It was a big prologue. There were an awful lot of people in these stage shows. Gabriel and Margarita did a few routines—pretty Spanish peasant dances and the Jeta, a very difficult folk dance. Rita was terribly scared the first time she went on, but she came off well.' Though not thirteen she looked considerably older on stage in her tight black classically-cut Spanish dress; her chubbiness gave the illusion of mature contours, and, like all good dancers, Margarita instinctively had the knack of showing herself off to the best advantage. The work in front of the mirror had paid off. Her bare shoulders were straight and white, her neck was long and graceful, even then she had beautiful arms and her hands and fingers were long and exquisitely delicate. When she smiled the corners of her mouth turned up and the little girl looked like a woman. *Back Street* was a smash and so was the engagement. To celebrate, her mother gave Margarita money to buy herself a new dress. Her father who had watched the performance from the rear of the orchestra would often tell reporters when Margarita had become a star: 'All of a sudden I woke up to the fact that my baby was no longer a baby, she had a figure! I realised then that staging prologues and attempting to operate the school was ridiculous. We can't wait around here, I thought. Here was a girl, my own daughter, with whom I could build a whole new dance act!'

Meekly, Margarita accepted her father's decision. Nobody asked her opinion. She'd been attending Alexander Hamilton High, but now she transferred to the Carthay High School so as to be closer to work, for after the engagement came to a successful end she was kept on either as a solo or with other students from the Cansino studios. Her stage assurance grew as she danced professionally in shows her father staged at military hospitals, out of town conventions, and even occasional fillers at swank nightclubs like the Ambassador Cocoanut Grove for the visiting Olympic champions. It was necessary to obtain working papers for her from the California State Board of Education and to make up whatever school work she missed because of performances with additional sessions of homework.

A complimentary postcard from the Foreign Club Café de Luxe, where Rita and her father danced. (Dorothy Valdespino Collection)

While the poor got poorer, and everywhere things were going from bad to worse, people still wanted to be entertained, and the rich were still rich. Night-life flourished.

There was one snag. Though Margarita had matured physically, so that people usually mistook her and her father for brother and sister, she was still a minor and the California State Laws did not permit minors to appear where alcohol was sold. It meant that their engagements were restricted to the notorious off-shore gambling boats and the easily accessible night spots below the Mexican border in Tijuana and Agua Caliente. Theoretically a health resort because of its hot water springs, Caliente proved popular with the Hollywood crowd becasue of its racecourse, its bullfights and the gambling in its flourishing, wide-open casinos.

Eduardo procured their first engagement at Tijuana's rococo Foreign Club Café de Luxe, a favourite watering spot for cinema bigwigs, through a contact with one of his students, who was also the mistress of the man who ran the club. The afternoon the booking agents for the Foreign club came to see him, he and Volga had gone out leaving Dorothy behind to look after Margarita.

'Rita had put on her rehearsal costume and I was playing for her. These were just practice routines—Flamencos and Farrucas that Eduardo had been getting ready when these two men càme up to see him. I knew that it had to do with one of the jobs Eduardo had gone for, but I didn't know when Eduardo would be back. So I said, "Would you like to see Margarita dance? She can change into a nice costume and dance for you." She wasn't the liveliest dancer, but she was skilled and pretty to look at, pretty

SPAIN'S FORMOST DANCER

EDUARDO

CANSINO

Assisted by
MARGARITA CANSINO

JOSE de ARRATIA
Leading tenor of the National Opera Company of Mexico City

PROGRAM

1. Aires Andaluces .... R. Gómez
   Salvador Sainz
2. Sevilla .... I. Albeniz
   Eduardo and Margarita Cansino
3. El Toero (The Bull Fighter) .... De Falla
   NOTE: This dance shows an amateur toréador encouraged by a furious bull.
   (This number is in memory of my dear cousin, killed in the Bull-Ring at Sevilla, Spain.)
   Eduardo Cansino
4. Ramito de Flores .... Popular
   Margarita Cansino
5. (a) Cuando al Balcón te iba a cantar ...... De Paz-Arratia
       (When I used to sing beneath your balcony)
   (b) Muchachita Mía (My dear one) ...... Noveo-Tabueria
   José de Arratia
6. Bolero .... I. Albeniz
   NOTE: This is a dance of the 19th Century, which was a kind of a competition between dancers. Dancers usually rested from the inter seat at that time.
   Eduardo and Margarita Cansino

INTERMISSION

7. Alegrías .... Q. Valverde
   Eduardo and Margarita Cansino
8. Farruca (from the Spanish Opera The three cornered Hat) ...... De Falla
   Eduardo Cansino
9. Chiapanecas (Mexican Folk Dance) .... Arreamena
   Margarita Cansino
10. (a) Macniola .... D. Macmorrough
    (b) Serenade .... F. Kelin
    José de Arratia

11. Canto Gitano (Gypsy Dance) .... Popular
    Eduardo and Margarita Cansino

INTERMISSION

12. Playera .... Granados
    Salvador Sainz
13. Gitanaza .... Larrañaga
    Eduardo and Margarita Cansino
14. O Amore! (L'Amico Fritz) .... Mascagni
    José de Arratia
15. Granada .... Albeniz
    Margarita Cansino
    NOTE: A dance from Granada, the land of the classical "Mantilla."
16. Malagueñas .... Albeniz
    Eduardo Cansino
17. Arioso (Pagliacci) .... Leoncavallo
    José de Arratia
18. Jota .... Font-Ant
    Eduardo and Margarita Cansino
    NOTE: The costumes are exactly the ones that the "Baturros" (peasants) of Aragón (Province of Spain) wear.

This program is subject to change   Costumes by Señora Zurtuche and Mrs. Muller

As Margarita Cansino she assisted her father, Eduardo Cansino, in a dance concert at the Ratliff Auditorium in San Diego. Rita was just fourteen.

face, pretty costume and that pretty sweet smile, and her dancing was lovely. She had danced two or three numbers for them by the time Eduardo returned. They were impressed. She and her father opened there on Christmas Day, 1932.

'The Foreign Club was in the middle of Tijuana—a beautiful place, a little like Las Vegas today. There were other acts there too, but the Cansinos were the headliners. It wasn't a staggering salary, though good considering the Depression was on, and what was more it was steady work. They had a fast routine—about twenty-six different numbers that were modernised versions of old Spanish classical dances and also folk dances from every part of Spain including Moorish dances and the Sevilla. One number that was a big success was the peasant number with its little country steps, the sort they'd do in small Spanish towns, and it ended up with them mouth to mouth, like wood pigeons kissing. Another number that went down well in Mexico was the Mexican hat dance. Eduardo might do a Corrida, that's a matador number, and there would be heel work, a Farruca. He was brilliant at that. While his daughter would be posing in the background doing beautiful castanet work Eduardo was doing this

The Cansino children with their Uncle
Vernon on an outing to Ocean Park. (Vernon Cansino Collection)

Eduardo (Sonny) Jr., a friend, Vernon and Rita by the hotel pool in Caliente, 1934.

flashing heel work. The whole act took twenty-five minutes to half an hour.

'Between shows Eduardo locked his buxom daughter in the dressing room to keep her out of harm's way, as he saw it, while he and Volga spent their time and money gambling, an occupational hazard of those who work club dates.

'They were there almost a year and could have stayed longer except for Volga's temper. And again it wasn't really her business. Apparently the wife of the man who had hired Eduardo had asked her husband's mistress to give him up. The girl refused, and when, soon after, the wife died, she left the way open for her husband to marry his mistress in what couldn't have been more than a week after the funeral. It was something of a scandal, and Volga felt she had something to say about the way the first wife died to the new wife. Well, they were out of a job! So they came back to L.A. Eduardo was saying, "If only she'd kept her mouth shut. Even if you feel that it's wrong, you don't say those things to the people you're working for, not if you want to keep your job."'

Soon after their promising start, which had looked as if it would stretch out for some time, Eduardo moved the family down near the border to the little town of Chulavista, a suburb of San Diego, so they could be together. After finishing the last show of the day at one in the morning, they would drive home; Margarita was rarely ever in bed before two. There was a noon show for the lunchtime crowd, followed by rehearsals for the new routines or lessons from private tutors. Though the Mexicans had no laws governing the education or working conditions of minors, her parents did not want her to neglect her studies altogether. Then there'd be another performance at four and a break till the evening shows which were at eight and half past eleven. If her brothers or relatives were down for a visit, she might be allowed some time to play and swim in the hotel's pool, or sightsee and shop in the town. Otherwise she'd remain in the dressing room. It was, to say the least, a frustrating period for her and she recalls it with a shudder.

All these impressionable years, in the centre of a sophisticated world, she was no more than a window-shopper of the life she helped to entertain. The irony did not escape her, and it drove a wedge of bitterness between her and her father which never quite healed and which Eduardo failed to understand. If anything, he became stricter. Dorothy came down to visit them in the middle of one of their engagements, and shared Margarita's bedroom.

'She was now a very mature fifteen. Other girls would have boyfriends at thirteen or fifteen, but Rita couldn't. Down in Tijuana, men looked at her a lot because she was so attractive, and I'm sure she noticed that when she passed all the eyes were on her. But her parents wouldn't let any of them near. Any boy who wanted to take her out always had to go through her father. It was a discouraging process because Eduardo had to know who they were, who their parents were, everything about them before he let her go out with them. I tried talking to her, thinking to give her a chance to open up and confide in someone but Rita never said what she felt, not even at night. When we lay in bed and talked it was only about her work. She liked her work, loved dancing in the Club, with her pretty costumes. Naturally a young girl would—a beautiful girl in all those beautiful cotumes. It's only natural. But nothing about how she felt.'

The régime was relaxed a few times. There was a date with a boy of her own age. He was persistent and respectable, so Rita sent him to ask her father. Eduardo arranged the table for them in the club, even bought them a bottle of champagne, then hovered like an old duenna at the next table, never letting them out of his eye during the entire date. Finally, the boy gave up and went home. There were no more dates till she got married.

Eduardo's next engagement was four weeks aboard one of California's floating casinos, the gambling ships moored three miles off the Long Beach shore just outside the state's jurisdiction. The problem here was that they could never get ashore and often found themselves literally fishing for their supper. Casting for fish Eduardo ended up with the hook in his finger and had to take to his bed with an infection. For the next three weeks Rita tried to carry on alone, but without a partner to show her off, and with her own insecurity a handicap, she failed to draw a feverish response. 'The management didn't think I had enough Spanish allure,' she told me. 'I was only fifteen at the time, and the only thing that really aroused me was food.'

This engagement set back their fortunes, until they got a booking at Agua Caliente. The brochure promised: 'A Dreamland in Old Mexico eighteen miles below San Diego.' This job was also due to one of his students—the celebrated Rumba dancer, Grace Poggi. She was now a headliner at the club, and the girlfriend of film producer and newly elected head of Agua Caliente Jockey Club, Joseph M. Schenck. She brought her teacher to Schenck's attention.

In Old Mexico at Agua Caliente, Margarita Cansino is a guest of
Carl Laemmle, Jr. (center) and Hunt Stromberg (right). Eduardo
Cansino is at the far left of the picture.

Booked for four weeks, the act was such a smash that the
engagement lasted for seven months, and while there, Margarita
was spotted by Hollywood producers and casting directors. Although her screen debut is usually given as *Dante's Inferno*, she had
already appeared in a couple of films, including a quota quickie
made in 1934 (probably *Cruz Diable*). Margarita, with her Spanish
features (her parents had deliberately emphasised her Latin
appearance by dyeing her brown hair jet black, parting it in the
middle and fastening it in a bun at the back), was mistaken for a
Mexican, and singled out for extra work as a street dancer outside
a bullfighting arena.

There was other film work. 'They were shooting one of those
musicals with everybody in it and there was this number that
Dolores del Rio had with lots of horses and riders and people in a
saloon. My father and I were in the background; you can't even
see me, it was a day's extra work—God knows what it was
called.'*

The rumour, often printed as truth, that she was a Mexican

* The film was *In Caliente*.

originated there. Early fan articles, to create drama, would often
refer to her as the classic illustration of the kind of Hollywood
know-how that could transform just another dirty-faced Mexican
kid into an All-American Dream. Many of the Hollywood agents
and co-workers I interviewed are still convinced that that was the
case.

At first, this assumption came in useful as most of her early roles
in films like *Under The Pampas Moon, Human Cargo* or *Charlie Chan
In Egypt* capitalised on her Latin appearance. It was to have
climaxed with the starring role in one of Hollywood's first
three-colour Technicolor films, *Ramona*.

More important from Rita's outlook was her love for Mexico,
where she always felt at home. These few minor film parts were
enough to encourage Eduardo in his conviction that there was a
future for his daughter in movies, and while he was cautious and
refused requests for dates with her, he saw to it that she sat at
tables with cinema bigwigs like Sol Wurtzel, Carl Laemmle Jnr,
Hunt Stromberg, if always only for a respectable minimum of time.
This caution earned him the jeering nickname 'Mama Cansino'.
But his tantalising strictness worked.

Max Arno, then casting director at Warner Brothers, arranged
her first screen test. 'I first saw her around 1933. I was sitting on
the patio of the Agua Caliente having lunch because they always
had entertainment. There was a band playing and the act began
when this very young, beautiful girl came down the steps of a very
high staircase, moving to the music like some marvellous big cat.
A man was in back of her, both in Spanish attire, doing this very
stylish act. I did nothing about her then because she was still
immature, but about a year later we made a photographic test of
her at Warners, just a head close-up—turn this way, turn that,
smile, no dialogue. She didn't say much and we thought she
couldn't talk English. In the end we decided not to sign her
because of certain hair problems she had. I was one of those who
passed her up at the time and let Sheehan get her.'

Winfield Sheehan, a short, paunchy, blue-eyed Irishman was
the vice-president in charge of production of the Fox Film
Corporation, and an old friend of Joe Schenck. Like many of the
Hollywood in-crowd, Sheehan was in Caliente for the weekend.
He knew Eduardo from his Vaudeville days, and hearing of his
beautiful partner, he went to see the act. Ever since *42nd Street*
with its spectacularly opulent Berkeley lollipop numbers, followed
by the sensational success of the Astaire-Rogers team, musicals

were back in a big way. Sheehan thought Eduardo might be useful as a dance director, for Fox had several big musicals lined up. While Eduardo, though he had been happy performing again, felt the need for a more secure job with regular hours, which would allow him to re-open the school and move the family back to their home in L.A. What's more here was the opportunity to launch his daughter on the career in films he and Volga had been hoping for.

Sheehan had apparently no idea that Rita was Eduardo's daughter. Watching her dance, he thought that there could be some use for her in the studio's Spanish-language features. After the show, Eduardo joined him and introduced the surprised Sheehan to his daughter.

At the same table was the gossipy Louella Parsons (later to become one of Rita's staunchest supporters). In her autobiography *The Gay Illiterate*, Parsons wrote: 'When she came to our table she turned out to be painfully shy. She couldn't look at strangers when she spoke to them and her voice was so low it could hardly be heard. Hardly, it seemed to me, the material of which a great star could be made. Yet when we were returning to Hollywood the next day Sheehan told me: "I've signed her to a contract!"'

Parsons didn't encourage Sheehan, but he decided to go ahead, though he hadn't quite offered Rita a contract. What it amounted to was an expenses-paid trip to Hollywood for her and her father plus a small salary while she made some more screen tests. There were two tests—one for dialogue, to see how she could handle words; the other a photographic test. By rare good fortune, both were photographed by the already legendary European cameraman, Rudy Maté. His love affair with the Hayworth Image which would light up the screen at Columbia in the 'forties began here. Designed to show off her features—good and bad—the tests exceeded Sheehan's expectations. He offered her a short-term contract with options for renewal in six months at an increased salary if she agreed to a rigid star-grooming programme. There would be a daily diction and drama class with other starlets to improve her voice, mature her and give her poise. She gladly agreed. As she was still under age, Eduardo signed for her.

She celebrated her sixteenth birthday a few weeks before work began on the film. She was a long way from being one of the beauties of the world. There was still growing to do, baby fat to shed, hair to be removed and dyed—all that was still to come.

Shipboard scene from *Dante's Inferno* with dancers Rita Cansino and Gary Leon, 1935. (Fox)

None of what she would be in the future was yet visible, but she had tremendous potential.

On December 3rd, the studio began production on their inspirational epic of sin and last minute redemption. It starred Spencer Tracy and Claire Trevor and was entitled *Dante's Inferno*. The playwright, producer, author and screenwriter, S. N. Behrman's account of it is funnier than the film—but then, the film wasn't supposed to be funny.

'The major story premise was that, if you spent all your time reading *Dante's Inferno* no harm could come to you, that the future would be swathed in felicity. The scene is Coney Island. It is a father-and-son story. The son runs the carousel concession; the father sits home and reads Dante. The sorrow of his life is that he cannot get his son to share his pre-occupation. He pleads and pleads but the son just won't read it. He prefers to hang around his carousel. The father's worst fears are confirmed. At the climactic point the carousel goes up in flames. It is a holocaust. It is a real inferno done with great realism. But it has a salutary effect. When the disaster is over the son, chastened, begins reading Dante.'

Besides the carousel, the plot included a gambling yacht, like the one, though a lot larger—this, after all, was a Hollywood epic—on which Rita and her father worked. This floating den of iniquity had a spectacular floorshow with Rita and Gary Leon, which Eduardo, too old to be her screen partner, staged. For her week's work she was to be paid the quite enormous sum of $500. Because of an accident to her partner, their sequence took five weeks to complete. Since the deal for the film had been made before she signed her contract with the studio Rita was paid the full weekly rate. The critics for the film, previewed in August 1935, were unanimous, they roasted it with glee. Spencer Tracy referred to it as the worst mess he'd ever been in, but added about Rita's debut: 'Anybody who survived that deserved all the recognition that they got later on.'

It's hardly surprising that in a film that offered some sort of Dante, hell and holocausts, a couple of dancers would be lost in the reviews, but the *Hollywood Reporter* noted: 'The others are standard excepting a dance by Rita Cansino and Gary Leon which is splendid, although it slows up the finale.'

The music they danced to is a series of arrangements of Ernesto Lecuona's song 'Mario de la O'. At one memorable accidental moment as she whirls around the dance floor Rita's tightly wound-up hair breaks loose and floats in a dark mass around her. It is at this significantly fitting juncture that a drunken customer tosses a heating plate at a curtain and starts the fire that consumes the boat. (The finale was inspired by the *Morro Castle* fire disaster off the coast of Louisiana.) But viewed with eyes only for Rita, what there was to come was foreshadowed there. The sensation of freedom that Rita conveys when dancing, a release so uniquely hers, catches one, as it always will, with an emotional thrust for which nothing that goes before prepares one. It is the moment when a star transcends his/her limitations as an actor, to become part of a much greater mystery, unique to films. It is the quality she must have shown, however subdued, as her father's partner but that Sheehan sensed or saw that time in the club. And when, in later years it was understood and exploited in her movies, it set her apart from her generation to make her the symbol of it.

She may not have been a dedicated or a great dancer, yet as a dancer she was something infinitely more exciting than many great and dedicated dancers can ever hope to be—a primitive force in evening gown and high heels. When she danced she cut through the banalities of her plots with a dramatic gesture that has so often been absent in her scripts. Freed from the scenario, she stands revealed as a *force majeure*. Rita was a harbinger of a type the cinema would not come to terms with until the 'fifties when a more mature, less inhibited public attitude to sex combined with a decline in receipts at the box-office eased a relaxation in the strict censorship governing movies. When the new wave came, the parts they brought were played not by Rita Hayworth but by European stars like Anna Magnani, Sophia Loren and Jeanne Moreau.* But Rita had prepared the way.

Dante's Inferno was finished early in 1935 but the release was held up because Sol Wurtzel, head of the studio production felt that, 'You can't release *Dante's Inferno* in the summertime!' It went out in the autumn of that year.

---

*The Italian cinema, and Italian stars like Virna Lisi and Sophia Loren, not only acknowledge the impact of Hayworth's personality on their career, but have played parts that copy Rita's *Gilda* in a number of films, including *Better a Widow*, and *The Gangster's Moll*. In the latter, Marcello Mastroianni falls in love with Sophia Loren only because she looks and dresses like Hayworth. When he finds another girl who looks even more like Rita, he deserts Sophia for her.

CHAPTER II

THE IMAGE MAKERS

Does the eagle know what's in the pit,
Or wilt thou go and ask the mole?
Can wisdom be put in a silver rod
Or love in a golden bowl?

William Blake

The 'thirties saw the apex of the studios' power, and what they all sold, packaged with countless different labels, was always the dream. Everything was possible in America. When, on a rare occasion, life mirrored this celluloid fantasy, in the case of an unknown discovered sitting at a drugstore soda fountain or behind the wheel of a truck (as were Lana Turner and Rock Hudson) it was a publicity department dream come true. They wrapped the nugget of truth in these 'discoveries' in studio flack tinsel until, like the proverbial five loaves and two fishes, they managed to feed the illusions of millions with just a few stories. This myth served as the basis of *A Star Is Born*, one of the few good, if uninspired, movies Hollywood made about itself. It has been re-made three times so far, besides inspiring any number of ever more fantastic spin-offs.

It was one of the much-touted myths popular with the old czars and assiduously promoted by their college-educated publicity managers that the omnipotent studio was the star-maker. This half-baked fantasy arose out of a concerted effort by the big studios to prevent the stars from fully understanding, and what would be worse, wielding the power which their popularity with the public gave them. The classic cases put forward to hold up the studio as Pygmalion were such luminous Galateas as Ann Sheridan, Veronica Lake, Gary Cooper, Turner, and, inevitably, Rita Hayworth. Implicit in this self-praising boast lay the threat: the studios that had made you could easily break you, should you get out of hand. Numerous examples come to mind to illustrate the

One of the first batch of studio publicity photos of Rita Cansino by the studio's ace stills man Frank Powolny, 1935. (Fox)

often petty exercise of executive power. When sultry brunette songstress Dorothy Lamour grew restless in her sarong-wrapped image and wanted more dramatic roles she would find look-alikes carefully loitering along her way to the set or cast in small parts in the same film.* Similarly, at the peak of Betty Grable's popularity, there were never less than half a dozen blondes being groomed under her nose with the clear intention of filling her shoes should she shed them or walk out. Not surprisingly, such unsubtle tactics from the top often exerted a pernicious pressure on a highly emotional, susceptible, often immature personality. Some spirits were inevitably broken. A few hardy ones, like Veronica Lake, chucked in their careers and got out. Sad to say only a few of them realised that this myth, like all the others

*Patricia Morrison and Yvonne de Carlo were just two of these.

surrounding their business, was ballyhoo. Studio heads might be able to afford a whim and promote a personal favourite, but there was no way they could make the public pay to see them. If anybody had stumbled on the ingredients that made a person a star with the public, they would have tripped over the philosophers' stone on the way.

'A star is made by an audience not by a studio,' said the director Allan Dwan. A pioneer of the industry he still lives in Los Angeles where he has soldiered on for more than sixty years as one of the most respected craftsmen in his field. He's seen more than his share of hopefuls and was instrumental in helping some to make it. 'You see, when they put you in a film, word filters back from the exchanges and the theatres: "There's a pretty girl. She was good. Who is she? We'd like to have more of her." And the fans would write little postcards to the theatres, which they'd drop in the boxes they used to have standing in the lobby, and the managers would let the booking exchange know that they were getting a lot of cards about Rita Cansino. That's what the studio wants to know. Then they'd say to the directors on the lot preparing films, "Can you use her, 'cause she's catching on?" Then they'd start to work it out, but cautiously, 'cause you can't just stick some kid up on the screen as a star, she's not ready for that yet, she'd stumble if you did that. They'd give her some good roles she could handle to make the public ask for her. After all, it's all dependent on public acceptance. He's the fellow that buys the ticket.

'The big trick was to go into districts and create fan clubs. That's what the big public relations men we had were for, to go out and create the interest. Not just get the press to print a picture, but to have the ticket buyers themselves ask for her. The studio would give somebody in the neighbourhood a lot of stills and free tickets to one of their theatres for starting a fan club, and get them to go round to all their girlfriends and say, "Do you want to be a Rita Cansino fan? We're going round tonight to see her and we got ten tickets." Ten women go, and that's the fan club started. Then they get them to write a letter or postcard to the fan magazines and how they'd like to see more about their favourite. And then it sweeps. Once one city hears there's a fan club, another starts one, and pretty soon all over the United States and all over the world, there are fan clubs, communicating with the star herself. The Studios send out thousands of photographs of her, some of which she'd autograph, most of which they'd hire some secretary to stamp with her name, and these photographs would end up in somebody's room, pinned up on a wall. Pretty soon thousands of letters and postcards praising her and wanting to see her next film arrive, and a star is born. In the old days, stars moved into the people's homes, into their hearts. Movies were the only source of entertainment.

'A star was something that floated high in the heavens. Above the rest. When Rita Cansino walked into a café, reasonably dressed up, all eyes would follow her while Claire Trevor could walk in and nobody would follow her. Later on stars were taught to be conscious of their worth by their agents. When a star might say, "This role doesn't suit me," it's usually because he'd been told to say that. No actor in the world ever read a role and said, "This doesn't suit me." It might not be any good, but that's something else. If somebody came up to Ty Power and had said, "I want you to play this one-eyed pirate with a wooden leg," and he'd say, "Great, I'd love it," his agent would quickly tell him, "The hell you would! No beards on your face. And no wooden leg. That's not the part for you."

'A studio can help to project you, but the girl must put forth. There's lots of cases where they'd put a beautiful girl on the screen and she was just beautiful—nothing happened. Photographically she must deliver on film what the studio have been promising in their build-up. When the women in the audience write in after saying how they liked her best in the scene where she cries after her mother dies because it made them realise how they felt in a similar situation, then you know that the girl has a great sympathetic streak which can be developed in her next role. But if the audience isn't interested whether she's laughing or dying up there then there's nothing you can do to make them stars. Spending more on them wouldn't change anything, you'd simply be throwing good money after bad. You've got to have what Hayworth had. Whatever role she did, Rita was always sympathetic, so the women liked her. And she was so glamorous that all the men were crazy about her as well. It made sense that they would be that way in life as well. Her marriage to the Prince was the climax of most people's memory of her. Like Grace Kelly. That, to fans, is the ultimate. It fits in with all their illusions. Stars can't be messy, they have to have style and glamour in private as well.'

Studios could not create the star ingredient. But neither would they wilfully destroy a successful one. Humanitarian instincts invariably fall by the wayside when they conflict with material

ones; the image of a profession controlled by vindictive megalo-
maniacs who ruled and destroyed at the flick of an intercom switch
is just another convenient myth. There is no shortage of cases of
recorded feuds between star and studio. Who, at Warner Brothers,
ever liked Jack while they were working for him? Some like Bette
Davis went so far as to take her employer to court, but she
returned to work after she lost her case to become the studio's
biggest star. It was rare for a movie mogul's private feelings to
override his common sense and jeopardise the welfare of his
golden goose. The Jack Warners, the Harry Cohns and the Louis
B. Mayers had not only their own feelings to take into consideration, they had also to account to the hard-headed front
office, composed of financiers, bankers and stockholders who were
interested in profits not squabbles. If a star had draw, he or she
remained. Personal gripes that had festered over the years might
be settled when the star started to slide. But it would have made
no difference if the falling star had been the most popular guy on
the lot. If 'Good Old Joe' wasn't pulling his weight at the
box-office, he found himself out in the cold as fast as 'that bastard
Harry'.

Take away the studio system and no doubt there would have
been no Shirley Temple, no Gary Cooper, no Gable or Crawford
or Marlene Dietrich, nor, for that matter, even Garbo. These were
strictly movie stars. On the other hand, without stars, one could
argue that there would have been no Hollywood. A lot of its
glamour and world popularity was due to them. Stars were the
life-blood of the industry, the money in the vaults, the glinting
bait to hook the fish. In the spring of 1935 the fish swallowed all
the lure they could get. Half-way through the decade Hollywood
was riding the crest of the wave, but the rest of America was still
submerged in the high tide of the Depression. And this was the
year that Rita Cansino's film career began.

When she had become the reigning Love Goddess and her
image towered over her past, audiences who were not expected to
remember were led to conclude that, like some latter day Athena,
Rita had sprung fully formed from the head of a Zeus-like Harry
Cohn. The truth might be more prosaic but Rita's slow, hard road
to overnight success began then and is a classic case of what a
potential star was made of and how they grew.

Sheehan was behind Rita. Along with a batch of girls* then being

*Helen Wood, Astrid Alwyn and Mona Barrie.

Her first dramatic scene—with Warner Baxter in *Under the Pampas Moon*, 1935. (Fox)

The caption reads: 'Four great ballerinas in the making at Fox Film studio. From left to right: Barbara Blane, Rosina Lawrence, Frances Grant and Rita Cansino—all of them studying ballet work under the direction of Eduardo Cansino, prominent Spanish dancing master.' (Powolny/Fox)

The caption reads: 'Heredity or Reincarnation? Queen Nefertiti of Egypt has a modern counterpart in Rita Cansino, who plays the part of an Egyptian girl in *Charlie Chan in Egypt*. She happened to pause before a statue of Nefertiti which is used on the set, and the resemblance was nothing short of uncanny.' That's for sure! Once the retoucher got to work on her profile. (Powolny/Fox)

groomed, now forgotten, she was set to posing in tutus and swimsuits, wearing big picture hats and slinky dresses. Her name was shortened from Margarita to Rita, her age was played down, her Latin looks played up. *Dante's Inferno* was still shooting when Rita was put to work in the first film under her contract, another of the studio's expensive expendable efforts, *Under The Pampas Moon*, starring Warner Baxter. Shooting began on February 25th, 1935, and the completed film was previewed, reviewed and released by the end of May. As Carmen, a waitress in a tango dive, she had a small scene and made her entrance down a flight of stairs doing something they called a Zamba. The story, yet another variation on the adventures of O'Henry's happy, heart-breaking gaucho whom Baxter had first played six years earlier in *In Old Arizona*, was now set in the Argentine. This time round he was chasing after a French actress and his racehorse; the order of priorities was doubtful and along the way the film inadvertently insulted every minority one can think of. The critics had a picnic roasting it. For once, time has confirmed a first opinion. Everybody had an accent. Ketti Gallian's was French, the rest were supposedly Spanish but no two people had the same one, and Rita's low, soft-spoken delivery is the least dubious. She is beautifully groomed and photographed and the intense concentration she directs on Warner Baxter's problems lights up her little scene.

Whether in front of the cameras or not, Rita worked to improve herself, listening, watching and learning. She stored it all up, the good with the bad. On her first day, she was taught one of the cardinal rules for a beginner: not to be late, and she experienced the paralysing anxiety that faces many a newcomer.

Rita remembers: 'Oh God! I was fifteen years old. They told me to be there at nine o'clock—that was my call, but I didn't know what a make-up call meant. This was my first part in a film and I got there at nine o'clock. I wasn't made up and the whole set was ready and they were waiting for me, I was rushed into the make-up and they said, "Oh, you're late," I was so scared, "We'll have to make you up fast." Somebody came in and screamed, "Don't you know when I say nine o'clock you're supposed to be ready and made up!" So I got back on the set trembling and shaking. I apologised to Mr Baxter, I told him it was the first time I'd ever had a call and didn't know what it meant. He said, "Don't worry, just quieten down." And this other man, not the director but some assistant, came back in and started screaming. I was supposed to say about ten words and I couldn't get them out. I was so nervous. That was a terrible day. Mr Baxter kept saying, "Just relax. Don't let them bother you." He was nice; a real sweetie like a big mommie cat. We used to work long hours. An eighteen-hour day wasn't at all unusual. But I loved the work.'

From tenth billing in her second film she jumped to fourth in *Charlie Chan In Egypt*. It began shooting on April 8th, ready to be previewed on May 31st, and released in time for the school holidays. It was eighth in the popular Fox series built around the avuncular Oriental detective, created by Earl Derr Biggers, who went about solving the most improbable cases in the most unlikely places all the while spouting cryptic homilies that were more confusing than Confucian. Mr Biggers had written six books devoted to the slant-eyed sleuth but this trip to Egypt wasn't in them. The film was inspired by the popular interest in archaeological digs among the tombs of the Pharaohs. Rita played a red herring called Nayda, a slinking, native *amah* with three lines. The best was 'Yes,

Effendi' while the longest, 'Mistress will take medicine,' could
have been meant as a question but delivered without any sort of
vocal inflection it came out so cryptically that even Chan takes
another look at the speaker. 'Inconspicuous molehill sometimes
more important than conspicuous mountain,' as Chan would say a
little later.

The primary motive in casting Rita for her glorified walk-on
was to give her exposure and build up her confidence. The studio
was using the series for the time-honoured tradition of grooming
new contract players. If she or the film was bad, little notice
would be taken; meanwhile she could take advantage of the
studio's facilities to learn about grooming, acting and all the
things that would stand her in good stead later. Other stars who
had received their early breaks with Mr Chan included Jon Hall,
George Brent, Ray Milland and Cesar Romero. Several years
later, over at Columbia, she played a glamorous foil in that
studio's successful grooming series—the *Blondie* pictures.

Her diets and exercise were paying off. She lost weight and
began to look svelte. And, as she said: 'I developed a burning
ambition—as only a too-fat seventeen-year-old can burn—to
become a good actress. I got to know a few of the other girls Mr
Sheehan was also grooming and I felt each of them had advan-
tages I did not. This was an added incentive for me to work twice
as hard. I paid strict attention to the acting coach and to the
woman who trained me to project my voice. At home I'd lock
myself in the bathroom, stand in front of a mirror over the sink,
and practise for hours. I learned to correct flaws in my posture
and pose for pictures in the studio gallery for hours without
complaining. It didn't require my being a genius to realise Fox
was spending a great deal of time and money on my behalf and I
intended for them to get their money's worth!'

Fashion spreads featuring her began to appear in the fan
magazines. Then there were items in the columns. With the studio
behind her, a wider public was beginning to notice Rita and her
family began to detect a change in her. The time spent at the
studio, away from her father's close surveillance, began to prepare
her for the subsequent transfer of her dependence to other men.
She still didn't go out on dates her father didn't okay—but she
started to do other things for herself, and she had an independent
career that promised bigger things. As part of her diet regime, she
took up tennis and riding. She loved the former, and though she
developed a lifelong aversion to horses her ability to ride well

came in extremely useful in the Westerns she was to make. With Vernon she could let off steam from pressures she acquiesced to elsewhere and show off what she had learnt.

Vernon: 'She'd take me out to play tennis till she found out I could beat her and boy, she never played again, not with me. I guess she didn't like to get beat. That's not pride, that's an older sister! The same thing happened with swimming. She got swimming lessons in case she got a part in which she had to swim. She was taught properly and she was a real hard worker, so she looked very graceful in the water. I came along one day and she asked, "Do you want a race around the pool?" Very innocent. She'd had all these lessons but what she didn't know was that I had the strength of an ox. I beat her so badly and kicked water in her face so hard, she could hardly swim! She came out spluttering, "You're not swimming, you're just splashing! I don't consider that a race, you're not even swimming. How horrible you look in the water!" The very next week she said, "Vernon, would you like to come riding?" I'd never been on a horse in my life but I'd seen plenty of cowboy movies y'know and I thought Jack Holt was God. That guy could really ride a horse. She got me fixed up with a horse John Wayne couldn't have handled! She nearly got me killed y'know. And she says, "You're not so hot, are you?"'

With three films behind Rita, Sheehan decided she was ready for her first lead in a Jane Withers' comedy, *Paddy O'Day*. Shooting began on September 9th, by which time her other films had been seen. Withers, a popular spunky child star, played an Irish youngster who arrives from the old country with her dog, a prop put in ever since Laurette Taylor dragged him into *Peg O'My Heart*. She's kicked around by the immigration department and about to be deported when she escapes from detention. Paddy goes to the house where her mother cooked, only to find her mother died while Paddy was on her way to America. Pinky Tomlin, as the bookish nephew of the owners of the home, takes a liking to her and hides her. Later he falls in love with a Russian dancer called Tamara Petrovitch (Rita), who came over on the same boat and whose brother has a Russian café but no cash. With Tomlin's help the café becomes a popular night spot just as his spinsterish aunts are about to have Jane and Rita deported, only to discover that their nephew has married the dancer and adopted the orphan. After a big operetta type musical number with everybody dubbed it's all over.

Rita carries her role as the romantic lead with an assurance far belying her years or her experience. Today, when one sees these little known films in which her work is usually written off because of her hairline, one is continually surprised to discover that Rita's rapport with the camera was ever-present. Her vulnerability becomes an attractive modesty, her shyness a regal stillness; there is no sign of uncertainty or self-doubts and the camera converts her desire to please into provocative poise. There is no sign of the introverted girl people knew off the set. Of course a great deal of work was still to be done to help her project through her voice the qualities she had as a woman, but the seductive timbre was there as well. She never needed to punctuate her conversation with space for a breath for she spoke on breath—the effect was quite alluring.

Pinky Tomlin, Rita's first screen romance, had been a popular vocalist and composer who had just made it big with a song he'd written called 'The Object of my Affection'. At the crest of his popularity he freelanced around Hollywood and met Rita.

Tomlin: 'I always thought it's easier to get big than to stay big. She got to the top on her own. But it couldn't have been easy. When she began there was a beautiful Spanish actress around, Dolores del Rio, and the word I got was that they had ideas of making Rita another del Rio type, and that they were going to star her in a remake of a silent del Rio film *Ramona*.

'I wasn't impressed by what she did, there wasn't much for her to do and she didn't project like a hot potato, it was more of a "don't touch" remote quality. So I didn't feel there was any great ambition there. But her beauty was already there. She was exceptional even then. Her dark complexion brought out the whiteness of her teeth and her eyes had a sparkle and a snap to them which her coal black hair set off terrifically.

'As far as work was concerned she was always on time, always ready, always knew her lines and was certainly willing to work hard. I didn't realise how young she was at that time—because she was a very buxom lady. The studio cooked up this scheme to get Rita, the film and me some publicity by making up a romance between us. They fixed for us to be seen at various hot spots, and furnished us with a nice car and a chauffeur. Of course the first place we used to go to in those days was the Copa Grove. They knew me there pretty well and pretty soon they were playing a couple of my songs and taking pictures of us while we made this regal sort of entrance down four or five steps and across to our table. I recall this so vividly because she was so damn gorgeous

Rita and co-star Pinky Tomlin on the town in 1935.

and photographed like a million dollars. Well, I ordered whatever we drank at the time and when she asked for the same I thought nothing of it. The waiters came and brought a bottle of wine and then another and then an after-dinner drink and I figured since it was cooked up by the studio they knew what they were doing and if there was any responsibility to be placed, they'd be responsible.

'After that we went to the club Alabam and had a couple more drinks. Lo and behold, when we got up to leave Rita was bombed. We get in the car, she gets ill. In the meantime she's told me about her father and that he was very strict if she stayed out late. I found out that I was the first date she'd had without a chaperone. I got to thinking that if her father was a Spanish dancer he was probably a knife-thrower as well.

'Now I'm sure her folks knew that the studio had cooked this up for publicity but anyway we go by my apartment first—I lived over on Hayworth Avenue, would you believe—so she could wash her face and freshen up a bit. I followed the gentleman's code and didn't take advantage of the situation. By now she'd become very quiet. I took her down to the pool and she hung her feet over the side and splashed water on her face. We sat there for a while and talked. It was getting on for two in the morning. So we drove to a place near where she lived. She still wasn't in very good shape so we walked for about an hour and then when we got to her home she asks me to walk her up the steps. There were no lights on in the house—she took her shoes off and disappeared.

'We didn't have a scene together the next day but the day after when I walked in she rose. She didn't apologise but was more on the thankful side, thanking me for the lovely evening and more or less taking care of her because she didn't realise she'd had so much to drink. And I said, "Hell, did you never have anything to drink before?" "Nothing but wine," she said.

'After that she'd sort of confide in me and ask me for some advice about her future. She seemed to lean heavily on the idea that since I'd come from the middle west I had common sense. She had several different routes she could take as springboards for her future and she'd explained that she had had several propositions from producers, and that one in particular had indicated that if she'd do what he told her he would promote her accordingly. She asked me if I thought that was the right way to go.

' "Well," I told her, "frankly if I had your looks and your possibilities and your youth I don't think I'd agree to any kind of proposition or knuckle under any threat of that sort. You've got everything going for you to make it on your own. Besides you don't even know how serious the man who made the proposition is." In those days all the studios had schools in which they developed your potential and I told Rita she should concentrate on that. She thanked me for the advice and that was about all there was to it. We never had another date.

'I remember her crying a couple of times in a corner by herself because she was embarrassed by something she couldn't do or something that hadn't worked. I only figured that she was ambitious because of what she told me that one time, not by her actions. You felt that she was doing this because of her father and because they had a background of show business.'

Between the first preview of *Paddy O'Day* at the end of October and *Human Cargo*, her first film to be released under the new Twentieth Century Fox logo, three months had elapsed in which time three important events relating to her career would occur: first, she made a colour test for the lead in the studio's most important film for the coming year; secondly, she was to meet the man who would become her first husband; and, thirdly, the ailing Fox studios would merge with the small but successful Twentieth Century and as a result Darryl F. Zanuck would assume control of the studio, and Rita would be unemployed.

Human Cargo, directed by Allan Dwan, began shooting on February 10th, 1936. It had also been a Sheehan project and since Rita's part, though pivotal, was small, Zanuck left it alone.

'That's the one where I hide in the bathroom,' remembers Rita, and that's about all one ever remembers about it. It was a smuggling melodrama, the sort of story the newspapers love to sensationalise, with Rita killed off half-way through in a classical 'thirties manner as she's about to name the culprit. As Carmen, she got feature billing, had a brief dance and a highly emotional scene. It's an interesting sidelight that in her early career Rita, a genuine Latin type, was cast in Latin roles. It was more usual to find all-Americans like Barbara Stanwyck playing Cubans.*

Dwan had a knack for spotting potential in people long before they became stars. He had found Carole Lombard and Olive Borden and later Linda Darnell. 'Rita was one of those. People always wanted to do things with her, which isn't the same thing as doing things for her, but if she'd never made a movie and just gotten married to some nice Spanish boy she would still have had that quality. A lot of people don't recognise it, I know, but if you have it, and you're in the movies, it's fortunate.

'Zanuck didn't see it, but then he wasn't an artist—he was a businessman. He was a guy who got money from some source and sat at meetings and made decisions, but he didn't have to do what we had to do. It's a different point of view. They are thinking of the dollar while we are trying to develop something human.

'I saw her for the first time when she was still dancing with her father, and thought she was a very attractive little Mexican girl. The picture had something to do with smuggling aliens without passports into America. We needed such a person who was also a dancer.† I remembered her and then found she was already on our lot. She was very nervous, terribly emotional and when she

---

* Prior to Zanuck's arrival on the scene she had been scheduled for a prominent role in *A Message to Garcia*, as Barbara Stanwyck's younger sister. It was begun on November 18th, 1935, but for one reason or another she was not in the film when it was released in April 1936.

† There's a brief shot of Rita cascading down a flight of stairs on to the nightclub floor before the camera reverts to two bickering journalists (Brian Donlevy and Claire Trevor) at a ringside table.

The caption on this 20th Century-Fox still reads: 'Garden Beauty—Rita Cansino, Spanish-Irish contender for stardom, sets off her brunette beauty with a cornflower yellow mousseline frock ruffled in coral organdy, with a large picture hat to match. She has just announced she is giving up dancing in favor of straight dramatic roles.' (Frank Powolny, 1935)

1935: a family reunion soon after Eduardo's father, Antonio, had returned to visit his children and grandchildren in California. (Frank Powolny)

got frustrated battling with the dramatic expressions required in some of her scenes she'd be inclined to burst into tears. She'd fly apart and hide her face and cry and we'd have to coax her back and get her to do it again. But she'd do what you asked her as soon as she got over her self-consciousness. Acting wasn't her bag at the time and for that reason it was an effort as it is for anyone, unless it's a child. Rita wasn't a child but she didn't have much experience in life either and it was difficult for this girl to express herself except when dancing. That came automatically. Then she was a woman.

'She was very beautiful then, very regal. You can see it in the film stills they took of her—she could be anything, the Queen of Society or a tramp, or all the mysterious women in history. Whatever you like, it's all there. She looks as if she has the knowledge of everything when in fact she didn't know a damn thing. She was probably just an innocent little virgin, but on the screen she's always a woman. There was more depth in her, more emotion than you'd find in most of the others. This is an honest girl—the others were phoney. There aren't many like that, not then and today's girls are nothing like that. You had to fight through to get to a girl like Rita. That was her attraction, it was something worth fighting for. Today they lack mystery—Rita had it.

'The principal reason Rita made it? Well, first she had all that Latin temperament, terrific things pent up in her which she was controlling, and which is great, sort of like a volcano. It keeps everybody on their toes in case she might blow any minute, but it keeps you watching as well. Also, she was terrifically graceful so all her movements were good and that's very important for the camera.

'Rita could make it now if she were the same girl. Matter-of-fact girls like her are rare, most of them are imported from some place like Italy. And with her remarkable photogenic qualities she'd be great in any age. The whole thing about her is that she's international; she could pass for Spanish, Italian, Russian, the dark English girls—that's the Irish in her—she fits in anywhere. That's very unique. When I think of it now, one of the greatest assets at the outset was her lack of expression—that created a mystery. You'd tell a girl that in this scene she loved this guy, would die for him, but she wasn't to tell him or show it and yet she had to convey it to us for the sake of the story. Now an actress would ask me how the hell she was supposed to do that but

Rita, she'd have this plastic, placid expression on her face and she'd probably be thinking of a doll she used to own and loved dearly, and with that doll in her mind she'd look at the man and her eyes would have the quality you'd want but her face would show no emotion, and that's exactly what we wanted, and you'd ask her after what she was thinking of, and she'd have been thinking of her doll. Whereas if I'd said, "Look at that man with love," she'd probably say, "How do I look at a man with love. I'd like to hit him on the head with a hammer, he's an egotistical pig, this guy you hired to play this lover of mine." So she thinks of something else she loves. Much simpler that way.'

However the results were achieved her reviews, though not many, were good. *Variety* said: 'Rita Cansino, as a dancer who's mixed up with the gangsters, is a good-looking brunette and not bad on performance.' The *New York Herald* inferred that to miss the picture would be a negligible loss but they too commented favourably on her. She was clearly going to be an exploitable asset to the company.

Yet by the time the film went on release in July Rita was dropped from her contract and had started a period of freelancing. The reason for this did not lie in anything she had done wrong.

That Darryl F. Zanuck was to drop her is puzzling if one accepts his reputation as a star-spotter. But this is another of those carefully calculated myths. He also dropped Marilyn Monroe because he saw nothing in her and wasted such star potential as Loretta Young and Gene Tierney, while concentrating a great deal of time and money promoting Simone Simon, Bella Darvi, Juliette Greco, Genevieve Giles and the like. A more likely reason for Zanuck dropping Rita was his personal disagreement with his predecessor, and since Rita was Sheehan's protégée, this was his way of showing it.

Dwan thought: 'The only reason I can think of why she was dropped was because she wouldn't play the game. A lot of the big guys didn't like girls who wouldn't come to their parties and if a girl said "no" they could exercise their power by dropping her and getting somebody more congenial.'

When Rita signed with Fox, that company, once a studio giant whose claims to fame included the first publicity-made star, Theda Bara, had been ailing. Zanuck was brought in to save it.

Only thirty-three at the time, Darryl had been one of Hollywood's resident boy wonders, looked upon as one of the heirs of Irving Thalberg. He had been self-made with no relatives in a business where nepotism was taken for granted. After publishing a novel at sixteen he became a gag writer for Chaplin and Mack Sennett, progressed to scripts, and got his big break writing for a German shepherd who was one of Hollywood's most durable stars—Rin Tin Tin, the first of many stars, though the only canine, to save the ever-precarious fortunes of the Warner Brothers. In 1924 they were still not certain of survival and were beset by the usual internecine family problems. They proved the perfect set-up for an ambitious workhorse like Zanuck. He quickly became Jack Warner's protégé and close friend. By 1927 he had graduated from scriptwriter to head of production. During his tenure he had supervised the film that revolutionised an industry—*The Jazz Singer*, revitalised the gangster film cycle with *Little Caesar* and brought musicals back with *42nd Street*.

He left Warners after a private dispute, and co-founded his own company Twentieth Century, with Joe Schenck, over lunch three days later. Initially releasing their films through United Artists, which took a large share of the profits, he was soon on the lookout for his own distribution set-up and Fox, with one of the best distributing organisations in the world, was ideal. Although Fox was the older and richer of the two companies, Zanuck insisted that the name of the new combine would be Twentieth Century Fox. Now that he was all powerful he began to clear house.

Zanuck's biographer Mel Gussow wrote:

> Like an inspector general, he [Zanuck] immediately pitched temporary headquarters at the studio and began surveying the property and the properties. He called in all scripts, read them, rejected twelve out-of-hand, and cancelled six movies that had already begun production. On a Saturday he cancelled a picture that was supposed to begin on Monday. He fired people left and right—from producers to policemen to prop boys—and replaced them with his own people, writers, directors, and stars like Loretta Young.

Winfield Sheehan had been the last remnant of the William Fox days and was one of the first to go. He resigned, albeit with a golden handshake. While negotiations for the merger—which began in April 1935 but were not finalised until late autumn—were going on, Sheehan, who for understandable reasons was opposed to it, was still head of production, and went ahead with his plans to star Rita in the studio's first Technicolor feature.

As Ramona, the Spanish heroine of Helen Hunt Jackson's classic romance of early California, Rita was perfect casting. It was an ambitious project—Henry King was to direct and Gilbert Roland, with whom Rita did the colour tests, was to be her co-star. The importance Rita laid on this promised leap to stardom can be gauged from the fact that, forty years later, Rita felt she could still recite the lines of the script from memory.

As a major project, one that Sheehan had initiated, it was one of the first Zanuck cut down on. He saw Rita's tests and footage from her previous films and decided not to risk so important a film on a beginner. His decision hit her like a bolt from the blue; for a time she was inconsolable.

Rita: 'I did a lot of tests for it with Gilbert as Allesandro. We did whole scenes from the script. I was very nervous, I didn't know what was going on. I'd only had a few lines in some pictures at the time. "Yes, Mr Chan, No, Mr Chan"—that sort of thing. This might have been a great break for me, but maybe it's better the way it happened.' Clearly she does not think so, but it's all so long ago and she does not like to think about the past. Prodded, she continues, 'Gilbert was so sweet and so nice; they had all the costumes made for me; the sets were ready, then the whole scene changed. There was Mr Zanuck, and he didn't want me, he had somebody else for the role. Sol Wurtzel called me in one day and he said, "I have to tell you something, things have changed due to the merger and our policies have changed, so we'll have to postpone *Ramona* and when we do it Loretta Young is going to play it. Mr Zanuck has decided on that and he's head of the studio now and we're not."

'I cried and cried so hard. But that was it. I tried not to take it personally but I was very disappointed. When you're disappointed at sixteen, you're really disappointed. You don't get over it very fast.'

The next blow followed on the heels of the first when one of Zanuck's minions phoned to tell her there was no need to show up at the studio. Her contract had been terminated. Before, she had wept. Now she got fighting mad—it was the best thing that could have happened. All through her adult life whenever Rita has had enough, she moves. It's usually dramatic, invariably surprising, and not always as beneficial as this occasion proved to be.

Rita: 'Zanuck just didn't have the time, or so he later said, to

meet me face to face and tell me his decision. I vowed I would
show those people they'd made a terrible mistake. I *would* become
famous and successful in films without them and they would be
sorry.'

Four years later Zanuck had good opportunity to mull over his
mistake when he had to borrow Rita from Columbia for the plum
role of Donna Sol for his lavish Technicolor production—*Blood and
Sand*. Not only did he have no one under contract who could play
the Spanish siren, but he had to pay five times her current salary
to get her, and even more grating, to watch as the role catapulted
Rita to the top—and the benefits go not to Zanuck but to a rival.

In her home things were better. Eduardo, who did the occasional
film job as assistant choreographer or dance instructor and
appeared with other members of the dancing Cansinos for a
sequence in the 1936 film *The Dancing Pirate*, had gone back to
teaching, at Ernest Belcher's ballet school. Taking his own classes
for a percentage of their fees as his salary, he stayed there until the
war broke out. With the enthusiastic dance revival that had come
through the success of the Astaire-Rogers musicals, there was once
again no shortage of students who could pay. On top of that Rita's
small but steady salary had come in handy. A sizeable percentage
of it was spent on her; more would be needed now that she no
longer had a studio to provide the lessons and create publicity, but
there was still enough left for the Padre to rejoin the family before
the Spanish Civil War broke out. It was the first time that the old
man had seen his American grandchildren since they were babies.
He spoke no English. They understood hardly any Spanish but a
strong bond sprang up between him and his 'little Margarita'. He
adored her in the way grandparents do. He was proud of her
appearance, of her ambition and hard work, and she adored him
in the uninhibited emotional way she never could her father.

Zanuck was the first strong man in Rita's life who failed to spot
her potential, but there was another nearby who saw it. Edward
C. Judson, a middle-aged, seemingly wealthy man-about-town
was acting as a front man for a Texas oil promoter who was
looking for financial backers. As a result of this he came to
Sheehan's attention. He had an appointment to see Sheehan on
business the day they were screening the tests for *Ramona*. The
shrewd promoter was sufficiently excited by what he saw of Rita
to ask Sheehan for an introduction. When they met sometime

after, he made a strong impression on her. He was successful, suave, sophisticated, courteous and almost forty—old enough to be her father, *but* not her father. And he would believe in her at a time when she most needed it. People have fallen in love for less. Discreetly Judson asked her father for permission to escort his daughter.

Perhaps Eduardo sensed a kindred soul at first—here was a man apparently with contacts in the film world who wanted to help his daughter's career—at any rate he agreed. Only Volga disliked him from the start. Just as Rita's private life had taken a decisive new direction so her career now took on a renewed lease of life with Judson as the guiding force. Rita still lived at home but now she had an official escort who knew his way about, had contacts with some of the right people, and took obvious pleasure in squiring her around town. It was the first step in a gruelling schedule to make Hollywood sit up and take note of her—for neither then nor later was Rita an extrovert. Judson advised her on what clothes to wear and the best places to be seen. He had been a successful car salesman, and a shrewd—some said shady—promoter of other people's goods. With Rita's burgeoning eagerness to get ahead, her acquiescence to suggestions for promoting her at this period—and at eighteen, with her broad shoulders, the graceful bearing that made her appear older and more sophisticated, and the ever more striking beauty as diet and nature helped her to shed the last of her baby fat—it was merely a matter of time before they would succeed.

Less than two months after Zanuck dropped her she began to freelance. Of greater significance was another calculated step that would eventually take her out of being a Latin typecast. She undertook the expensive, painful and long course of electrolysis to widen her brow and dramatically emphasise her features. Much has been made of Rita's early hairline, most of it exaggerated to read dramatically. In fact, the change, though spectacular, was subtle. Depending on whom you hear everybody seems to have had a hand at advising Rita that the way to improve her chances was to change a thick Spanish head of hair for a lighter, flowing style. Perhaps because the legend sounds better, or because most people had begun to believe the stories themselves, if there were no early photographs around of Rita, one would be left with the image of a pretty Neanderthal whose hair grew down her forehead until it reached her nose. All agreed that it was thick and there was too much of it.

Hair with women is like a mane to a horse; it catches the wind, it is their crowning glory and though in itself non-sexual it figures prominently in man's erotic fantasies. Even the plainest woman will spend more time, care and money on her hair than on any other single feature. Though Rita's hair became justly famous and launched numerous styles after each film, it was in truth only one complimentary aspect of her appeal, deriving its erotic potency less from the cut, colour or electrolysis, and more from the excitement Rita generated within, which acted on the public's imagination like an electrical conductor. In this context her hair, like her hands and mouth, was a prominent asset. But, unlike Veronica Lake's peek-a-boo bob, Dorothy Lamour's long tresses or Jean Harlow's platinum blonde fleece, Rita was not identified with a particular look at the outset. Her most famous style, the one which typifies her 'forties look, was created by Helen Hunt for *Gilda*—and that was not until 1946, well after she had been established as the nation's Love Goddess. Throughout her early 'forties films her hair would be swept up in one film and let loose in another.

The long drawn out process began when Rita joined Columbia in February '37, where the studio's hair stylist, Helen Hunt, played a major part in the Americanisation of Rita. She wrote about it in a letter on December 10th, 1974:

When Rita first came to the studio she had black hair and her hairline was very low. Her first picture, *Criminals of the Air*, was filmed mostly across the street from Columbia, which is now a parking lot. She was there under contract with about five other girls with the idea of coaching them for stardom. Rita was going out with Eddie Judson who lived on a small allowance an oilman friend gave him for some past favour. Eddie was a car salesman before, in Tennessee, I believe. Good-looking and intelligent. He realised Rita's potential so he started on a publicity campaign for her. He is the one who asked me to find a good electrolysist and start the treatments—which I did. Eddie paid ten dollars each for about one year. This was slow work. Eddie went to the top jewellery shops and borrowed jewellery for Rita, and even evening gowns—he took her to the finest restaurants—saw that she was seated in a good view. All this time she was unnoticed by Columbia and I was dressing her hair—still black. Finally the New York office called Harry Cohn and said you have a beauty with loads of publicity—why don't you capitalise? Harry Cohn then gave her some tests. The cameraman said that her hairline was still too low and too black—so I suggested putting a bleached streak across her forehead. We tested, it was a success. This was for the picture with Jean Arthur and Cary Grant [*Only Angels Have Wings*, 1939]. Jean was asked to pose with Rita in some stills and she refused, saying, 'She's too pretty for me to stand with her.' The streak across the front of her hair was copied by many. My daughter was a student at U.C.L.A. at the time—her girlfriends were begging me to give them the streak. One day I talked to Harry Cohn about making Rita's hair red so we could do away with the streak. When she was in a picture I always shampooed her hair every morning and brushed it completely dry and very little pincurls were necessary to give the luscious flow of shiny hair. At this point I told Harry Cohn about what Eddie Judson had paid out of his small funds on Rita's electrolysis and asked that the studio take it over. He agreed and I started in again. I worked with the electrolysist, drawing lines on a still picture showing the line we wanted. Now the treatments were fifteen dollars each but never more. This lasted another year until the work was finished. Achieving a new design for Rita's forehead entailed a long and very painful process. Each hair had to be removed individually, then the follicle deadened with a charge of electricity.

Rita was acutely sensitive to pain, but her determination to succeed was stronger. As Vernon said, 'It must have hurt her like hell but she never moaned about it.' She underwent the prolonged ordeal between films, until by 1940 she emerged with her graceful brow. To Rita the talk about her hair is irrelevant—a look of 'Oh, God' is the best she'll give to the subject nowadays. When she was not working on another film, on lessons to broaden her range as an actress, on her hair or on her wardrobe, she and Judson went out to Ciro's and the Trocadero—the glamorous Hollywood night spots where stars went to see and be seen.

Later to become music director at Columbia, long before he worked with Rita or they became friends, Fred Karger noticed her: 'She had a tremendous magic back then. She used to come into a club with Judson where I was working with an orchestra—that was around '39. I had never seen anything so beautiful in person and you've got to remember the town was full of beautiful women. She had a tremendous magnetism about her, walking into

Trouble in Texas with Tex Ritter and stuntman Yakima Canutt.
(Republic)

a room, an aura really. Lana Turner was gloriously beautiful, too,
but she didn't have that magic. Rita made you stop what you were
doing and take a deep breath.'

It was partly due to Judson's manipulations that Rita secured a
small part in her first film after leaving Fox which turned out to be
at Columbia, *Meet Nero Wolfe*. The plan was to make this the first
of a series based on the popular detective created by Rex Stout,
but since Edward Arnold, who played his hero, was not under
contract and not available for more, the idea lapsed. Of its kind it
had superior production values and was critically well received.
Rita's role was minor and Harry Cohn was unimpressed.*

There was no shortage of other parts now as Rita freelanced all
over town with Judson acting as agent. She had the feminine leads
in a succession of modest westerns shot on a shoestring; none of
them took more than a couple of weeks to make. Rita's pay
averaged $200 a film. There was *Hit the Saddle* starring The Three
Mesquiteers for Republic; two others, starring a popular cowboy
star Tom Keene, were released by Nat Levene, an independent
distributor who bought his second hand car from Judson; and

*The film has another interest to film historians. Its leading lady Joan Perry, a model
who had been brought out from New York, retired from the screen soon after to marry the
studio's boss. It's the only time the two most important women in Cohn's life, his future
wife and his future star worked together.

another western, *Trouble in Texas* starring the singing cowboy Tex Ritter, was made for Grand National. Usually cast as a Latin, Rita had to ride a horse, but they provided experience and more important, exposure. When anybody in the trade press bothered to review them, they took note of Rita Cansino. She was several notches above the run of leading ladies in similar oaters and it was always mentioned.

While any agent could have done the same for her, what Judson did was to broaden her outlook. The columnists reported seeing them at the fights, the tennis matches, the smart clubs; he took her to concerts, to art exhibitions, to museums. For Rita the age difference did not seem to matter. She badly needed confidence in herself, and a guiding hand that was sensible of her emotions and feelings, a man thoughtful of her whims, yet also able to instil a sense of authority in her. And there was no other man in her life—no boys her own age had a chance to compete for her. She had no previous experience by which to judge.

On one of his business trips to New York, as Rita drove him to the station, he asked her to marry him. They had been going out now for over a year and Rita said yes. When she told her parents it hit them like a blow. Her father was furious, her mother in tears, but Rita's mind was made up. She felt, with good cause, that Judson had her interests at heart, had helped her career, loved her for herself and was just what she needed. And something more—while she would never have said it—here was the longed for chance to leave the nest. Judson offered a means of escape, a key to freedom. The marriage created a rift with her parents that hurt her as much as them but if in most other respects Rita was ready to bend over backwards to comply and so to avoid unpleasantness, when it touched on her private emotions, she listened to no one.

Vernon: 'My mother could never take that marriage. Judson was as old as my father and Mom could not stand him. It seemed to me that he used to come over to the house just to torment Mom because he knew she didn't like him. She even slapped him on several occasions in my presence. It made for a very bad relationship while Rita was married. After Rita left him things eased up. 'Course Rita was in love with him and when she was married to him she had to take his side. But that's Rita, she's very loyal. Once she makes a decision she really sticks it out, no matter what the guy's like or what people say.'

Things did not improve. Indeed, a friend told me the relation-

Rita Hayworth and husband Ed Judson at Ciro's (1941).

ship between Rita's husband and her family deteriorated even further with his demand to them of a complete accounting of all of Rita's past earnings from the time she signed with Fox to the time she left home, or else he would take legal action. It took them months to go through all their old records to sort out what her share of the earnings were and how much of them had been spent on her behalf etc. They paid back every cent. Because of her family's attitude it could not be a church wedding. On his return from New York on May 29th, and after finishing her day's work at Columbia where she was now under contract, she drove by his house, sounded her horn, and when he came up to the car said,

'This is the day.' They were married that night in Las Vegas. She was eighteen, he was forty.

While it would be naïve to imagine Rita failed to appreciate what Judson's efforts were doing for her career, nothing in any of her relationships with the men in her life ever leads one to assume that she married them because of what they could do for her career. On the contrary. If any of her husbands used her in a film it was due to the strength of her name and not theirs. Had she been calculating enough to accept the proposals that were pressed on her by some of the richest and most powerful men, not only in Hollywood, but in the world, she would be a much richer woman than she is. She married Judson because she responded to his attentions with love. The reasoning of her heart sometimes seems the great weakness in her life but in it is undoubtedly a large part of her vulnerability and enormous appeal on the screen as well. Rita gave, and perhaps only the public ever truly appreciated what she had to offer.

The Judsons' first home, a small house in Brentwood, was bare of most things—like food and furniture, except for a picture in a beautiful frame of Rita in a wedding dress, taken for an ad for 'Community Silver', the only sign in her life that she might have longed for a good old-fashioned Catholic wedding with all the trimmings.* For the first year they simply kept an electric train set on the bare living room floor to play with when Rita was bored and because they had no furniture for it anyway. The money she had went on her grooming, her clothing and publicity—the fuel that set everything in motion. Certainly her salary would not have been enough to pay for all—at one point Rita was taking diction and voice lessons four times a week and dramatic lessons five times a week, at ten dollars a lesson. After her new contract, they stepped up the process and Judson hired one of the best press agents, at seventy-five dollars a week. They invested heavily in clothes bought at top Hollywood couturiers, like the exclusive and stylish Howard Greer. The point was to make the people who mattered notice. They went to all the right clubs where photographers were sure to be, and the photographers invariably began to take her picture because in her exclusive dresses, that averaged $350 each but proved their worth in free publicity, she was usually the smartest young woman in the room. By 1940 there had been more than 3,800 stories filed on her and her photograph had been reproduced over 12,000 times.

*Reference to Ruth Waterbury's interview with author.

It was only after the wedding that Rita discovered her bridegroom had been married twice before, and that a good deal of his
sophisticated taste in food and clothing came from his second
marriage to Hazel Forbes, who had been a cultured Follies
beauty. Any hint of uneasiness on her part was smoothed over by
her husband's plans for her career, their future together, the home
they would have, and by the fact that it was he who had arranged
for the seven-year contract, starting at a salary of $200 a week,
that she had just signed with Columbia Pictures.

CHAPTER III

ENTER COHN!

Q: What does it feel like being the president of a studio
for twenty-five years?
A: It's better than being a pimp.

Harry Cohn, 1957

The first time that Harry Cohn saw Rita, she had a minor role in one of his company's features, and he didn't even notice her. The next time she came to his attention, she was Edward Judson's wife, and Cohn signed her to a studio contract that was to last for twenty years. At the end, she shook off the studio's claims on her life and never looked back. Nor did she see Cohn again. After all that had gone before, it was a surprisingly quiet conclusion to a professional relationship that, for better or worse, had infiltrated every aspect of her life: the public and the private.

And yet . . . and yet. . . . There are those once close to both who were certain that Harry had proposed to Rita, had wanted her enough to make her his wife and was even willing to help her obtain her divorce from Judson. Certainly his involvement in her life went beyond what even the head of a studio would normally allow himself in order to protect his investment. Rarely has Rita said anything to shed light on the more personal side of her relationship with Cohn. Then recently during a public question and answer session at the San Francisco Film Festival, Rita unexpectedly, albeit discreetly, opened up: 'I signed a contract with Harry Cohn when I was about eighteen and I went on suspension so many times I can't really remember them all. And although I can't prove it, I think Harry had all the dressing rooms bugged so he always knew what was going on. And even while I was his biggest box-office star I still had to punch a time clock! But you want to know something about him? I think if he could ever have been in love with anyone, he was secretly in love with me.'

Columbia's Boss in a rare studio portrait taken in the '30s by A. L. 'Whitey' Schafer.

One has to know something about Harry Cohn to get an insight into the life of Rita Hayworth. Bob Thomas gave a lucid and colourful account of the man's rise to all-powerful movie mogul:

> The immigrant hordes that packed into Manhattan's East Side during the closing decades of the nineteenth century produced millionaires on both sides of the law; hoodlum empires and industrial fortunes were spawned amid the tumult of the city streets. Harry Cohn, born in New York City on July 23rd, 1891, chose to operate in a legal manner. Although in later years he enjoyed entertaining Frank Costello and other mobsters in his New York hotel suite and often hinted darkly of underworld connections, Cohn was impeccable in his business dealings. His income tax return was a model of rectitude. His stewardship of Columbia Pictures Corporation, of which he was founder, largest stockholder, and chief officer, was thoroughly honest. When disgruntled stockbrokers charged mismanagement in a lawsuit, Cohn satisfactorily answered each of the accusations.
>
> Cohn adopted the speech and mannerisms of a gangster, but he did not operate like one, since he could not face the possibility of being caught. He was the son of immigrant parents who believed in unceasing toil and scrupulous honesty. If a Cohn son swerved from that code, he was thrashed severely by his father or mother, or both.
>
> He made his professional debut as half of the singing team, Edwards and Ruby, in 1912 but when that tumbled he became a trolley bus conductor before going back to music as a song plugger in Tin Pan Alley.
>
> The life called for energy, resourcefulness, and nerve; Harry Cohn possessed all three. His day began when he reported in the morning to his employers. Along with a score of other pluggers, he learned which songs were being pushed by the company; they might have been *I hear the voice of Belgium, Becky to the Bombay*, or other tunes by one of the prolific partners of the firm, Irving Berlin.
>
> Through his older brother Jack, already in the film business working at Universal, they sold the studio's founder, Carl Laemmle on undertaking a series of song shorts employing Universal stars. These proved a success, and 'Uncle' Carl was impressed by the energy and resourcefulness of the younger Cohn brother. In 1918 the astute Laemmle hired Harry to be his secretary at the

studio in Universal City. He left a few years later to join his
brother and form their own releasing company, C.B.C. Film Sales
Co. in New York. By 1920 he was back in Hollywood as a fully
fledged partner for a producing company—even if it was in
Poverty Row.

By the time Harry Cohn arrived, the procedure of a Poverty
Row producer had already been ritualised. The foremost consideration was the money needed to begin the enterprise. He
found his banker and at once started producing.

One had to be tough to survive in a cut-throat business where
nobody gave an inch unless it was to a relative. He learnt fast—at
first it was just him and Jack but by the mid-'thirties the humo-
urist Robert Benchley could joke that Columbia was like a pine
forest, 'Because there are so many Cohns in it!' From two reelers
Harry graduated to features and fashioned his first feature film,
More To Be Pitied Than Scorned in 1922. It was produced for
$20,000 and made over $130,000 in sales. The studio's growth was
rapid.

On January 10th, 1924, C.B.C.—known in the trade as Corned
Beef and Cabbage—officially became Columbia Pictures. By
1926, Columbia had become the pride of Poverty Row. Expansion
was needed if the small company was to compete with the
unlimited resources of the major studios. The partners agreed that
Columbia should offer shares to the public on the stock market.
Harry Cohn insisted on the purchase of a studio. Round the
corner on Gower Street was a small plot that included two stages,
and a small office building, and this, when bought from its heavily
mortgaged owner, began the establishment of Columbia as a
respected part of film future.

Born in the heart of Poverty Row, Columbia never moved. It
resisted the impulse to transfer to more spacious quarters in
outlying areas, as had bigger studios. Instead, it merely swallowed
up Poverty Row, parcel by parcel, until it occupied most of the
long block between Sunset Boulevard and Fountain Avenue and
between Gower Street and Beachwood Drive. The area was small
by major studio standards, but it was crammed with sound stages,
offices and shops. In 1935, because the studio prospered and
exteriors were needed, Columbia bought the first forty acres of an
eventual eighty-acre ranch for outdoor sets in nearby Burbank.

Harry also defined his own image in that image-conscious
profession, characteristically finding his inspiration in one of the
biggest bullies of the decade—none other than Il Duce, Benito

Mussolini. In 1933 Columbia had released a documentary feature called *Mussolini Speaks*. It had cost $10,000, but at a time when America was still impressed by a man who could make the trains run on time, it grossed a million. Il Duce was pleased with the publicity and offered to decorate the president of Columbia Pictures. Cohn travelled to Rome for the ceremony and while Mussolini's ideology may have gone over his head, the dictator's style impressed him profoundly. Back in Hollywood he spoke awesomely of the legendary Mussolini office chamber, with its vast length and the platform on which the dictator sat. Bob Thomas quotes Cohn: 'By the time I arrived at his desk, I was whipped.' What was good enough for Italy was good enough for Columbia. He set about creating a structure modelled on it.

'The outer office was occupied by a receptionist, who admitted visitors to the inner office, where the head secretary and an assistant or two were located. It was here that visitors waited for admittance to the Cohn chamber. The length of the wait was judiciously calculated by Cohn. A writer, director, producer, or actor in disfavour might be detained for two or three hours. One who was being wooed by Cohn was admitted immediately,' writes Thomas. In later years, Glenn Ford noted discoloration of the doorjamb at mid-level; it had been soiled by the sweat from innumerable palms of those who had passed through to an audience with Harry Cohn. In keeping with the Mussolini tradition, the Cohn office was massive and elongated, with the desk at the far end. The visitor marched down the thick carpet to the huge semi-circular desk, slightly raised above floor level. Cohn remained in the shadows while the visitor was clearly lighted. Behind Cohn rose the gleaming symbols of his achievements: the Academy Awards, eventually numbering fifty-two, won by Columbia films.

Cohn treated most of his producers with contempt. Directors—the better ones—received more consideration. He permitted the best of them to work without interference, if they so demanded; his attitude towards mediocre directors could be indifferent or brutal. Actors whose fame had been achieved at Columbia were considered possessions by Cohn.

A studio's style did not develop overnight, nor did it come by chance. Columbia's style was born in the 1920s, and it grew to a large degree out of necessity. But style must also be nurtured and directed, and that was done at Columbia by the man who guided its every move.

With each of the major studios developing as specialists in a certain genre of film, Columbia's features seemed to be peopled by beauties in long gowns and handsome men in dinner jackets. They thrust themselves into outrageous situations, always maintaining their *savoir faire*. Columbia became the home of the sophisticated film, an astounding surprise for the many people in Hollywood who considered Harry Cohn the complete vulgarian.

From the start, lacking a Clara Bow or a John Gilbert, Columbia relied on cast-offs from the big studios: stars who had been let go because their box-office appeal had seemingly been drained. With the passé stars, Cohn combined newcomers, often borrowed at a bargain from major studios. 'We get 'em on the way up and the way down,' he said.

By 1937 he still had made no stars, though several of the best writers and directors in Hollywood were working for his company. His films made money, collected Oscars and belong to the classics of the era. Most of these were the work of Frank Capra. More than anyone, it was Capra's arrival at Columbia in 1928 that marked the beginning of Cohn's ascent to first rank status. Their partnership lasted over a decade and when they split, it had brought both enormous fame and prosperity. Capra's films—beginning with the five he made with Barbara Stanwyck establishing her as one of the great stars of the 'thirties; his homespun philosophical comedies starring Jean Arthur, and of course, *It Happened One Night*—were artistic and box-office triumphs. The last not only saved the ailing careers of Claudette Colbert and Clark Gable and won Oscars for both of them, for the film, for Capra and the screen writer, but also made a fortune that secured the studio's position and set the screwball genre on its whacky way. It was on the strength of such blockbusters that Cohn was able to sell the rest of his annual output.

The only thing Cohn lacked in that star-conscious age to rank him with the majors was a star his studio could claim to have created and developed. He had tried but till now, whenever a big star was needed for one of his 'A' products, they would be on loan-out from other companies. It rankled with him that it was common knowledge that for them these loan-outs to Columbia were usually considered punishments by their own companies. To add salt to the wound, since he had no star to offer in exchange, he had to pay vast sums to get them. The queen of the Columbia lot in the 'thirties was Jean Arthur whose screen career revived with a bang after she starred in Columbia's John Ford comedy *The Whole*

Town's Talking. She was unquestionably one of the legendary box-office stars of that era with her smoky voice, wry look and whimsical humour, equally suitable for romantic and comedy roles. She had come to Cohn, after establishing herself as a great success on Broadway which placed her in a position to dictate her terms. These included not only director and script approval and the freedom to make films of her own choice for other companies but, what was more, the fees for these loan-outs would go, not to Columbia, but to her. Having initially agreed on these points, Harry Cohn grew to resent them. Eventually the situation between them deteriorated into a state of constant litigation. Jean Arthur feared and loathed him.

Physically Cohn presented a compelling figure to the opposite sex. He was brawny but possessed a lightfootedness that made him a dream to dance with. He was fastidiously clean and well-groomed, sporting the snappiest new styles from Broadway haberdashers. He had large, classic features, dominated by large, intensely blue eyes. Most women would have found him attractive, but he failed singularly to charm either of his biggest female stars, Jean and Rita.

Coincidentally these two worked together only once though they hardly spoke unless called for in the script. But this arose out of shyness and not some spurious feeling of resentment Jean Arthur might be thought to have felt on seeing a younger woman taking the spotlight and most of the publicity. For, if such a thing was possible, Jean was even more introverted than Rita, and it was due to her well-known avoidance of the limelight that the studio's hard-put publicity director Lou Smith first turned to Rita in an effort to gain the newspaper space the studio lost because of difficulty in capitalising on Jean Arthur. The parallels between Cohn's stars and their similar attitude to their employer merits discussion at some length. On both of them his bullying tactics had the reverse effect and instead of giving him either the fight or affection he could have understood or needed, he only succeeded in driving them further into their shells. His coarseness frightened them at first, then revolted them. Rita might be in his office on business but Cohn would think nothing of relieving himself in his private toilet with the door open. When he talked the air turned blue. While Arthur could refuse to deal with him directly, Rita would not be in that position for many years, but her dislike of the man had begun early.

The two women were alike in other ways. Like Rita, though ten

1939: studio fashion art shows Rita in a wedding dress. (A. L. 'Whitey' Schafer/Columbia)

years earlier, Jean began her film career with Fox, was dropped soon after and survived in freelance westerns. Originally a brunette, the decisive change in her career came after she dyed her hair and became a blonde, while Rita's career took off after she became a redhead. Both women were pathologically averse to publicity. At the outset of their respective careers the two women complied with the publicity gimmicks demanded by the studio publicity department to keep a star's name before the public. They attended premières, were photographed posing in bathing suits, bridal gowns, on car bonnets, out in fields of clover or the middle of a stream with skirts pulled coyly over their knees. They were made up as bunnies for Easter, posed with turkeys for Thanksgiving, astride rockets for 4th of July stills and made up as unlikely Santas for the Christmas layouts. It was all part of the job.

But it was the giving of interviews that was possibly the most painful public occasion for either. As soon as they had the power to do so, they would do their best to avoid them. Arthur refused them altogether. Naturally this sort of behaviour only brought resentment from within the industry. It was one thing for Garbo to refuse to meet the press and pose for cheesecake—she was foreign, and such behaviour had long since been integrated and accepted as part of her enigma. But this, coming from two apple-pie American types, was another matter. Invariably the two women headed the annual lists drawn up by the Hollywood Press Corps of the most un-cooperative stars.

These then were Cohn's greatest stars. When, many years later, he placed the studio's machinery behind another newcomer, Kim Novak, his and the studio's last star proved to be a personality much as her predecessors, shy, withdrawn and not overly fond of the man who found her.

Harry Cohn had another idol he emulated, M.G.M.'s boss, Louis B. Mayer. Like Mayer, he too enjoyed a long shot, to which many of his studio's projects testify, and which may have influenced his initial signing of Rita. Apparently it was Judson who convinced him that Rita would be a good investment. Her previous experience was certainly sound enough to make her a safe bet for the string of 'B' features produced by one of the minor units on the lot, run by Irving Briskin. For more than a decade Briskin had pushed out 'B' films whose only real claim to fame was their speed and the cheeseparing way in which they were shot. The motto was 'one take and run'. But they always earned back costs and showed a profit. A young girl could sink or swim in them without affecting the film or anyone being any the wiser. And while it could prove a handicap to become typed as a 'quickies queen' many an ambitious career got started in them. Meanwhile it was steady employment.

In the next two years Rita would make thirteen films, ten of which were for Briskin, none of which had much effect on developing her career—but her thirteenth was to be her lucky one—*Only Angels Have Wings*.

Cohn's contribution to Rita's first phase at Columbia was to remove the last trace of her Latin links by ordering the change of her last name from her father's Cansino to her mother's Hayworth, half-way through her first film under contract—*Criminals of the Air*. Depending again on whom one listens to, the 'Y' was already part of the spelling or was added so as not to confuse her

Premature shades of Gilda can be seen in Rita's dress and posture when she played a thoroughly disagreeable chanteuse in *Who Killed Gail Preston?*

The last role for some time as a Spanish dancer in *Criminals of the Air.* (Columbia)

This time ice-hockey was *The Game That Kills,* with Rita taking over co-starring honors from Jacqueline Wells opposite broad-shouldered Charles Quigley (June 9, 1937). (A. L. 'Whitey' Schafer)

with her Uncle Vinton Haworth, who had made a name for himself as a character actor at R.K.O. (where his other niece, Ginger Rogers, was Queen of the Lot), and as the star of the long-running radio serial *Mert & Mardge*. Either way the new name was considered suitable by all concerned.

She got third billing in the film and her last Latin or dancing role for some time. It was also the first of five with Charles Quigley, whom Rita inherited as leading man from Rosalind Keith, the film's leading lady. The roles that followed were a succession of all-American goodies, baddies, vamps, tramps and imperilled heroines. In *Girls Can Play* she was the captain of a girls' softball team whose crooked boyfriend bumps her off by putting poison in her baseball glove!!! In *The Game That Kills* she played the girlfriend of a hockey star and the New York critics called her a promising young actress. The publicity promised, 'Murder on the ice ... as cold terror grips 10,000 hearts.' Don Terry, a former Olympic boxing champion, played a secret agent investigating the dance hall racket in her next film *Paid To Dance* with Rita as one of the hostesses at the Paradise Dance Hall. She ran a circus in *The Shadow*, but as the Hedy Lamarr look-alike lady in the title *Who Killed Gail Preston?* her reels were numbered. While she lived she was the best thing on the screen. It was only the second time Rita had had to sing in a film and given the limited time and budgets these films were allotted, since she was not a trained singer with the sort of voice the role demanded, it was thought expedient to dub her. Her last two films shot in 1937, *Special Inspector* and *Convicted*—'Terror stalks to sizzling swing'—were inferior quota quickies shot back to back in Vancouver, Canada.

Her 1938 films were much the same, but she was as American as apple-pie with names to match in all of them. Her last Latin role came on a loan-out to R.K.O. for a George O'Brien western, *The Renegade Ranger*. She played Judith Alvarez, a Spanish lady Robin Hood out to revenge the wrong done her rancher father. By now her transformation into an all-American is almost complete. Her hair photographs noticeably lighter and no attempt is made to make her look Spanish. The part demands little more than for Rita to look proud, brave and feminine while getting on or off horses and changing out of trousers into dresses. The usual standard of female support opposite cowboys was so low that by contrast, Rita's contributions made the critic in *Daily Variety* cheer her as, 'one of the finest femme sagebrush performances seen in a long while. Ideally cast, she displayed both acting and riding

Rita and George O'Brien in *Renegade Ranger,* August, 1938. (RKO)

skill.' To work with, Hayworth was as modest and self-effacing then as before and as she ever would be. Years later George O'Brien reminisced that, unlike most actresses who work in 'B' westerns on the way up, Rita never gave herself airs, unfailingly asked for advice when in doubt and '... walked and moved with *such* grace! Cliché though it might be, she was poetry in motion.'

Back at work for Briskin she was only a lab. assistant at police headquarters in *Homicide Bureau.* But her efforts had not gone unnoticed for then came her first role in one of the studio's superior programmers *The Lone Wolf Spy Hunt.* Ida Lupino played the Lone Wolf's daughter and Warren William was the best of the actors who had played the retired safe-cracker gone straight. For the first time, Rita was given her own stand-in, and, more important, instead of the usual cast-offs from the wardrobe department, the studio's ace designer Kalloch created dresses especially for her. She wore sleek and decidedly sexy gowns and furs as head of an international gang of thieves with the challenging insolence of one who comes naturally to good things. The fan magazines featured her prominently.

There had been an earlier plan to cast her in *Holiday*, an 'A' film—directed by George Cukor—in the role of Katharine Hepburn's sister. Cukor considered her too immature for that role, but had been impressed, which further contributed to the ground swell that was making impressive people take notice of her.

The story of how she got her next role, the one that would drastically change the course of her career, is like her hairline. Everybody seems to have a different version. But the important thing was that she got it. *Only Angels Have Wings* began shooting the day before Christmas, 1938, and from the outset it was intended as Columbia's blockbuster for 1939. As soon as she heard about it Rita, so one set of stories goes, set out to campaign for the part of 'the other woman'. The role was small but stars have been made from less. Reading interviews describing how she got the role, one gets a picture of a determined, calculating and self-confident young woman. As with most articles published in fan magazines, elements of truth undoubtedly run through it but the style of presentation and the personality they convey is not the one they went to interview, but the one the public was thought to want and the studio fostered. Admittedly, on occasion the two do go together but, invariably, the long quotes from Rita were first made up in somebody else's head then put into Rita's mouth.

It's possible that she did go to the restaurant the night director Howard Hawks and Harry Cohn were having dinner there; it's possible that she spent $500 on a special outfit for the occasion, described by a woman writer for *Photoplay* readers as 'a grey charcoal coat, form-fitted, pinching her waist in snugly and flaring from the thighs down, combined with a dream dress in three shades of grey and fitting like silver fluid poured over her body, topped off with a hat, one of those tall startling things that was meant to be carried on a head held high.'

Rita told her:

I paid $500 for the outfit and I had a few uncomfortable moments thinking of my extravagance. Not a cent in the bank—and $500 for one outfit. But when I saw myself in the mirror I felt reassured. I had never looked like that before.

The first evening I wore it I went to the Trocadero. That was no accident. It was done deliberately. At that time the Troc. was the hang-out of the stars and star-makers. It was the beauty-jaded moguls of Hollywood I was trying to reach.

The fantasy ring hanging over the piece starts to clink when one realises that the outfit described is remarkably like the one she wore in the film, but then the Rita they interviewed is a twin to the character she played in it. It is the endless two-way mirror that blurs reality and fantasy until, with time, it becomes impossible, for public *and* star, to distinguish between the two.

Howard Hawks, the director of that film, was established with a string of hits that gave him complete control over all aspects of its production. Cohn had secured his services with this understanding and would have been powerless had he wished to argue a point. Hawks had told him a story and sold it on the basis of ten pages of yellow foolscap written beside his pool. Recalling the events leading up to the shooting, he was, like his films, dry and to the point.

Hawks: 'The film is based on a true story that happened to some people I knew. I'd been flying in Mexico with a bush pilot whose face had been burnt in an accident. His eyes were the only thing left that smiled. He was a very hard guy and I got this story from him. He took me to this anniversary wedding dinner for some friends of his, a pilot and his girl, and they told me how they met, and that was the part of the story with Cary Grant and Jean Arthur. And the incident about the fellow who jumped out of an aeroplane and left his partner to crash and was blackballed later on, well I'd seen him jump. And I saw the guy he left behind lying on a slab in the morgue. And I watched the other guy trying to do horrendous things to prove himself because nobody would talk to the bastard anymore. So I put these stories together but it was all based on true incidents. The film came about when I was going over to Columbia to see Frank Capra, and of course, you couldn't take a step in that studio without Cohn knowing. He asked me to see him and since he had two stars waiting to work and no story, he asked me if I had a picture for him. So I said, "Here's ten pages of yellow paper on which I've scribbled the story." I was still down in Capra's office when Harry called down and said, "When can you start, can you get going in a couple of weeks?" I told him it would take me longer than that to build the set and it would cost him a lot of money. But he said it would cost him a lot not to do it since he had two stars hanging around and he had to pay them and if he didn't put them to work soon, they'd go off on other commitments. Years later some French guy who says he likes my films writes that I have too much imagination and that this is the only phoney picture I ever made.'

Rita: 'Harry Cohn called me to his office, and I think the

casting director, whose name I can't even remember now, was there too, and he said, "Howard Hawks would like to make a photographic test of you for a picture we're going to do here." I said, "Fine." I didn't do a scene from the script or anything, just an expensive photographic test. Then they photographed a lot of people and in about two weeks they decided that I was to do the role. They told me it was going to be a small part in a film and the stars were Cary Grant and Jean Arthur.'

Jean Arthur played a show girl who, en route to an engagement in Panama, is stranded in an airbase in one of the banana republics where she meets Cary Grant, daredevil flyer and woman-hater. A young pilot crashes his plane and dies attempting to land at the fog-shrouded airport to keep a dinner date with her. Hopelessly in love with Grant, she remains as his uninvited guest. Richard Barthelmess as a renegade flyer who once broke the code of the sky bailing out of a plane, leaving his mechanic to crash to his death,* arrives as a replacement for the dead flyer. With him comes his wife (Rita Hayworth) who is none other than Grant's ex-girlfriend and the reason for his present misogynist attitude, while his best friend, Thomas Mitchell, is the brother of the ill-fated mechanic. Barthelmess, hated by all the men, draws the airline's toughest assignments. He flies a doctor to a remote mine high on a narrow plateau in the Andes, goes aloft with a cargo of nitroglycerine, and takes Grant's place flying a big tri-motor job through a narrow mountain pass during a violent storm when Grant is accidentally shot by Miss Arthur. Barthelmess almost crashes but makes it through to win back his flighty wife and the respect of the other fliers.

Given that the story is based on real life incidents, the world Hawks creates on the screen is a boy's own land, where men are men and women, all women, are a convenience at best, but most often the wedge in the wheel of male camaraderie the rest of the time. As a show girl, for all her personally endearing sincerity and charm, Jean Arthur is miscast in this world, but Rita's entrance, if far-fetched—like Harlow's in *Hell's Angels*, or Monroe's in *Asphalt Jungle*—was the kind to make one sit up and take notice.

Half-way into the story she comes down a flight of stairs into a room of brawling men, who stop what they're doing and stare as if frozen to the spot. A mid-shot takes in the room, the stairs and her legs from the waist down, the silver grey jersey clinging to her hips

---

*This character was the reverse of a similar role in an earlier film he had made, *The Last Flight*, where he went down with his plane so as *not* to leave the mechanic.

With Hayworth every movement was a perpetual creation—it gave her a romantic mystery. Here she is in *Only Angels Have Wings*, 1939. (Lippman/Columbia)

and fanning out into a swirl around her knees. The camera moves closer to take the rest of her in, everything clings—the dress to her body, her impact on the mind. She holds her shoulders straight, carrying her body with that clear-striding, forthright sexual quality she had and which she knew she had. It was the way girls like her were put together; it was a readiness or acquiescence to use the body for all the pleasure it could give, a readiness they picked up from their mothers, in the Hollywood malt shops, out of the air. When she walked into that South American airport she was, in fact, home. Helen Hunt reported that at the first preview the audience broke into whistles and applause.

Hawks: 'I have a theory that the camera likes certain people and not others. Well, she had a face I knew I could photograph, no problems about that. She was very attractive, very nervous but she got over that during filming. She moved so easily and she listened to every blooming thing you'd tell her.

'She was a quick study. She tried. Her very first scene was one we shot between her and Grant. He was sitting behind a little desk in his office and she was outside and I told her to go in. She came in so fast Grant and I started to laugh. So I told her, "Hold on, try it real slow. Come in again, this time lean back against the door, look at him, slow." She did it and I said, "Wait a minute Rita, your dress is all moulded to you. Why?" "Well, I guess to show off my figure." "Okay!" I told her, "Lean back and show it and look at Grant as if you were telling him what you're thinking." And she did and she looked awfully good doing it, because she had the dancer's quality of assuming a position. I asked her what she was thinking and she said, "Well he was looking at me in a peculiar way." So I told her to ask him if he liked her hair this way. We made up scenes as we went along this way. Everything she did after that had a sex connotation to it. The sex was in her. All we had to do was to get it out and use it right.

'She worked hard. There was a scene she had to cry and she worked almost too hard there, so I moved it out of doors and had the rain put on, rain was pouring all over her face. It calmed her down but you still got the feeling of the emotion in her. I only do something in a film that somebody can do well. When they can't I change it so they can. She was supposed to get tight in the scene where she's behind the bar with Grant. It was a fairly long dialogue scene and she hadn't experience enough to do it. Finally I said to Cary, "What do you think's the matter with her?" He said, "I don't think she hears what I'm saying. She doesn't take it in." So I said, okay, and

Rita, Cary Grant and Jean Arthur in *Only Angels Have Wings,* 1939. (Lippman/Columbia)

called for the prop man to bring me a pitcher of ice-cold water, gave it to Cary and told him, "When you feel the scene going dead on you, just look at her and say, 'You don't know what I'm talking about, do you?' And she'll react to that and then you pour the bucket of ice over her head. Then he took a couple of her lines, dries her hair and sends her out blowing her nose. Those scenes she did well. Damn well! But she couldn't play a drunk, and I wouldn't ask her for things that were beyond her at the time. She was just a kid and scared, and here she was working with a bunch of the best actors in the business. This was the big league.

'She was grateful for the help—if she hadn't been she'd have been a silly ass—because everybody tried to help her. She was the baby of the picture and they were all good actors, willing to help any newcomer, especially when they could see how hard a time she was having. I've worked with girls who didn't appreciate that, and they lost because of it.

'At her best Rita was slightly unreal. She belonged in some kind of fairytale story—she had that kind of beauty, which isn't the sort of film I make, so there was never a part for her in any of my other films.'

Hawks's draconian measures to get the performance from Rita he felt was there, certainly brought results. From the start her success had been assured. The problem was when. From now on it was only a matter of months. For all that it set her career on its road, Rita remembers the film more because of her nervousness, her fear, her pain. She was just twenty.

Rita: 'It was a difficult film for me. I hadn't been in a big "A" picture before and I was really frightened. Cary Grant was so lovely and kind to me. He said, "Don't worry, it'll be okay!" He knew I was frightened and he took time to put me at my ease. There are people in this business who are so kind, who help people, and Cary was one of those. Those are the lovely things to remember. It doesn't happen often! Mr Hawks asked me to do certain things that I was very unhappy about, but between Cary and Hawks I did it. Cary is more genteel about things. Hawks is quiet. You can hardly hear him speak when he talks to you, but he's kind of hard. But, I got through what he wanted me to get through and I DID IT!'

Things were different on the other side of the mirror. But again, this is all that mattered. Her discomfort while filming is not on the screen and no signs of it appear in the articles that were sent out to promote a confident Rita.

Photoplay: April 1939: '*Photoplay*'s Own Beauty Shop' Carolyn Van Wyck, reporting:

Modern way to beauty—Rita Hayworth finished a difficult scene with Cary Grant for *Plane No. 4* and walked off the set. I had watched her rehearse the scene several times before this last take, and the terrific amount of energy it required to do the same thing over and over again until it was done perfectly had practically exhausted me, even though I had nothing to do with it.

But Rita wasn't exhausted. She didn't even look tired. As a matter of fact, she looked more glowing and lovely than I had ever seen her.

'Nice going,' I said. 'I needn't ask you how you are. You look wonderful.'

'Oh, I feel marvellous,' she laughed, 'even though I'm working so hard. You know, this is really my big chance. It's the best part I've had, playing second lead to Jean Arthur, and I've just got to feel well and look well.'

'How do you do it?' I asked. I felt positively haggard in contrast.

'It's simple,' she said, 'and you can see what it's done for me. I don't let myself get run down or tired. You know the importance of vitamins to health and beauty. I just supplement my regular diet by taking vitamins in concentrated form. They do wonders for you.'

The film was given its preview on May 11th, 1939 to an ecstatic reaction—first in Los Angeles, and subsequently echoed in most of the New York papers. Only Jean Arthur, in a role that required a Carole Lombard type, received less than enthusiastic praise. Rita seemed to catch everyone by surprise, including Cohn, who had suggested her to Hawks for the part. Hawks advised him to husband her until the film came out and reaction to her had a chance to develop.

Despite the favourable reaction to Rita that came back from the previews, the Columbia hierarchy developed doubts about exercising the option on her contract which would have raised her salary from $250 a week to $300. If it was an example of the usual power play studios tried to keep from paying more money, it was certainly idiotic timing. Had they dropped her at this stage she would have been snapped up by Warners or Metro or Twentieth Century Fox, all of whom were beginning to bid for her services. Somebody, probably Cohn, must have realised this for a compromise was reached; the extra $50 would be paid, not to Rita, but on her behalf to a dramatic coach, Gertrude Vogler, with whom Rita was now studying on Cukor's recommendation.

Rita's genuine desire to please, and her willingness to co-operate with the studio was a God-send for Columbia's Public Relations man, Lou Smith. Rita arrived at a most opportune time. The recent elevation over at Warner Brothers of another 'B' features star, the Texan red-head Ann Sheridan to Empress of 'Oomph!' through a clever promotional stunt by her studio's Public Relations was the talk of the town. Sheridan's 'overnight' road to stardom had taken her seven years but these were lost in the glare of publicity which made her, along with Hedy Lamarr, one of the hottest new properties in movies. It was bound to intensify every studio's search for new stars, especially with another decade about to end. Now Rita was being groomed as her studio's bright hope.

With a choice between the exotic allure of Lamarr and Sheridan's home-spun, down-to-earth sex appeal, Smith settled for emphasising Rita's qualifications for the latter. There were striking physical similarities between the two, though Rita's features were more refined and graceful, and Sheridan was a much more outgoing person, but when, by another of those

April 30, 1941—'Which twin has the Toni' is a question that could be aptly applied to this picture of when Rita and 'Oomph' gal Ann Sheridan met.

Rita and co-star Tony Martin in *Music in My Heart*, 1939. (Columbia)

coincidences that populate the lives of stars, Sheridan walked out
of the title role of *The Strawberry Blonde* because she had grown
tired of playing so many similar parts, it seemed natural that Rita,
whose height and measurements were similar to Sheridan's,
should be asked to take over. This proved to be another important
step in her rise, and occasioned the final change of Rita's hair
colouring.

Lou Smith's department meanwhile went into full gear and
Rita spent long hours with the studio's ace photographer 'Whitey'
Schafer in Columbia's photogallery posing for glamour and pin-ups
in various settings. Besides the photographs that went out to the
newspapers and magazines, there were two stacks reserved for
written requests from fans. The ones that went to men showed
Rita alluringly posed in a bathing suit, while her female fans were
sent photos of her wearing a sport outfit and walking her dog. All
part and parcel of the selling of a dream that money could buy—
for the price of a ticket.

When Rita began her next film, a musical co-starring Tony
Martin, *Music In My Heart*, more than six months had elapsed as
Hawks had suggested. There was nothing of the 'B' feature star
left about her. The problem now was the lack of product the
studio had set to go that could take advantage of her. Meanwhile,
though she continued in programmers like *Music In My Heart* and
Blondie On A Budget, it is apparent that great care was taken with
the scenes in which she appeared. She was well groomed, alluringly dressed and stunningly photographed. Her first film in 1940
was to be another 'B' film teaming her with a newcomer, Glenn
Ford, when the first of her significant loan-outs intervened, and
with it, the final stage in the rise to international stardom.

1940 was her year and it began auspiciously. M.G.M., advised
by George Cukor, borrowed her for the all-star society comedy
drama *Susan and God*, starring Joan Crawford. The film, based on
Rachel Crother's play, was heavy going but had the ultra-chic of
the Metro production organisation. Everything was the best. The
cast had a starry sparkle. Rita playing an adulterous actress who
arrives as a weekend houseguest with her older husband and
younger lover in tow, was exceptionally vivacious.

Cukor: 'She added to the film's ensemble playing with her
youth and her beauty and charm. She had a marvellous way of
wearing clothes. She was a real creature of the movies, possessing
the quality of involving the audience in her problem, like all the
great stars. And she possesses a great deal of style, a quality of

A portrait by Columbia's gallery man, A. L. 'Whitey' Schafer in 1940,
captures a last stage in the metamorphosis from starlet to star. ('Whitey'
Schafer/Columbia)

femininity and womanliness that is rare. The studio couldn't make
what she had that attracted the public. They could sustain it and
produce it and help it along but only if it's there in the first place.
There's an awful lot of shit talked about movies and stars. Rita
was an extremely good actress. Like Gary Cooper. They said the
same about him, that he was just himself. But that's not so. They
had discretion and taste and a quality nobody could provide for
them.'

After seeing the film, Louis B. Mayer was so impressed with
Rita he considered her for the showy part of the scheming minx in

Boom Town, but eventually gave in to Hedy Lamarr's campaign for the role, since she was under contract to the studio and with two flops behind her was desperately eager to get a good part that would redeem her standing.

Mayer wasn't the only one after Rita. Producer Arthur Hornblow Jnr was hoping to get Rita for the role in his aviation drama, *I Wanted Wings*, that made Veronica Lake a star instead, and Cecil B. De Mille wanted her for the colourful, scene-stealing, half-breed in his lavish Technicolor saga, *The North-West Mounted Police*. That part went to Paulette Goddard. These had been three of the most coveted female roles of the year and all of them had been offered first to Rita. Cohn could swell with pride at his good fortune. Rita was still only earning $250 a week, but was now worth a hundred times that in the loan-out fees Cohn could obtain for her services. The films she made at Columbia at this point were still not vehicles built around her, but they were interesting films for all that. She had the female lead in a very charming little film *The Lady In Question*, and in the literate Ben Hecht comedy-drama *Angels Over Broadway*.

The former was, in fact, built around the comical but oddly touching moustachioed bicycle shop owner (Brian Aherne), whose moment comes as a jury member where his zeal saves a girl (Rita) on trial for murder, and then almost lives to regret it. Charles Vidor, who directed, had seen the original French film *Gribouille*, the name of the leading character, when it was shown in the United States the year before as *The Heart of Paris*. Raimu was the star and Michele Morgan was exquisite as the pathetic little French girl on trial. Vidor had talked Cohn into buying and re-making it. It was the sort of story that had been dipped heavily in Gallic sentiment and dripped humanity and whimsical humour. But Vidor's grip was firm and affectionate and the cast was an accomplished one. Brian Aherne, temporarily given a chance to forsake romantic leading roles, played the father; Irene Rich, a great star of silent films, played his wise wife; Evelyn Keyes, also being groomed by Columbia, was perky as his daughter; and Glenn Ford, in his first film with Rita as romantic *vis-à-vis*, was all boyish appeal as the son. As the unhappy cause of so much domestic upheaval, Rita, playing a character of her own age and type, was enchanting. All in all, *The Lady in Question*, was one of those 'little' films with which everybody is delighted, makes back its cost and winds up on most critics' year's-end 'ten best films' list.

December 16, 1940—The first time one of the screen's great love teams was matched, but some time before the sparks flew. Hayworth and Glenn Ford in *The Lady in Question*. (M. B. Paul/Columbia)

Of course what gives the film its special piquancy for Hayworth fans is that it commemorates her first teaming with Glenn Ford. On the screen their sizzling sado-masochistic affairs in films like *Gilda* and *Affair in Trinidad*, made them one of the cinema's classic romantic teams, like Garbo and Gilbert and Harlow and Gable. Here they were both young, on the threshold of their careers with his part significantly smaller than hers and the sparks that would ignite later slumbering. Ford puts the reason for the change to his time in the Navy, from which he returned after the war, no longer a boy. As part of the Columbia stock company, along with Rita and Bill Holden, his memories are mellow and affectionate, for all of Cohn's interfering.

Ford: 'In the early days at Columbia they used to throw us into almost anything that came along. That kept us really hopping, we'd do maybe six or seven films a year that way. It was all part of the studio's building system, which, unfortunately, they don't do any more. We had the great luxury of exposure, of experience, like you do in a repertory theatre. We *had* to work and do everything and not complain. We didn't get to choose, otherwise you'd be on suspension and you couldn't afford that on what they paid us. Oh, we resented it terribly, but we complained and kicked up our heels and did terrible things. As I look back on it now I suspect it was a great luxury. I think if I was starting in the business now I would like to have that to look forward to, being under contract to a studio with the protection of a studio which they used to give us in those days. They took marvellous care of us, looked after our relations with the press, with the exhibitors. They sent us out on tours with the films—we went all over the world when our pictures were shown, which was marvellous. I stayed with Columbia for nineteen years.

'When I first got there they used to put what they call corrective make-up on me. My nose was crooked, one of my cheeks is a little bigger than the other, and my eyes are too close or something. I've still got the chart of my corrective make-up from the old days which I framed. They shade here and they highlight there and they move this and that and it's terrible. Can you imagine what they must do to the women! I tell you, I've worked with some you wouldn't recognise in the morning when they first arrived in the studio.

'Even though Cohn was a hard taskmaster—he'd come down to the set and if he didn't like what he saw in the rushes the night before, he'd tell you so in no uncertain terms, but he kept you on your toes. Consequently Harry is the one I have to thank for everything I have today. He was right and it's been proven—Columbia has never been the same since Harry died. It just went down.

'The only thing that really griped me was when he tried to interfere with my private life. Then we had a few little tiffs. Harry was just Harry, he thought he could tell you how to dress, what to do, what to eat, who to be friends with. If you were friends with somebody he disapproved of, the only way he could find to stop the friendship would be to call your wife. When Rita was doing a picture he'd bar the men from coming on the set. When I was doing a picture he'd forbid the starlets from coming on my set. When Rita and I did a film together, I think he bugged our dressing rooms. It was the same with Bill Holden.

'I guess he was just a very "moral" man,' Ford says jokingly. 'The trouble was a lot of the actors got cowed by him. The time he respected me the most was when I went into his office after he'd interfered in my personal life to a point when it was rather ridiculous. He had a baseball bat behind his desk—I think Babe

Ruth must have given it to him or something—I went around and grabbed the bat and hit the top of his desk so hard that it broke and said, "Don't ever do that again, Harry!" and walked out of the room. He shouted after me, "You'll never set foot on this lot again!" Of course I was working the next day because I had a star part in one of his pictures. From that day on he was great. I used to have dinners at his house and take him to football games.

'He used to call us his "three children". He specially favoured us, I don't know why except I remember one night shortly before he died I was narrating a documentary at Columbia—Rita had left the studio by then and so had Bill—and he came down to the set with tears in his eyes—he was a very strong man, a bull—and he said, "Glenn, you're the last, when you go, that's the last of my 'three children'." I thought this was kind of poignant.'

Rita went straight from *The Lady in Question*, begun in May, into *Angels Over Broadway* in June. It was an original screenplay Ben Hecht had written and wanted to direct, and together with the ace cameraman Lee Garmes, and the actor Douglas Fairbanks Jnr, he took the idea to Cohn.

They all knew Cohn socially. Years before, when Columbia was still a Poverty Row studio, Fairbanks had starred in Frank Capra's second film, *The Power of the Press* (1929).

Fairbanks: 'Cohn was not only bull-headed but a monster, probably one of the most detested men in the hierarchy, and while one doesn't mind coarseness and vulgarity in its place, one doesn't want it all the time. Somehow, when we did *Angels* he was always charming and respectful. Possibly because Hecht was such a sharp wit and didn't give a damn and Cohn was frightened of him.

'Somehow we managed to get Cohn to give us a free hand; he probably judged this project as a good business deal as he lacked other contract people who could make something off the beaten track and who'd work for a reasonable price and with their own salary at a minimum. It wasn't a case of his being courageous but a fairly safe gamble. We had complete control, but I remember him saying about Rita, that since he had this new, young girl on the lot, why didn't we use her. There was no meeting about it, it happened indirectly on a phone with someone suggesting Hecht take a look at her. Cohn never came on the set which surprised everyone at the time since no one outside of Frank Capra got away with so little trouble. But we all agreed on the casting.

'I remember that she was *so* shy that our first reaction was, "Is she acting dumb or is she shy?" She seemed so incredibly innocent

Ben Hecht discussing a production point with Douglas Fairbanks, Jr., and Rita on the set of *Angels Over Broadway*. (M. B. Paul/Columbia)

and naïve to the point where even a rough-neck like Hecht was careful about his language in front of her. If someone said, "Damn," Ben would nudge them—which was unlike him. He used to tease in a rough-house undertone to me about her figure, that he didn't think she knew she had one. We finished the film without ever knowing her really at all.*

'What I remember most about Rita was the striking contrast of her personality—she might have just come out of high school for all I knew—versus this very sexy figure. It was all there on the screen but in life she didn't exude anything very sexy.'

Playing an out-of-work show girl, Rita, as photographed by Garmes, looked more stunning than ever before in this strange mixture of reality and fantasy, in which she was picked up by a down-on-his-luck gambler (Fairbanks) and in the space of one eventful night wandered through the back ways of Broadway,

*Hecht was sufficiently impressed with the results of Rita's work that it spurred him to try and activate a film project he had in mind based on the life of the famous dancer Isadora Duncan with Rita, but when he proposed it to Cohn, it was turned down as being too arty-crafty. Years later there was talk again of Rita playing Isadora for a French production company. It is regrettable that neither project materialised.

joined by a man contemplating suicide and a drunken playwright (Thomas Mitchell) who played God with their lives, sorting them all out before the dawn. Rita comes across with a chaste, doe-like quality, that gives the film a delicacy which complemented the fantasy, otherwise noticeable in the literate, sparse screenplay, the striking architectural look of the sets and the sombre lighting. She possessed that remote fairytale quality Hawks referred to and which one occasionally saw in some of her musicals. Hecht's concern and affection for her had borne fruit.

So, Rita was whizzing along to her breakthrough as an international star of the first magnitude, and Cohn exploited her to the hilt. But the films that would establish her were both on loan-out: Warner Brothers' *The Strawberry Blonde*, and Twentieth Century Fox's Technicolor tale of bullfights and Spain and death in the arena, *Blood and Sand*.

The veteran director Raoul Walsh's chef d'oeuvre, *The Strawberry Blonde* was a nostalgic gaslit comedy, set in turn-of-the-century America, with beer halls, brass bands and barber shop quartets. James Wong Howe's photography turned the studio into a richly shaded world, and to single out for praise the set decoration or costumes would be to disturb the delicate harmony in which all are equal partners. Neither could a single member of the cast have been improved on. There's pugnacious, tender-hearted Biff Grimes—Cagney at his best; militant melting feminist (Olivia de Havilland) who realises that a girl who speaks her mind ends up with a lot of free time on her hands; wheeler dealer Hugo Barnstead (Jack Carson), a wise guy born to politics with the conscience to match; and Rita as every young man's unobtainable fancy, Virginia Brush, the Strawberry Blonde of the tale. Though the film was shot in black and white, Rita's hair, apparently at the suggestion of Warner Brothers' make-up wizard Bud Westmore, was dyed the lighter shade of red to fit the part. The film is told with such delightful humorous and human touches, that it remains an extraordinarily fine entertainment. It was adapted from a play which had already been filmed before and which Walsh was to direct again as a musical, but this version is definitive.

There were few dissenters when it came to praising Rita's contribution, for at this blossoming stage the critics still treated her as an actress, capable of creating a role and not as a manufactured presence, as they would when she was enthroned as a symbol and became an easy target for their barbs. Soon Rita's

Unretouched photo of Rita as *The Strawberry Blonde*. (Madison Lacy/Warner Brothers)

Director Raoul Walsh and Rita on the set of *The Strawberry Blonde*, 1941. (Madison Lacy/Warner Brothers)

roles would be limited by her image and not her capabilities but here it was what she brought to a part that mattered. Ironically, her success in these early films helped to form the image that would stifle her as an actress.

Walsh drew on his own memories of the period with affectionate gusto; he is one of the few directors of 'men's movies' who was also capable of treating the women in his films as three dimensional characters, neither idealised nor denigrated, but equal and worthy reasons for making the world go round.

Walsh: 'Regarding the lovely, vivacious and talented Rita Hayworth—she came off magnificently despite the fact that she had two of the greatest actors, Jimmy Cagney and Olivia de Havilland to compete with.

'When Ann Sheridan turned down *The Strawberry Blonde*, Jack called me to his office and said, "Irish, we're up against it. The film's ready to go, the costumes are made. Who can we get at this stage?" I told him—the most beautiful girl in pictures, Rita Hayworth. He got her at once, and when I first talked to Rita about the part and how she saw her, her questions and answers convinced me that she was the perfect choice.

'This beautiful girl was a bit nervous at first, but I cleared the set of all those not working in it. I would take her aside, hold her hand, look into her beautiful eyes, and tell her I was more than pleased at the way she was playing the part, and that one day she would be a great star. She looked at me for a second, kissed me on the cheek and *The Strawberry Blonde* went merrily on its way.

'Of course, Jimmy and I were old buddies and while they were lighting up the set, I would get Rita and the three of us would sit down. She loved to hear the stories that Jimmy and I told of the early days in pictures. Some of them a bit Rabelaisian and Rita would roar with laughter.

'Many of the pictures I made later, I would surely have liked to have Rita for. But then her studio said no more loan-outs for the beautiful girl. I only remember her, and the one film we made together, with great affection.'

Jack Warner was so pleased with the results that he immediately asked Cohn to loan her for another film—a screwball comedy, *Affectionately Yours*. Rita had been billed below the title in her previous film; now she was given equal billing with the other stars, Merle Oberon and Dennis Morgan, but she would have done better to have avoided it. *She was Irene Malcolm, a newspaper gal chasing after newsman Dennis Morgan, who fools

*Merle Oberon was paid $85,000 for her part; Hattie McDaniel, in a supporting role, was paid $500 per week, for a total of $3,500; Rita, on loan out, was paid $6,500, at a weekly rate of $927.85 for seven guaranteed weeks of work.

Between takes of *Affectionately Yours* on the Warner Brothers Burbank lot, the four stars look happier than one might expect. The film turned out to be a turkey. (Jack Elliott/Warner Brothers)

around on foreign assignments but is still in love with his domestic wife, Merle Oberon, who wants to re-marry. Since the other man was Ralph Bellamy, one knew from the start there was no way Morgan could lose. Bellamy always lost the girl. On paper the idea read like a farce, but on film it was farcical. Because of her freshness and perhaps because hers was the smaller part, Rita came out of the shambles best—Merle Oberon just missed getting pie in her face but everything else tumbled her way. The best moments came from the supporting roles, for the film picks up with the irreplaceable Hattie McDaniels and Butterfly McQueen as maids who steal their scenes with the raffish nonchalance that comes when you know the burden of blame doesn't rest on your shoulders.

Affectionately Yours began shooting on January 10th, 1941, as did *Blood and Sand* over at Twentieth, but Rita's work was finished in time to play the role that was the final rung in her ascent: Dona Sol.

Scores of actresses, including Maria Montez, Gene Tierney,

Lynn Bari, Dorothy Lamour and over thirty others had been seen, and over half of them tested. Zanuck was pushing his own favourite, curvaceous Carole Landis, who was being groomed by the studio as a blonde sex bomb. The director, Rouben Mamoulian, was not satisfied with her but the problem was solved with her temperamental refusal to allow her blonde look to be changed into the required red one. The day Rita walked into his office, Mamoulian knew he had found his Dona Sol, and there was nothing for Zanuck to do but bow to the obvious.

Since the film was a major investment, and the actress who played the pivotal 'vamp' would benefit from the studio's extensive and profitable build-up, Zanuck got an agreement from Cohn that he could have Rita's services for two other films as well—with the proviso that she would be given top billing in both. Cohn could only beam at seeing one of his stars getting $150,000 of free publicity and one of the most coveted roles of the year from another studio, and agreed.

The film was adapted from the novel by the popular Iberian novelist Vincente Blasco Ibanez and had already been a famous silent film in which Valentino had one of his greatest roles as Juan Gallardo, the ragged urchin who becomes his country's greatest matador, forgetting his childhood sweetheart, Carmen, and loosing his heart, his strength, his courage and eventually his life because of the beautiful temptress of the arena, Dona Sol. The caustic critic of the bullring, Curro, to whom the success of others is the only attribute worth knowing them for, sitting in the stands surrounded by his accolytes, points her out as she arrives in her box and says, 'What I could tell you about that one would fill a whole book. Several books.' Then with a dismissive nod to the bullring before looking back at her, 'If this is death in the afternoon, she is death in the evening.' In short, an almost impossible role. In the silent version when vamps were still stock movie characters, Nita Naldi could come on as Dona Sol, eyes pooled in kohl, a stifling network of veils trailing from head to foot like a storm cloud, having only to point her finger for strong men to fall hopeless victims to her.

By 1940 the book's freshness had faded, conventions had changed, and audiences had grown too sophisticated for a simple re-make of the old story. Rouben Mamoulian realised the problems he was up against and set about solving them in his highly original way.

By using the full Technicolor, Kodachromatic range, Mamou-

With vanquished matador (Tyrone Power) Rita plays
Dona Sol in *Blood and Sand*. (Fox)

lian turned the dated imagery of the book and earlier film into a
complex modern psychological drama. The new film pulsed with
colour and held the eye even when the pace lagged and the plot
became tortuous. The colour heightened the emotional and
dramatic effect: in the nave of the chapel attached to the arena, as
Juan prays before entering the ring, the El Greco composition is
rent by the entry of Dona Sol whose dress of mourning purple,
with almost vampirically moist red lips and nails, strikes a
deliberately discordant note amid the soft blues and greens. From
the start she parades her intent. Sol intends to appropriate Juan
and all his glory.

For the scene of Juan's seduction later the same day, set in the
garden of Dona Sol's elegant mansion of cool, marbled blues and
whites, Mamoulian strikingly employs Velazquez's sense of space
and light against which the red carnation on the table in the
moonlight and the brilliance of her scarlet fingernails beating out
a tattoo on her guitar as she sings to Juan, chills the very heart
it heats. Juan's poverty-stricken childhood draws on Murillo's

bronzes, browns and blacks; Goya is drawn on for the bullring and the turbulent cafés; the luxury and glory of Juan's dressing room, hung with his suits of light, the colourful capes and mantillas, owes much to Titian.

The furniture, costumes and sets were most carefully worked out ahead of time to assure the right colour harmonies. There was nothing incidental in anything, everything was premeditated. Mamoulian had a collection of spray guns with different colour shades in them so he could more easily spray an item, a shirt that was too white, a chair or curtain that didn't blend properly, and which looked terrible to the eye but looked great on film. Any effect he couldn't achieve with the lighting he achieved by using the spray gun, painting a shadow on the wall the way the painters did in their pictures. Not surprisingly his set decorator became really scared by this.

Mamoulian: 'Because in Nacional's (John Carradine) death scene, we had this hospital bed, white sheets and white high walls, and it looked so shiny and new, not at all like a hospital, and I thought if El Greco had painted it, it wouldn't look white, it would look green and grey, so I sprayed all the sheets and painted shadows on the walls. It looked absolutely appalling to the eye, and it really shook me because I thought I'd really ruined the set, but it came out beautifully. So at the end of the bullfighting which, colouristically of course, is the chromatic climax of the film, with all the reds, and then I have to follow it up with Dona Sol's house, I thought to myself, what do you do after you've used all those colours in the preceding scene? So I decided to do it in black and white, as close as you can in Technicolor. I discussed it with the set designer, with the property man about the furniture, etc. Everything was arranged. I came on the set and there it was, in the style of Velazquez. A beautiful set. Of course all the guests had to be in black and white and we had white flowers in the centre of the table, but naturally the leaves were green. And the beautiful armchairs round the table, highly valuable props that Twentieth Century were proud of, they were golden frames. So I told the set designer to spray the frames white and meanwhile I took the black spray and sprayed the greenery so it goes with the white flowers. And when we'd finished it looked dreadful again. While we were doing this, the studio manager walked in and looked at what I'd done and said, "Mamoulian, are you all right? Do you find it hot in here from the many lights?" I said, "Yes, it's hot." Off he went.

'Five minutes later there came a message from Zanuck asking
me to see him after I'd finished shooting. The big boss! So, after
the scene was over I went to his office and he asked me, "How are
you feeling?" I said, "What is this, everybody is concerned about
my health today?" He said, "It's hot, isn't it?" And I said, "Yes, it
is." And he asked, "Does the heat affect you?" I said, "Yes,
normally." So he said, "Then what on earth are you doing on that
set? I understand you are ruining our props, you are spraying
green things black. What on earth is that?" "Darryl, I can give
you an explanation in thirty seconds or one that takes half an
hour. Which one do you want?" He asked for the short one first.
"I've been shooting for a week now. You've seen the rushes, what
did you think of them?" He said, "I sent you notes telling you that
it was the best colour photography I'd ever seen." "So that's your
answer. I sprayed."'

As the doomed hero, Tyrone Power takes it upon himself to act
the part. His own screen presence would, in this instance, have
served better, for his digging for depth drained him of the animal
magnetism needed to raise Juan to heroic stature. Linda Darnell,
as his devoted sweetheart and suffering wife, might have stepped
out of a Piéta, but while her tranquil acceptance of fate and her
pure love deserve our sympathy, she is too static for her unhappi-
ness to matter. Inevitably this lack of spirit further dulls the
drama. In the scene building to the confrontation between the two
women, Carmen arrives gowned in a black taffeta and lace dress
with a black mantilla which accentuates her wraith-like appearance but makes her a bride in mourning before she even
begins. As she stands in the bright palatial room leading out into
the garden she shrinks to a small weak shadow. Sol's entrance is
the sun eclipsing the moon. Her red hair streams loose, her eyes
are flushed with success. She has just finished playing matador to
Juan's enslaved bull. A pale chiffon robe floats breezily around
her with flashes of a darker fleshy pink beneath provocatively
tracing her contours. Except for a ring she wears no jewellery but
her nails and lips glisten like bleeding rubies. With porcelain
graciousness, she asks her lover's wife, 'Anything I can offer you?'
Unaware that her husband is in the garden, Carmen asks as a
suppliant to a feudal lady, 'Yes, my husband,' but then, with a
show of proud spirit, adds, 'I've heard that you've been all over`
the world. That you speak many languages. That you have known
a great many men.' The novelettish dialogue like Linda's Carmen
could have come intact from a Victorian melodrama. Admittedly,

Dona Sol waiting in the cool marbled entrance hall of her elegant mansion to receive her guests. Though the still is in black and white, one can get a sense of Mamoulian's striking use of space and design. (Fox)

goodness and mercy are great virtues in life but they rarely get their just share of our interest on screen. Villains always have more fun. But Rita's Sol, a first cousin to Prosper Merimée's *Carmen*, is poised on the sharp edge of her own insatiable hungers—not merely another siren without a heart, but a dramatic multi-faceted creature. She roams the earth to find the love that will give her peace, doomed by a nature that destroys those who would love her. The animal magnetism that was Valentino's as the matador is Rita's as the mantis. She arrives on the screen half-way through the film and from then on dominates not just her own scenes but the memory of the film and what has gone before.

Her casting now seems so simply the only choice, that it's hard to believe there could have been thirty-eight other possibles. But then seeing her on film one forgets that in life Rita is the shadow of her screen self.

Mamoulian: 'Was it Oscar Wilde who said, "The sphinx is an enigma which has no solution." That's Rita. Casting her was a hunch, something I felt rather than saw. I've always been strong on my impressions of people, usually first impressions. Nobody else could have played it, because you couldn't *play* Dona Sol, you had to *be* it. Garbo is the only other woman who could have done it. Now this isn't necessarily Rita Hayworth in life, but that inherent thing that comes out on the screen when she performs. Why do you think men like Orson and Aly married her? She had something that attracts, something you cannot define and if you could, you probably wouldn't have it. Bankhead might have played it but there would have been no enigma, no subtlety, no secret. You wonder why this person does what she does. But there is no answer. The fascination lies in asking the question: what is it about them that makes you ask about them? The quality she had was rare, there aren't many people like that. Rita possessed sophistication and then, the beautiful way she moved which makes Dona Sol very attractive. The rarest thing on stage or screen is a beautiful walk. On the screen there is Greta Garbo, Katherine Hepburn, Cyd Charisse and Rita Hayworth, and after that ... period.'

During the filming and just as her career was taking off, Rita's marriage to Judson was entering a crisis, but into the picture came a man who was to remain one of her closest friends, Hermes Pan. Pan is one of the handful of brilliant choreographers of American film musicals. He'd worked with Astaire on all his 'thirties films and also later. When the Astaire-Rogers team broke up and Astaire began to freelance, Pan accepted an offer from Twentieth Century Fox where he spent most of the 'forties creating numbers for the Betty Grable and Alice Faye musicals.

Pan: 'I'd just started at Fox the time I first met Rita. That was probably the first time that she made an impression on people, 'cause she played the heavy in a way that brought across her slumbering sensuality. She is like that, very shy and quiet and then she explodes suddenly. I remember the time when I was going to dance with her in *My Gal Sal*—at rehearsals she was very easy going but as soon as the camera started she went "WHOOM!"'

There are two kinds of introverts; the extroverted introvert and Rita's kind, the introverted introvert. But even in such an extroverted profession as show business, where introverts are surprisingly common, Rita's type is surely unique. Such a nature might be death at a party but is a gift to the camera. The loving lens plucks secrets from the human face like petals from a flower being shed in search of truth. Played by an extrovert, such as Maria Montez or Carole Landis, Dona Sol would have been a one-dimensional vamp because there would have been no basis for understanding either her psychological make-up or motives. Given the role, Rita develops from the inside out. At first there is a terrifying stillness, then the dormant self wakes and there is a volcano.

Technically, as the years went on, she became increasingly proficient as an actress, capable of deploying her assets so that she would be seen to advantage even without a worthy part or a sympathetic director to woo her. When a director like Howard Hawks, understandably fixed on exacting his own demands, collided with her he failed fully to realise what she could have given because he frightened her. Given a Raoul Walsh the results show that there isn't a nuance in the part Rita failed to bring out. She brought to life a woman who could remain one man's dream even while she revealed herself as another's quarrelling shrew. What a fascinating Kate she would have made. What a shrew to tame!

In the run of her movies Rita had to carry the burden, for these moments only happened when she danced.

Pan: 'Sol didn't have to be a dancer. But there was something which was meant to be seductive, just moving around the room pretending to be a bullfighter. Mamoulian told me he didn't want it to look like a dance number, just an impromptu sort of thing where somebody is being seductive. He worked very closely with me the way he does with everybody on his films because he had an overall feeling for what he wanted. I'd never seen Rita dance before, as a matter of fact I don't think I'd ever heard of her before then. We used to have lunch together and talk, and we became very good friends. Of course I found out about her family, and that she was an accomplished dancer, but I didn't see much of any of them on the set, and since she was having trouble with Judson at the time, I don't remember him coming over much, maybe once or twice. I only met him once and never her father but I got to know her mother and her brothers. She looks like none of them. You couldn't imagine it's her brother when you saw him. On the film things went smoothly. Mamoulian is a fine director. At the time I thought it would be Tyrone Power and Linda Darnell's movie, 'cause he was the star and Linda was

Rita as Dona Sol, 1941. (Gene Kornman/20th Century Fox)

under contract to Fox, but when Rita came on she was just dynamite. You couldn't believe the excitement when we saw the rushes. Not that she was conscious of the impression she was making, but the studio was.'

Shooting, including exterior long shots made in Mexico City of the bullring that were superbly matched up with the close work of Tyrone Power, was completed on May 3rd, and the finished print released to the critics on May 22nd.

Mamoulian: 'The film was never previewed, which is quite unheard of. Zanuck saw it in the projection room and I asked him where were we going to preview it. He said, "No preview. It's the greatest film I've ever seen. Ship it." And we shipped it like that. As a matter of fact if it had had a preview I would have cut it a little but it never had one.'

Despite lethargic patches and tired plot, the film was raised on a crown of hosannahs. About the only ones to get panned were the author and the bull. Travis Banton, whose dresses had given the 'thirties star ladies their style, came in for deserved cheers. So did the stunning art direction by Richard Day and Joseph C. Wright. Alfred Newman's lush score and the classical guitar solos by Vincent Gomez were singled out. The colour photography by Ernest Palmer and Ray Rennahan won the Oscar hands down. Mamoulian's established position among the industry's most innovative and admired artists was further enhanced. And had Rita read the papers she could have basked in her personal triumph, but Rita hardly ever read the papers—at any rate, not about herself. Her happiness was private and came a short time later when she took her family to an evening performance in a Brentwood cinema, sitting as part of the audience in the balcony, totally unobserved, a situation that only lasted until her image appeared on the screen. Padre, understanding not a word but seeing with his heart in his eyes, burst into "Olés!" at every move his granddaughter made, and kept them up despite the pro- testations of his family and the audience around.

Overnight, Rita had become the hottest property in films, and even the clouds on her silver lining couldn't dim that.

But *Blood and Sand* not only launched her into the stratosphere, it had a long-reaching and directly personal affect on her life no one could have foreseen. Among the millions of men who saw the film and fell asleep with her image in their minds, few woke to think they stood a chance of their dream coming true. After all, she was every G.I.'s sweetheart and the world's Love Goddess; but one man saw it who was in a position to make his dreams come true. In Cairo during the war, Aly Khan attended a party where they showed the film to the guests. The rest of the sophisticated party found it amusing, but Aly, a compulsive movie addict, hushed their laughter, telling them, 'Don't disturb me—I want to see this wonderful girl.' Their romance when it began would cap a decade in a career that had begun so sensationally with *Blood and Sand* eight years earlier.

On film and in life the 'forties was her era.

CHAPTER IV

THE TIME, THE PLACE
AND THE GIRL

The system contains, the fountain overflows.

C. G. Jung's *The Four Archetypes*

The time, the mid-'forties; the place, the El Morocco and the girl—Rita Hayworth. One evening, the story goes, Hayworth came in and moved to her table, the focus of all eyes. Nearby a jealous rival turned to her roving-eyed escort and inquired what he saw in Rita. After all, Grable had better legs. He agreed. 'Lamarr is much more beautiful.' He nodded. 'Lots of girls have better bodies and Ginger is a better dancer.' 'Yup.' 'Besides,' the actress threw in caustically, 'she wasn't born a redhead.' Still eyeing Rita at her table, he assented. 'So,' she repeated sourly, 'what's so special about her?' He thought, then said: 'I guess it's just the way it all hangs together.'

War had broken out in Europe in the autumn of 1939 when Hitler sent his Panzers into Poland. America, fresh out of the Depression, kept a neutral face at first, hoping perhaps that if she ignored it, it might go away. Under one of a series of neutrality acts designed to keep the U.S. aloof from European affairs, it became a statutory offence for Hollywood producers to make films slanted on either side, even if they had been so inclined. Considering that by and large the film industry had managed to ignore the Depression, there was no reason to suppose they couldn't have carried on ignoring somebody else's war. Another major cause for hesitation in warning the free world of the Nazi threat was the importance of the German market, the most lucrative outlet for American films in Europe.

However by the spring of 1940 a change in attitude could be

"A girl is...a girl. It's nice to be told you're successful at it." (Bob Landry, *Life* Magazine) © 1941 Time Inc.

detected in the American consciousness. For one thing, the war hadn't gone away, and Hitler seemed about to take possession of Europe; only England held out. The Atlantic Ocean separating the continents no longer appeared quite so large or so safe. Last doubts about America's active involvement were squashed by the brilliantly timed Japanese bombing of Pearl Harbor on the morning of December 7th, 1941. Now everybody wanted to do their bit to save the world for democracy, whether it was trying to make do with a scarcity of hair pins and glass eyes on the home front or sending sons and husbands off to fight overseas.

Now Hollywood also began to do its share. Stars travelled into the very heart of battle to entertain the allied forces in the hugely popular U.S.O. shows. They appeared at monster rallies to sell war bonds, and took turns appearing nightly at the popular Hollywood Canteen in Los Angeles, or the Stage Door Canteen in New York. Here, soldiers on leave could have free food served by their favourite stage and screen star, and have Rita Hayworth ask them for a dance.

The entry of the United States into the conflict had also transformed a minor cycle into a new genre. War films became a major staple of a studio's output, shredding the last traces of isolationism and pacifism in a hail of bullets and enemy atrocities whose popular appeal outlasted their morale-boosting function. No sooner was an invasion launched, a victory scored or an heroic defeat suffered by their own men, than Hollywood, just a step behind the headlines, dramatised it. Robert Taylor died heroically in *Bataan*, Bogart saw *Action in the North Atlantic*, Flynn was busy on *Operation Burma*, John Garfield and Cary Grant in *Destination Tokyo*, Brian Donlevy on *Wake Island* and Gary Cooper as the World War I hero, *Sergeant York*. In *Back to Bataan*, John Wayne walked in triumph where Taylor had trod earlier and died but not in vain.

Not a phase of the armed services, male or female, on land, sea or air, whether in the Atlantic or the Pacific, went unsung. *So Proudly We Hail* was a tribute to the nurses. *Keep Your Powder Dry* remembered the W.A.C.S., and *This is the Army*, *Air Force* and *Pride of the Marines* said what they had to say in the titles. Even the musical, the least war-like genre imaginable, found itself drafted. *Here Come the Waves* had Crosby as a singing tar; Astaire was recruited as a pilot in *The Sky's The Limit*; Betty Grable went dramatic over *A Yank In The R.A.F.*, Alice Faye sang a classic lament, *No Love, No Nothing* for the girls left behind in *The Gang's*

What *Life* captured, Hurrell enshrined. (Hurrell)

All Here, and Rita Hayworth raised morale as a Windmill girl during the London Blitz in *Tonight and Every Night*.

Once more Hollywood thrived on the need for escapist entertainment that this time the war created. Here were the audiences: the G.I.s in their cold water bunkers; the teenagers—a new label to describe adolescents now that spending money had given them consumer respectability in the eyes of Madison Avenue merchandisers; the club women—ladies too old for industry but too active to sit idly by—another wartime product, and all those in between—the wives, mothers, sweethearts, who worked and worried all day long and wanted to go out in the evening to forget. Musicals, which had been in something of a slump, revived with a bang, lit up by Technicolor and situated in exotic, untroubled South American locations for escapist glamour.

Stars trailing enigmas were out, so was Continental sophistication or screwball comedy and, for that matter, anything else that wasted time on thought not connected with the war. The mental and emotional climate was such that the inner ruminations and soul-searching of a Garbo or the finesse of a Shearer would have seemed wasteful if not downright unpatriotic. As the last films of these two stars show, their voluntary retirement was the only sensible way out, for neither was able to fit herself into the extroverted 'pin-up' mould that was now demanded. Their image—refined, perfected—was a golden chain around their creative necks.

Rita, who for all her Latin heritage, was strikingly like the silent Swede in temperament, had no established reputation to break from; her past was a launching pad. Her personality was directed to the new era. Her body suited the bathing suits, as it did the clinging dresses in which she looked down from grim barrack walls, like a vibrant Varga girl out of the pages of *Esquire*, a Hurrell dream or one of the pretty 'Petty girls' come to life.

'Pin-up' and 'Cheesecake' became new words in the nation's vocabulary, and with them came a whole new breed of stars. The 'forties was the era of bouncy, straightforward women like Betty Grable, Betty Hutton, Dorothy Lamour, Paulette Goddard, Lana Turner, Veronica Lake, Jane Russell, and of somnambulistic men like Victor Mature, Alan Ladd, Dana Andrews and Orson Welles. Most of them better known by such catchy labels as: The Hunk, The Threat, The Genius, and The Sweater, The Sarong and The Peek-a-Boo Bang, or The 'Ping' Girl, The Body, and The Girl with the Million Dollar Legs.

Rita seemed so much to personify all the good things of life worth fighting for that no label would suffice until *Life* magazine, whose favourite cover girl she became, turned up with the right one: the Love Goddess. One stunningly erotic shot taken of her by Bob Landry* became one of the most popular photos of the war. The caption, discreetly describing Rita's black lace and white satin negligée as a 'nightgown', suggested that the photo had been taken in her spare time when she had crouched in her own nightgown on her own bed in her own home. In fact it was taken during a break between filming, on a prop bed that stood on an empty stage and the negligée was not hers but came from the wardrobe. Rita's bemused, over-the-shoulder look was spontaneous. It held a direct promise few films could do more than toy

* *Life*, August 11th, 1941.

The business of glamour—what the public saw was head and shoulders and a soft cushion suggesting a bed. The jar of cold-cream on the side and the price tag still left on the flock lace, ensure the allure. It's all in a day's work. (A. L. 'Whitey' Schafer/Columbia)

with. By the end of the war, over five million copies had been sent out (a record exceeded only by a shot of Betty Grable in a white bathing suit), and its spurious fame was guaranteed when the United States Navy, detonating the first atom bomb on Bikini Atoll in 1946, paid their homage by pasting the picture on the bomb.

Hayworth's screen persona contained the ingredients of all that wartime taste dictated: she was desirable, yet could be a sex symbol for servicemen without offending the women back home; she possessed an air of romance that made it possible for her to exude those elements of mystery, formerly the stock-in-trade of foreign *femmes fatales*, without reminding the wives and sweethearts of the sort of women their men might find overseas; furthermore, she was an American classic; a heady mixture that enthralled the world.

Rita and Fred Astaire, co-stars of *You'll Never Get Rich*, relax off-set with old vaudevillian-turned-director Sidney Lanfield and the film's composer, Cole Porter. (Columbia)

It was therefore, as a gilt-edged security that she returned from her loan-outs to Columbia. The studio was prepared. Her very first film had the smell of success all over it. It was a musical with songs by Cole Porter. It had girls, gags and glamour galore, and the extra attraction of Fred Astaire. Shooting on *You'll Never Get Rich* started on May 23rd, 1941.

Except for the few films of Grace Moore, Columbia had put together very few star vehicles, and it showed. Take away Astaire and Hayworth, Porter's songs and the humorous Bob Benchley, and a trifling story remains about a Broadway dance director (Astaire) who lets himself get drafted in order to avoid the problems created for him by his producer's romantic entanglements with showgirls. As a vehicle for the talents of Astaire and Hayworth, it illustrates the old showbiz wheeze about the performer so brilliant that he could read the phone-book and make it sound good. However, Astaire had known worse pegs on which to hang dances and it was a notch above musicals of that time with the army slant a positive morale-boosting asset. More important,

Fred and Rita—the perfect team. (A. L. 'Whitey' Schafer/Columbia)

every department at Columbia was mobilised to offer the Hay-worth the public craved. The script was strung together on excuses for the star to change her wardrobe and her moods, to show her exchange caustic quips with fellow chorines and romantic ones with Astaire, and to present Hayworth as nothing less than Fred Astaire's best dancing partner. That was a cause for cheering.

Astaire was unquestionably the best known and best paid hoofer in the world. His fee per film was approximately $150,000 or one hundred times Rita's salary at this moment. In 1941, despite several films with other partners, he was still closely—and jealously—identified in the public's mind with Ginger Rogers. After their split in 1939, Ginger had gone on to success as a dramatic actress, while Fred continued in musicals, though now his partners were either temperamentally unsuited or inadequate as dancers. While this was not yet serious enough to create a crisis in his career, Astaire—who was then as now one of Hollywood's top self-deprecators—entertained thoughts of retiring. At this timely moment Columbia's Harry Cohn hired him to co-star with Rita in two films designed to boost both their careers and establish her as a major musical star.

At first, Astaire was uneasy about accepting. He was known to be morbidly sensitive about his physical appearance though women had found him romantic and men likeable ever since he had appeared in Vaudeville. Then there was the matter of height, always a delicate subject with male dancers. In his autobiography, Astaire wrote:

I asked her how tall she was as I stood alongside of her. This was always an important item to me because if the lady happened to be about 5 feet 7 inches minus shoes, and came up to the set with 3-inch heels, she'd be just a bit above my 5 feet 9½ inches ... As we stood there, both in flat heels, I was easily 3 inches taller and I told her I hoped she didn't have to wear very high heels with me. She said very quietly that she didn't think she had to. We then danced around the mirrored room in impromptu ballroom fashion, as I wanted to get an idea of how we looked together.

Recently, Astaire expanded on the subject of their work: 'She knew from experience what this dancing business was all about; that was obvious from the moment I started working with her. She was very nervous and shy when we first met in the rehearsal hall at Columbia. When I arrived, Rita was already there, sitting in a corner with Judson. That was the only time I saw him—I never saw Cohn on the set and Eduardo only came once and that was to see me. Creating an original dance routine is hard work, and we took seven or eight weeks to compose and perfect the dance numbers for the film before shooting began. The film took another two months after that.

'I never thought much about why I did something; you just did it, you know. If you don't do it like that, but try to intellectualise every step you take and every step your partner takes, you keep on doing the same damn thing the whole time, which is the only thing I was against. That's probably why I don't remember particular things to do with a film or a number or a person.

'Sometimes they'd come and be nervous like Rita was. I remember that because she mentioned it to somebody, and we talked about it to get her to relax. I usually have a lot of fun on a picture because I kid around a lot and if things ever got serious we'd discuss it, because I don't fight with the people I work with and certainly never with Rita. She had a lovely sense of humour. We used to play tricks on each other in rehearsals, always clowning around, like I would put my hands into iced water and then say to Rita, 'Let's try this step,' and she'd take a hold of these freezing hands that she wasn't expecting and let out a yell. Things like that. Silly things to keep tensions away. Laughs.

'She worried about herself, about her work; she was that much of an artist. Always a pro and very anxious to do things right. She was a good dancer, easy to work with and a quick study. She learnt steps faster than anyone I've ever known. I'd show her a routine before lunch. She'd be back right after lunch and have it down to perfection. She apparently figured it out in her mind while she was eating. But she was better when she was "on" than at rehearsal. That's when she really came alive. I asked Hermes, who'd just worked with her, about her and he told me that at first you said to yourself, "Is she going to get this? Will she be able to do this?" And then she gets before the camera—Wow! And that's true. In fact, sometimes she would do so much that I would say, "Whoa, hoah!", because she got more movement in than we needed or expected at some point. But she was doing her own thing.

'Mostly, you have to draw things out of Rita in rehearsals, then she lights up when she comes on. Of course, for me she used to light up everything because she was such a beautiful girl to be around. That's why she shines so. That's why she's a star. She had a saintly quality, you know. She had plenty of fire too—a lot of that, but there was this other quality about her. I don't know how to tell you any better, it's just that we used to say she's like a saint sometimes.

'It's a shame the two films we did were in black and white—colour would have been so much better, but I think it was something to do with wartime rationing. You couldn't do those kind of movies nowadays. They were too light. Not like the ones you see now or like the great, big-budgeted musicals I did later on at Metro. These were nice little musicals, they did all right and they still look good. You used to be able to make big musicals with a nothing story and a lot of numbers. They must have had some merit because people still like them, but that was our day, and that day is past.'

Rita's happiness at working with Astaire in two films she considers jewels in her career was marred by one thing—the studio was promoting her as a musical rival to Metro's Garland and Twentieth's Grable, but her singing voice was dubbed. It was to become a source of gnawing resentment to her that Columbia who starred her in a succession of musicals did not make the effort to train her voice so she could sing for herself. Although her ghost voices were skilfully selected to go with the image she conveyed, and so well synchronised that for years only those closely involved knew it was not Rita, she felt exploited and embarrassed. When she did sing for herself, as in the war benefit edition of the *Charlot Revue*, once even on film, no one noticed any difference between her and her dubbed voices. This suggests that she would have been capable of doing her own singing, given the patience and help she had every right to expect as the studio's prize asset.

Fred Karger, who joined Columbia as musical arranger during *Cover Girl*, put the studio's case: 'You expected a great voice from Rita, the way you didn't from Betty Grable for instance, simply because it started that way when they first tested her and felt she couldn't do her own singing. I once made and intercut eighty-four takes of a song with Rita singing, I think it was "Amado Mio". The effort was certainly made and Rita worked hard. She was going to Kay Thompson at the time, and recently she went back to Kay to develop some new ideas.

'But great research went into getting the right voices for her. The dubbers would come up and watch the number while Rita was working on it. They'd work with her, especially Anita Ellis

and Jo Ann Greer, who were very conscientious and would
develop a rapport with Rita. Lovely and unassuming as she was,
she would learn the number thoroughly, where to breathe,
everything, so that you believed it was Rita singing. She did a
superb job of lip sync. A lot of thinking went into it, so you got a
very nice soundtrack recording of it.

'Of course she was victimised a bit by the times. The thinking
then was, "This is an expensive picture and everything has to be
perfect." Today you'd want to use Rita's voice from the start, the
visual would overtake the audial. Today maybe, with the absence
of voices all over . . .'

Full orchestra rehearsals seemed like a useless expenditure, and
not only in an economy-minded studio like Columbia. It was
expedient to dub performers who had untrained voices; this was
top secret at the time, indeed it was one of the last facets of movie
making that the studios made public. The fact that she was not
allowed to sing with her own voice was humiliating for her. Jack
Cole told me that, during the making of *Down to Earth* Rita
informed an interviewer from *Life* magazine that she usually did
her own singing in films. She was, of course, being loyal to the
studio rather than merely protecting a badly bruised ego. Even
today, this is one technique of corporate image-making that she
finds hard to accept.

Rita Hayworth: 'I wanted to study singing, but Harry Cohn
kept saying, "Who needs it?" and the studio wouldn't pay for it.
They had me so intimidated that I couldn't have done it anyway.
They always said, "Oh, no, we can't let you do it, there's no time
for that, it has to be done right now!" I was under contract, and
that was it.'

You'll Never Get Rich, opening at the prestigious Radio City
Music Hall in New York, was a smash. Especially with the critics
who outdid the studio's own flacks to claim that Astaire and
Hayworth were the screen's finest musical comedy dance team.
Time magazine devoted its cover to Rita at a time when to put a
movie star on their cover was still a special accolade, and opened
their story, 'California Carmen' with:

> It was news in Hollywood that a new star had been made. But
> it was news throughout the US that the best tap dancer in the
> world, Fred Astaire, had a new dancing partner—and there
> could be no doubt that she was the best partner he had ever
> had.

All the reviews read as glowingly, which is surprising since Fred and Rita had only three major numbers together in a Cole Porter score which, while pleasant, was not top drawer. It is charitable to accept Astaire's reason when he says that the score didn't have a full chance to catch on because of a radio network strike during which no *Ascap* music was played for quite a long period. A much more likely explanation is in the Porter biography, *The Life that Late He Led*, wherein the anticipation of working on the project and the actual doing of the job were two quite different things.

> Cole found writing songs for a plot that utilised military life as the background for the familiar Hollywood triangle surprisingly difficult. Even his enthusiasm for the cast ... could not carry him through the assignment with ease. He had been accustomed to the lavish and Olympian rites of production as practised by M.G.M., whereas Columbia Pictures was budget-minded and practical. Cole was amused but slightly disconcerted, too, when studio head Harry Cohn insisted on submitting the songs to clerical workers to pre-test their appeal.

Basically, some of the film's success was attributable to the heavy promotion campaign behind it and to the paucity of really good musicals at that time, coupled with an insatiable demand for escapist entertainment. In the final tally, however, its success was a tribute to the talents and chemistry of the stars and that, when all is said and done, is what the director, writers, photographers, make-up department, set-designers, dressmaker, and hairdresser were paid for—to ensure that these shone to the best possible advantage.

As with Ginger, but quite differently, Astaire's personality gained an extra dimension from dancing with Rita. In their nine films, Astaire and Rogers epitomised the classless 'aristocratic' Americans of the 'thirties. Compressed in their two films, Fred and Rita bridged generation and age difference to embody timeless romanticism. Those two lovely introverts, so private in life, are transformed when dancing so that, like the lovers of *The Enchanted Cottage* whose beauty becomes singularly apparent only in their world, they, too, need never fear the stroke of midnight.

The film opens with a bang: a Broadway dance director (Astaire) is trying to drill a group of chorines into a snappy routine; the new girl (Rita) is out of step; to wry looks from the other girls, he gives her a private demonstration of *The Boogie*

Barcarolle, an explosive little mixture of tap and ballet, only to find her matching him, beat for beat, step for step, leap for joyous leap. If he is still a bit slow on the uptake, the point Rita was scoring isn't lost on another girl whose snappy line in put-downs echoes her sisters from the hungry 'thirties:

'Honey, don't kid yourself, he doesn't notice you. To a hungry man a lamb chop is a tasty dish, but to the butcher it's just another hunk of meat.'

But shortly after, Fred and Rita are thrown together again in a roof-top restaurant, where the two slide on to the dance floor and into a simple Samba that makes it obvious they were meant for each other even if the script has to find ways of keeping them apart for another hour, only possible through musical-comedy misunderstandings. Here, as in so many other films, the war's function was reduced to making the paths of love run less smoothly. No sooner is Astaire in the army than he lands himself in the guardhouse for a swinging buck and wing solo, backed by a steamy negro quartet, none other than the Delta Rhythm Boys playing 'Since I Kissed My Baby Goodbye'. Rita turns out to be the sweetheart of a captain on the same base which allows her to turn up in the army—not unreasonable, since we've already accepted that a girl with her looks and talent could also turn up in a chorus line. Continued confusion allows for more dances and leads to the best known number, a haunting Rumba, 'So Near and Yet So Far', sultry and elegant in rhythm, spirit and emotion. She brings him her youth, her beauty and her devotion; he takes her flying among the stars.

The production is smoothly packaged by Sidney Lanfield, an agile director who had also known Rita's father in Vaudeville. The eighty-eight minutes whizzed by and left one longing to see the two together again. But first, they had prior commitments to fulfil: Astaire to make *Holiday Inn* opposite Bing Crosby, and Rita on loan-out to Twentieth for the starring role in a Technicolor period musical, *My Gal Sal*, and for her contribution to the all-star portmanteau comedy-drama, *Tales of Manhattan*. Her episode opened the film and it was completed before she began work on *My Girl Sal*, although the latter was released first. Before reporting to Twentieth in November 1941, Rita, accompanied by her husband, was sent by Columbia to New York on a spectacularly successful promotional tour for the film. By now, it was becoming increasingly obvious to those close to the couple that the marriage was entering its last phase.

It was the first time in their five years that they had gone on a trip, or been together for any length of time. But at the arranged receptions and interviews, Judson remained discreetly in the background. It's quite probable, however, that this ploy had been suggested by the publicity department, so as not to detract from the allure of a beautiful young woman by the presence of a husband, especially an unglamorous older one. Her capacity for attracting the headlines was a Public Relations' dream; the resourceful publicity man in Columbia's New York office, Frank Rosenberg, suggested a stunt in the spirit of the times. Rita was to tour the city, whether opening bazaars, appearing on radio shows to plug the film, selling war bonds or going to parties in her honour, always in the company of a soldier, a sailor, a marine and a coast guardsman. That sort of stunt doesn't leave much room for a husband, but it made the front pages of newspapers and magazines throughout her stay, throughout the country.

Soon after her return to Hollywood and before she began work, Rita and Judson parted.

Making the move towards independence, she shifted into a new gear; as difficulties in her marriage increased, differences with her family caused because of Judson were patched up. Near the end of Rita's marriage she was calling her mother on the phone regularly. Dorothy Valdespino, visiting Volga, overheard one of their conversations.

Volga was so pleased, because since the marriage she hadn't seen much of Rita. She kept saying, "Yes, Rita? Oh, Rita, I'm so pleased. I'm so glad Rita ... I'm so glad.'

'I didn't know what they were talking about. Then when she hung up she said, "Now this isn't for the press, but Rita is going to file for divorce." Rita had told her that after the first six months she knew it wasn't going to work out.'

Rita was about to become the most sought-after girl in town. She dated many of Hollywood's most eligible bachelors—and while one might suspect the studio of cooking up headline romances, there's no reason to suppose Rita had trouble getting a date. She was seen at parties and openings with Tony Martin, David Niven, Errol Flynn, Howard Hughes, a budding Greek shipping magnate, Stavros Niarchos, and so on—some were fun but none were serious.

Meanwhile, there was her career. Her episode in *Tales of Manhattan*, a glossy Park Avenue melodrama with Rita as a two-timing wife who looks classy in a gaudy lurex gown and at

In all-star portmanteau *Tales of Manhattan* she is the reason for murder between two men, lover Boyer, husband Mitchell. (Fox)

ease whether pawn or predator, only took a couple of weeks to shoot. It was the first and most glamorous of five stories linked by the adventures of a man's dress coat in its brief transition from Park Avenue to its final service as a sharecropper's scarecrow.*

Each episode had its own team of writers. Hayworth's was based on a short play by Ferenc Molnar adapted for her by Ben Hecht, and needed all the dimly lit *savoir faire* its French director and cast could give it. She was cast opposite Boyer as her lover and Thomas Mitchell as her husband. The list of famous writers was as impressive as that of the starry cast, which read like a *Who's Who*, including Charles Laughton, Henry Fonda, Edward G. Robinson, Paul Robeson, George Sanders. Rita's cousin Ginger appeared, too, though not in the same episode. Julien Duvivier, fresh from similar French triumphs like *Un Carnet de Bal*, directed it.

*Although six episodes were filmed, the sixth, starring W. C. Fields, was deleted from the released print because its mood was felt not to be in keeping with the rest of the film.

Hermes Pan, a life long friend, partners Rita in a number he choreographed for *My Gal Sal*, 1942. (20th Century Fox/Frank Powolny)

Tales of Manhattan opened at the Radio City Music Hall to mixed reviews, but sensational business. Modestly, the studio claimed it was 'The Greatest Hit of the Twentieth Century'!

My Gal Sal was a typical Fox musical; that is to say it was biographical, set in an earlier period, shot in colour and revolved around one man and two women or two men and one woman—they all looked the same. In drama, Zanuck had brought the studio into the Depression, but in musicals they were still in the gay 'nineties which allowed their blonde stars to look ravishing in the gaslight and champagne costumes of that era. As far as the biographical data in any of them was concerned, few of the facts would stand checking; their heroes and heroines were only motivated by the exigencies of the next big musical number, which stretched credulity to coincide with events. *My Gal Sal* was no exception.

This film was based on the life of Paul Dresser (Victor Mature) and his stormy love affair with the Broadway musical star, Sally Elliott (Rita Hayworth) who was supposedly his inspiration for the title song. The story (credited to no less source than Theodore Dreiser's book *My Brother Paul*) narrated brother Paul's rise from the banks of the Wabash to the toast of Tin Pan Alley, but it all comes across as just a lot of lavishly decorated hog-wash. Most of the songs they used in the film weren't even his, since the studio evidently thought that few of Dresser's songs were sufficiently memorable for big production numbers.

The difference that made the difference was that the leading role was played by neither of the studio's resident musical queens, Betty Grable and Alice Faye, or even Carole Landis (in a humiliating supporting role), but by Rita. Gwen Wakeling's romantic period dresses in the style of *Strawberry Blonde* exploited every inch of Rita's figure; her hair was swept up in the mode of the time without diminishing her allure. Her performance, given that this was a role that could have been wrecked by an emotion heavier than a frown, was faultless. The unsure, uncertain, questioning Margarita Cansino was light years away from this assured celebrity.

It is her performance in films like this that enhances the fascinating incongruity between the woman and the star. To read the reviews the film received, one might be forgiven for thinking they were enthusing over a cure for cancer as they praised her acting ('Nothing less than sensational' *New York Daily News*); her looks ('She outglamors glamor' *Los Angeles Times*); even her dubbed vocalising by Nan Wynn, ('A pleasantly husky voice' *New York Times*); and her dancing. The numbers, choreographed by Val Russet and Hermes Pan (her partner in one dance) were the best things in the film. A lot of time had been allowed for them before filming began. There was plenty of high-stepping verve and sparkle to big production numbers like the old-fashioned bathing suit number, 'On the Banks of the Wabash', the glamorous 'On the Gay White Way', or the colourful finale that serves to re-unite the quarrelling lovers, 'My Gal Sal', where a long-stemmed Rita was surrounded by a chorus of top-hatted gents.

Rita was being wooed by chunky Victor Mature in private, but surprisingly little of this emotion registers on the screen. But then, true love rarely conveys the same excitement on the screen as it does in life. There was a great deal more chemistry between her and Astaire, with whom there was no suggestion of anything but a professional rapport. She had separated from Judson before she began work on the film.

Acting for the first time without other guidance, she started her divorce proceedings, charging Judson with extreme mental cruelty. Apparently in the belief that the court would keep secret the charges she was making against her husband, she accused him of treating her as an investment and demanding $30,000 to get out of

May 22, 1942—Rita with her mother in court after obtaining a divorce from Judson. 'The red-headed actress, who rose to screen stardom in the past year, charged cruelty and testified Judson nagged her constantly and interfered with her work. She is 23.' (Associated Press)

her life in return for the time and money he had spent on her. If she didn't pay, he threatened her with bodily harm and exposure to public contempt and ridicule. The court, refusing her plea for secrecy, published the case and the resulting publicity revealed that what had been announced as an 'amicable parting' was in fact a battle royal. This was not good for her career as far as the studio was concerned, and they stepped in to smooth things over. Though she did not return to Judson and there was no hint of a reconciliation, Rita withdrew her charges. Her ex-husband received his $30,000—from Harry Cohn.

'I didn't have any fun in those five years,' Rita declared. 'I never was permitted to make any decisions. He robbed everything of excitement.'

In spite of their domestic differences, Rita has never sounded bitter or ungrateful when she tells reporters: 'I realise how much Ed has done for me. I never had to do any fighting for myself with executives and agents. He fought for me. After we got married, running my career was his only concern, and he gave it everything he had, and his efforts paid off. Although we had our differences, he's entitled to a fair return.' Their divorce came through on Friday, May 22nd, 1942, after the kind of unpleasant publicity that would only make Rita withdraw more into herself.

Mature was by now her constant escort. They had first met when she was making *Blood and Sand*, at which point Rita was married and, except for the usual pleasantries, nothing had sparked between them. Now that she was separated from her husband, she was ready for some of the fun and glamour everybody assumed surrounded her constantly. The next few months saw, albeit only briefly, an extrovert glamour girl. She was not much different from the other romantic girls who took Mature in his first wave of success for a glorious hunk of masculinity. Added to which, he had yet to be drafted and had the field pretty much to himself. Known as 'The Hunk' ever since his biceps had smothered the screen in *One Million Years B.C.*, he was much in demand as a leading man on the screen and about town, collecting stars the way other boys collected stamps.

Rita was distinctly Hollywood's current favourite daughter, and their brief romance had all those elements that made for colour, excitement and conversation. Either because of Mature's reputation as a limelight-seeker or simply because of his Olympian disregard for the opinion of Hollywood's columnists, he was not popular with them. Articles like Ruth Waterbury's astringent 'The Romance Hollywood doesn't like' in *Photoplay*, November 1942, went out of its way to warn Rita off Vic by categorically stating that his best friends were an editor and a press agent. By this time, however, he was long out of harm's way, as a member of the Coast Guard. At any rate, Rita, who would listen neither to her parents nor to her powerful employer when it came to the man she loved, would be even less likely to listen to columnists on the subject.

When Mature was shipped to Connecticut by his outfit, Rita planned to visit him. Cohn heard about it and tried to get her to change her plans by having his dissuasive New York publicity head meet her at the train. After spending an evening of argument, she finally agreed that it would be imprudent for her to join Mature. The next morning, however, she felt differently and left to join him. All Cohn could do was fume. When Victor was given leave from the Coast Guard to attend the première of *Tales of Manhattan*, Rita was his date and wore a big ring which he had given her, though neither said it was an engagement ring.

Where others had failed, the Coast Guard succeeded. When he

was called up, still carrying a torch for Rita, she in turn promised to wait till he returned, but that was fan talk. Ruth Waterbury's article concluded with some friendly advice which she might have left out had she foreseen the future:

Rita has had one misfortune in love. In the year that must elapse before she could marry Vic, she may discover a man truly chivalrous, intelligent, and worthy, who would adore marrying her. To Hollywood, the man should not be Vic Mature.

When the right man presented himself, Rita had no trouble deciding, though the columnists, led by a vitriolic Louella Parsons, disliked him even more than Mature. Rita met him at a dinner party given by Joseph Cotten, and was as impressed and dazzled as everyone else had been by the genius who conceived, co-authored, directed and starred in *Citizen Kane*—Orson Welles.

He asked her out to dinner the following night, and she accepted. If the columnists were unhappy, Cohn, who saw every man in Rita's life as a spanner in his works, was furious and banned Welles from the lot. Rita was ecstatic. The press treated their romance in much the same humour as they were to adopt for another celebrated *amour* between a Love Goddess and an artist—Monroe and Arthur Miller. Wags referred to it as a marriage of 'Beauty and the Brain', but Rita was in love and, as always, like a little girl totally devoted to that one being.

Welles conversed brilliantly on subjects of which Rita had never heard. He did not make her feel small; rather, he outlined a course of study and furthered the education which her work had interrupted at an early age. She had never been more serious about anything in her life, as she gallantly essayed philosophy, politics, music and a wide range of literature. She volunteered to join Welles and Cotten on the Mercury Theatre radio show, and the magic act they performed for the entertainment of servicemen. So, nightly, Welles gave G.I.s the illusion that he was sawing Rita in half. Despite auguries to the contrary—what, after all, did a man of his portentous intellect see in a shy Love Goddess?—the romance bloomed. According to *Life* magazine, she had her moments of panic at parties full of his intellectual cronies.

'All those people are staring at me,' she whispered to Mrs Joseph Cotten, 'because they think I'm a dumb woman.'

Rita and Victor Mature attending the premiere of *Tales of Manhattan*. The ring was a present from Victor but she meant it when she told reporters that it wasn't an engagement ring. *(Photoplay)*

Rita and Orson on one of their several appearances together on the Lux Radio Show for CBS, on December 5th, 1941. (CBS)

'They're staring all right, darling,' admitted Mrs Cotten, appraising the situation realistically, 'but it's not because you're dumb.'

Paramount among her attractions for the opposite sex, perhaps more than her beauty, willingness to learn, her sweetness and generosity, was her gift for listening—an unsung but highly treasured art from which few men are immune. Happy in love, she was happy in work, and there were no difficulties at Columbia after returning from *My Gal Sal*.

Frank Capra had lifted Columbia into the major league and Rita had consolidated that move. In the next fourteen years, Cohn would countenance no more loan-outs of her services. Whenever Rita packed up to leave, it wasn't to make a movie for someone else.

Rita eagerly began on her new musical with Astaire, *You Were Never Lovelier*. In every respect, it turned out to be a small but brilliantly cut gem. William Seiter, who was assigned to direct, had previously made *Roberta*, one of Astaire's most distinguished 'thirties musicals with a score by Jerome Kern. He equalled its elegant sheen on this occasion. *You Were Never Lovelier* had been adapted for the American public from an Argentinian film of a few years previous (*The Gay Senorita*); it possessed a slight but smooth framework into which the songs and dances fitted with hand-in-glove ease to achieve that added dimension which musicals can, but do not always, possess.

In 1942, the Arthur Freed unit at M.G.M. and directors like Minnelli, were only just beginning their, for America, revolutionary strides towards marrying the song and the book. Their inspiration came of course from Broadway shows like *Oklahoma*, directed by Rouben Mamoulian. In the musical genre, virtually the only directors whose films achieved such a homogenous blend were those made by Mamoulian, all of whose work (including such straight dramas as *Blood and Sand*) was guided by a musical approach. To speculate on what a Mamoulian, a Minnelli or a Charles Walters might have done with the Astaire-Hayworth team is more frustrating than rewarding, for although they were all around at the same time, the combination never happened. Several years later, Astaire's career would reveal new dimensions working with all three of these directors; *Silk Stockings*, *Bandwagon* and *Easter Parade* are classics of the genre and highlights in the careers of all concerned. But there was none of this in 1942, hardly a red letter year for musicals. Against that backdrop, the skill, charm and harmony of *You Were Never Lovelier* becomes all the keener.

Astaire played an American dancer (Robert Davis) stranded in Buenos Aires after losing his money at the races. Against his own inclinations but out of necessity he goes looking for an engagement at a swank nightclub owned by the wealthy Senor Acuna (Adolphe Menjou), who already has Xavier Cugat and his orchestra working for him. Acuna is a crochety, domineering man who doesn't want Astaire; his main concern is the forthcoming wedding of the eldest of his four daughters. The youngest two also have boyfriends, but it is Papa's rule that they must marry in descending order of age. This complicates matters, since his third child, Maria (Hayworth) has romantic notions about a knight on a white horse sweeping her away, an idea which precludes most of the local male populace. To put her in a romantic frame of mind, her father secretly sends her orchids and unsigned love letters. By accident, Astaire, still hanging around for a job, is mistaken for a messenger and delivers the flowers to Maria who promptly mistakes him for her Lochinvar. To maintain the pretence and dispell his daughter's romantic illusions, Acuna decides to hire the American. At this stage, the soufflé story takes on a crust as complications mount.

The story's thinness is not a weakness; it's a perfect fairy tale. There's little of it, but what it contains is good. The songs are classic moments: Snow White's apple, Rapunzel's hair, Cinderella's slipper. They illuminate everything and thus were vital ingredients in the film's success. They were written by the father of contemporary popular music, Jerome Kern, and his lyricist was Johnny Mercer. Together they spun off a group of songs, most of which became instant hits and remain standards.

In his autobiography, Astaire wrote:

The Columbia lot was heavily occupied with production at the time, and it was difficult to find a place to rehearse. For a while, Rita and I had to work out in Hollywood at a civic auditorium. The rest of the time, until the picture started actual shooting, the only available place to suit our convenience near the studio was a room in a funeral parlor of the Hollywood cemetery on Santa Monica Blvd. This was a sort of meeting hall, a parlor, to be exact, on the second floor of the building, overlooking the vast sea of tombstones below. We had plenty of jokes about this

This is the show-stopping 'Shorty George' number as performed. (Lippman/Columbia)

amazing workshop where we were supposed to be inspired to turn out the gayest, most glamorous entertainment.

Every time a funeral came through the gates, we could see it from the windows, and naturally we'd have to stop until it moved well on past. One of the men from the office downstairs would come running up half whispering, 'Hold it a minute, folks, they're bringing one in.'

Oddly enough, we pulled some good dance material out of those weird surroundings ... and one of my best solos. A trick number performed while Adolphe Menjou was supposedly sitting at a desk in his office. The dance had a lot of tricks including one where I jumped up on his desk and on a certain two beats hit him physically on his head with my cane.

The following number is his first with Rita, the exquisite 'I'm Old-Fashioned', which she sings in the garden of the family estate

Just Joy. Rita and Astaire in *You Were Never Lovelier*. Rita's dress is by Irene. (Lippman/Columbia)

to still his arguments (unbeknown to her, being proffered under orders from her father) that he's not the right man for her. Every argument he puts forward she frustrates. He tells her he's a gambler. So is she. He argues that he's just a dancer. 'I *love* to dance too.' If ever an exchange begged to be put into action, this must be it. More and more in love with her he makes a last stab to prove himself the wrong man. 'I'm old-fashioned. You're streamlined. You're today. Sister, I was raised among the grasshoppers. I am strictly from corn.' We don't believe it; we're not supposed to believe it; so why should she. She vanquishes him with the most melting lyrical *coup de grâce*: 'I'm old-fashioned, I love the moon-light, I love the old-fashioned things.'

It's Kern and Mercer at their finest, phrase and melody wedding. What came first? Who cares anymore. They are all one. The big studio production plays around them; the sets are elegant moorish designs to create a garden for lovers—black and white filigree fences and doors. Astaire is in tails, Rita in a black lace dress by Irene that combines modesty with allure. They stroll as she sings, the verse ending with the two of them one, gliding dreamily down a tree-lined walk. The number is divided into stages showing their transition from mutual happiness at discovering they're in love into an exuberant bursting commitment and ending on a sensuous Latin American Samba arrangement, all of which encompasses the wooing, the wedding and the nuptials. (As an example of the transition from story to song to dance, this is as perfect as anything of its kind, reminding one of a similar arrangement for the 'Dancing in the Dark' number Astaire did with Cyd Charisse in *Bandwagon*.

Rita not only brought rhythm and precision to her work, but her rapport with Astaire was miraculous. Unlike many of his partners, one never for a moment feels he has to woo her to dance; the harmony between them is established from the first. The dance is their own private language. This is evident, too, in the fast-paced 'Shorty George' number—a dance where you beat your feet till your feet are beat. It's a foot-tapping, rug-cutting Jitterbug, which became a popular hit with the Saturday Night Jukebox set. It was the last of Astaire's 'The . . . numbers'. They had been a regular feature of his 'thirties films, e.g. *The* Carioca, *The* Piccolino and *The* Yam, among others which were inserted into the film to give his fans a new craze to follow. During rehearsals of this complicated fast-paced routine, Rita tripped, fell, hit her chin on the floor and was knocked out.

As a contrast, Rita then has one of the best known of Kern's melodies, 'Dearly Beloved', which she sings to herself as she undresses and showers to get ready for the party celebrating her parents' anniversary. While it's not quite a 'dance', she moves around the room in a dreamy daze, collapsing at last on to her bed. She is the quintessence here of those things she does best and for which the public loved her: reflective, romantic and ravishing.

Meanwhile, there is a misunderstanding in the Acuna household when Mother thinks Father wrote the letters to another woman, creating one of the film's funniest exchanges. Menjou

stomps out of the door, knocking into Xavier Cugat, kneeling
pop-eyed behind it. Snaps Menjou, 'What's·wrong with you?'
'There's something in my eye,' blurts out the embarrassed Cugat.
'The keyhole I suppose!' retorts Menjou with a cutting relish. To
sort things out Bob explains. Maria overhears and leaves. This
time, Bob, with full family consent, sets out to woo her back.

Hourly, orchids arrive. Kern spun out another of those beautiful romantic melodies 'Orchids for Tonight' sung by a group of
delivery boys in the hallway so Maria can hear them through her
closed bedroom door. Her resistance is weakening as the melody
switches to a *dolce* Samba arrangement played by Cugat's orchestra, but it's laughter that brings the lovers together, as dressed
in armour, he crashes from his horse, but steps out of the debris in
white tie and tails. To a reprise of the title song (abruptly cut
earlier), they swing away from the camera into the distance. One
of those little miracles. It's really all too short.

The film was released with a great deal of fanfare again at the
Radio City Music Hall, Rita's third there in a year. Perhaps
expectations had out-distanced what this film, any film, could live
up to. There was no dissatisfaction with the stars, the score was
liked, though it was felt not to be up to Kern's standard, but that,
too, is expectation blunting judgement. But the major complaint
was the same as on their previous outing—not enough dancing.
This was the standard complaint, even in those films Fred made
with Ginger. It wasn't that there were insufficient numbers, but
that they were so superior to what came before and after that they
showed up the proceedings.

But the gripes were mild. It was simply a case of asking for the
moon when, as in one of the decade's great tag lines, they already
had the stars. It was previewed on October 5th and generally
released on December 5th in time for the Christmas trade. Its
success was hotly to be followed with the studio's most ambitious
attempt to showcase Rita's personality. It would be sold on her
name alone. And to further emphasise her deluxe position there
would now be only one Hayworth picture a year.

She had time off to spend with her family, get to know Orson
Welles, and travel to New York. Mature was now well out of the
picture, but he wasn't the only person to have brought the war
closer to Hayworth. Her father still took evening classes, but his
daytime was spent working in the Douglas aircraft factory for the
Government; her brothers had been drafted—Eddie was stationed
in the Pacific, Vernon in Europe. Now Rita also saw more of her

mother, to make up for the years of estrangement caused by her first marriage.

Like her daughter, Volga was not a great socialiser, preferring to remain at home when Eduardo didn't need her to interpret. Added to which, ill health and worry over her absent sons only made her more nervous and prone to drink. When she wasn't visiting Rita on a set, or going with Eduardo to Rita's for dinner, She would stay in bed. From there she kept in touch with friends who dropped in, and with Rita by phone. To protect their mother from possible bad news from the front line, the boys arranged amongst themselves to name Rita as their next-of-kin. While this brought them closer together they could not have foreseen the problem of being identified as the brothers of a famous movie star.

'When you go into the service they ask who you want to be notified in case you are injured or killed,' said Vernon. 'Well, my brother was in the service, my mother was quite ill and my father couldn't read English that well, so the only person I could put down was Rita because I was afraid my mother would have a shock or something if she got the news first without someone to soften it for her. Of course it got out. The Army is no different

Rita's brother Vernon and his army friends look at a picture of his sister pinned up in his foot locker, 1943. (Vernon Cansino Collection)

from any other organisation—they wanted to exploit me so, of course, there was some resentment at first.

'For instance, I was in a camp near a small town in Kentucky and they wanted to show the town that the camp was full of fine young American boys and they needn't worry. So they wrote articles about Private Cansino and everything to get the townspeople to accept the camp. There is always a lot of resentment when an Army camp gets set up so they wanted good publicity for it. Naturally, the other guys get to ribbing you or try to use you to get introductions or photos from movie stars. I had a photo of her myself in my locker. After a time it didn't mean too much to the men in my platoon.

'As far as getting into a fight because of Rita, that only happened when the comments about her got so out of hand they were obnoxious. They weren't really saying things about her they were just challenging me; I wasn't really defending her, I was defending myself. Usually you let it pass because the guy is a jackass. And you can't go round fighting everybody. Eddie had it tougher because he took things differently and he used to get very incensed when people made cracks. Once a guy knows your weak point they've got you—but that was his nature. Was Rita aware of that? Oh yeah. But what could she do!'

In the beginning Harry Cohn had an idea and the idea had a title—*Cover Girl*. Rehearsals for the dance routines began early April: shooting May 27th, 1943. It was the studio's most ambitious production for the year and their first Hayworth film in colour. Along with *Meet Me In St Louis*, released the same year, it has since been credited with the arrival of the musical as an art. Actually, the idea for *Cover Girl* had been presented to Harry Cohn by Warner Brothers' publicity man Robert Taplinger, after his own studio turned it down. It was just the idea of doing a picture about cover girls. Since Rita Hayworth was on nearly every cover it must have seemed an inspired title to Cohn.

Writing in the 'fifties as programme planner for the British Film Institute, Karel Reisz stated the general opinion:

> In *Cover Girl* we can see the transition from the old to the new taking place. Though its story has the usual backstage background, many of its numbers are staged in the open air and characters dance in it for the joy of dancing and as an ex-

pression of mood, not simply as professional performers. (Astaire, it will be noted, always played a dancer in his films; Kelly did in *Cover Girl* but has since increasingly danced character parts.) The design of costumes and sets, moreover, is notably above the usual standard of the routine product. *Cover Girl* saw, too, the emergence of Gene Kelly as a choreographer himself playing the role which he has since played often again: he dances pieces of 'plot' instead of interpolating numbers and his style is that of a ballet dancer rather than that of a 'hoofer'. Already in *Cover Girl* the numbers choreographed by Kelly stand out in sharp contrast against the rest of the film, foreshadowing what was to come.

To see Kelly's highly vaunted choreography now is to observe the efforts of a talented man exploring new limits at the expense of a homogenous melding with his surroundings. What the film has not lost is that uniquely 'forties Technicolor lushness, the wry wisecracking of Eve Arden, the glow of Kern's score and the ebullience, the sheer joy Rita exudes so effortlessly. In private and in her work she had never been happier and the camera gained by it.

Rita: 'No problems while making that film! None, none. We had a sensational time with Gene and Phil (Silvers). I knew we had a rapport—they were both so great to work with. It was a happy time. I didn't know we were doing anything special, but you knew it was good because it felt good making it.'

What Rita doesn't say, and which explains in part some of her joy, was a secret she kept and which no one guessed until they read it in the papers—she had married Orson Welles.

When *Cover Girl* was still only an idea, songwriter Arthur Schwartz was brought in to produce it. He had originally approached Cohn to buy back a story he had written as a vehicle for Jean Arthur which Columbia had bought but never made. Out of the blue, Cohn asked him if he would like to produce Rita Hayworth's next film.

'I think there is some sort of typographical error there,' said Schwartz. 'You must be thinking of somebody else. I have never produced anything before.' Cohn said, 'I know you haven't but I talked to a lot of people and they said you are the sort of person I should have for it. We are having a lot of trouble with the script. Would you like to do it?'

Since Schwartz had heard about Cohn from his friend Jean

On the set of Columbia's Technicolor *Cover Girl* are (left to right) cameraman Rudy Mate, comedian Phil Silvers, songwriter Sammy Cahn, Rita, Gene Kelly, and director Charles Vidor. (Scott/Columbia)

Arthur he was suspicious, but the deal was finally settled and a salary of $1,000 a week fixed. Though he left at the end of the film because Warner Brothers came up with an offer that Cohn wouldn't match, he had grown to appreciate Columbia and its head:

'In spite of everything people have said about Harry Cohn, his vulgarity, his lack of education, neither of which was a unique characteristic among the men in his position—he had an instinct for quality. *Cover Girl*, as I made it, couldn't have been made at W.B.; Jack Warner wouldn't have had the taste somehow, while at Metro they would have overproduced it—too many girls and too many of everything.'

Story: Kelly plays Danny McGuire, who runs a small nightclub in Brooklyn with a budget chorus of five girls, led by Genius (Phil Silvers) as star comic. Though Rusty (Rita) is Danny's sweetheart, she's just another girl in his show whom he keeps in line with the reminder, 'You get there on your feet, not your face.' Rusty disagrees, enters a Cover Girl Contest sponsored by *Vanity* magazine, and wins. She does so because the magazine's distinguished publisher (Otto Kruger) remembers the woman he loved and lost forty years earlier—none other than Rusty's grandmother (also played by Rita), glamorous star of Tony Pastor's Music Hall. Dissolve to Pastor's and Rita in becoming period costumes. Cue for a delightful musical interlude not staged by Gene Kelly, and a song, 'Poor John!', not written by Kern, but by Fred Leigh, a popular turn-of-the-century tunesmith. Rita's period costumes were by Gwen Wakeling, who had done the same for *My Gal Sal*. Though contrived, the flashback (recalling Victor Saville's *Evergreen*) served a dual purpose—it enriched the plot and it satisfied the demands of Hayworth's audiences, who had previously queued up to see her in *Strawberry Blonde* and *My Gal Sal*. 'Poor John!' was a busker's number that allowed Hayworth some fun, incidentally illustrating her versatility as well as her professional approach.

It was Gracie Fields who taught Rita the Cockney accent required for the number. 'I'd never been to England and I knew nothing about the way they did it, and Charles Vidor was a Hungarian, so he couldn't help me with my accent for that part at all—and Gracie was in town. She was living at the Pacific Pallisades at the time and I used to go down there and work with her every day on that number.' Remembering the incident for me thirty years later, Rita lapsed into the song—'John took me out to see his mother'—the Cockney inflections loud and clear, the voice jolly.

The intimacy of Danny's Club suffers from an invasion of up-town socialites—including an impetuous Broadway producer (Lee Bowman)—who have become Rusty's admirers. When the infatuated Bowman offers to star Rusty in a Broadway show, Danny, not wishing to hold her for sentimental reasons, fires her. This cues Kelly's famous *alter ego* number. As Kelly himself recalled for Clive Hirschhorn's biography of him:

Right after I'd been jilted by Rusty, there was a spot where I wandered out into the street—alone and unhappy. At this point I wanted to express what I felt in a dance. And I wanted the dance to further the plot emotionally, and not just be a musical interlude. But unless you're in a ballet, you can't just begin to dance. You have to state your 'thesis' in a song, first, and then go into the dance.... I tell the audience in a song what I'm going to do, and then I do it. So, in *Cover Girl*, what I decided to do at this point was state my thesis not in a song, but in a few words which came over the soundtrack as if they were my 'stream of consciousness', and then go into the dance.

The film's ebullience comes across in this still of the three principals, Silvers, Rita and Gene Kelly in the finale, 'Make Way For Tomorrow'. (Scott/Columbia)

His *doppelgänger* deserved its acclaim. Rusty is an overnight Broadway sensation in a typical 'forties production number that featured *the* Cover Girls. Everybody's at the opening except the man she loves. After, she goes searching for Danny at the club—it's closed, he's gone, she's heartbroken, gets drunk and agrees to marry the persistent Bowman. But at the altar, she falters, takes a leaf from her grandmother's book and bolts from her would-be bridegroom to join the man she really loves. Instead of the usual expansive girlie production number, the film concludes on a bright burst of the three principals, Phil, Gene and Rita, dancing down the street to the sound of clanging ashcans and the exuberance of Kern's rousing 'Make Way For Tomorrow'.

The auspicious atmosphere conducive to everyone giving of their best was marked by the production line-up—either continuing or beginning Rita's working partnerships with some of the finest exponents of creative craftsmanship. Rudolph Maté, who had photographed Dreyer's *Passion of Jeanne D'Arc* before going to Hollywood was the principal photographer on *Cover Girl*. The Hungarian, Charles Vidor, who to everyone's surprise was assigned his first musical, had directed Rita's first starring film and was to direct her greatest successes. And this was also her second Jerome Kern score.

The costumes were by Travis Banton (*Blood and Sand*), Gwen Wakeling (*My Gal Sal*) and Muriel King. Less significant to the success of *Cover Girl*, but a happy factor in many of Rita's subsequent films, was band leader turned musical arranger and accompanist, Fred Karger, who was brought over on a loan-out from Twentieth because somebody at Columbia had heard he was good with dancers. While on the fringes, though not yet actively involved, were two men who would play a significant part in the Hayworth career: the designer Jean Louis and choreographer Jack Cole. There was one other vital ingredient to *Cover Girl*'s success—Virginia Van Upp, who fashioned a classic from what had been seven or eight bad scripts.

Virginia not only either wrote or produced Rita's subsequent films including *Gilda*, she also became a good, understanding friend. As a woman and a writer, Virginia was capable of transmuting her understanding of Rita into aspects that would fit with Rita's screen image, thus refining and adding depth to them. She felt for Rita and she wrote dialogue specifically for her. She'd be on the set, read the lines and change them to suit Rita. But her contribution was not only to the script, but dwelt on every part of the production from wardrobe up. Her value to the studio and Rita was such that Harry and Hayworth were both agreed that she should produce Rita's subsequent films.

When she joined Columbia, she had already had a great deal of experience with actors and producers at Paramount. Like Rita she had begun work at an early age—at five she was acting in silent films. Later she became a script girl, cutter, reader, casting director, agent, secretary, and writer of stylish vehicles for female stars. By the time she joined Columbia in 1943 she had become one of the highest paid screenwriters in the business. The screenplay she fashioned from Erwin Gelsey's story certainly allowed Rita to reveal many more facets than before.

She not only got on well with Rita, she was able to act as a buffer between Rita and Cohn, because her relationship with Harry was extremely good. He respected her professionalism and admired her ability to survive in what was, after all, a man's enclave without losing her femininity. In return she was stimulated by his prodigious vitality, understood his drive and his terror of being thought vulnerable. At the end of an exhausting day's work, Virginia would go to his office to recharge her batteries by listening to him.

While the production line-up was fixed and Rita was set as the female star, a leading man was still needed. Schwartz felt Kelly was the one to convey the cynical, bitter twist in the film. 'The problem there was that Kelly was my idea from the start but Cohn hated it. He said: "That tough Irish face! He can't be in the same frame with Rita, my Rita." The other problem was that Kelly was under contract to M.G.M. But I knew people there, told them a sob story to get him, then rushed back to Columbia, took a deep breath as I entered Cohn's office (I thought he might kill me) and said, "Harry, we've got Gene Kelly." He said, "Thank God!" That was Harry.'

The only problem now was with Kelly who, like Astaire, was worried about Rita's height. So, Rita took off her shoes and let Kelly sweep her off her feet.

Schwartz continued: 'Our attitude towards the characters in the story was realistic, a departure from the standard musicals being made then. The thought in the back of our minds was—would it work without the song and dance and if it did we went on. From the beginning we conceived the leading man as someone able to sing and dance. Rita could dance but we had a very good girl, Martha Mears to dub her. I don't think we ever bothered getting her to sing for herself. And I don't recall her making any fuss about it. It was pretty much taken for granted that she couldn't sing. I think she told me that she was constantly being asked to entertain the troops and that she was embarrassed because 'They don't know I can't sing'.

'Of course lots of people were being dubbed. Kern wrote a melody for Gene, to introduce 'Make Way For Tomorrow'—with an impossible range for Kelly. There was one passage that repeats, going higher each time till I wondered how Gene was going to be able to do that. Things like that give you grey hair. I asked our Musical Director, Morris Stoloff, what we could do, and he said, "Come to the recording session and I'll show you what I'm doing about that." There was a group of male singers around Gene immediately behind the microphone. When they came to this passage Gene stepped back to let another voice come in and do it. When the whole thing was finished they melded their voices into one so that you wouldn't have been able to tell the difference.'

'Jerome Kern was, in spite of being such a romantic writer, a very opinionated man,' reported Schwartz. 'When I couldn't get Dick Rodgers because of his schedule with *Oklahoma*, I got Jerome Kern who is the daddy of all of us. He and Ira Gershwin became the combination. Kern had already written the melody that became the big song 'Long Ago And Far Away' but without lyrics. He called these unused hit tunes his plums. He'd say, "I've got a plum for you." Because he was so involved with harmonisation, when he demonstrated the melody at the piano, there were so many inner voices I couldn't tell what the hell the melody was. I had to ask him to play it with one finger so I could hear it. The great thing about Kern was that he could write to order, a specific song for a specific scene. Most of the times that Kern wrote, the melody came first and the lyrics later. Ninety-nine out of every hundred songs he wrote had a melody first. The only time I knew that the lyrics came first was with 'The Last Time I Saw Paris'.

'There was one little song in *Cover Girl*, "Put Me To The Test"—it was just meant to be an incidental rhythm number, staged by Gene for the girls in the club. Well, apparently Jerry had been to M.G.M. and played a lot of the songs and they all told him how good they were and weren't there any left over. He called me up later that night and asked: "What are you doing with that song? I want it done more prominently." "What do you mean?" "Well," he said, "I've just come from M.G.M. and if you

In the middle of shooting *Cover Girl,* September 9, 1943,
Rita eloped with Orson Welles. The press had a field day
describing it as the marriage of Beauty and the Brain.

don't want to use that song they'll use it." That's the way he
talked. In the end he was satisfied with the way we did it. He
could be finicky, very difficult. I don't think anybody stole as
many melodies as Kern except for Romberg—if you ever mentioned this to him he'd say: "I know, I'm just quoting." But he
was so gifted, so prolific, he created American musical comedy.
Jerry adored Rita. He used to like to come on the set just to look
at her.'

The only other person to drop in now and then for a similar
reason, although he had no involvement with the picture or for
that matter with the studio, was Orson Welles. It was fairly well
known he and Rita were dating, the columnists took care of that,
and Louella Parsons who'd been given wind of a possible marriage, even wrote an article publicly advising Rita against it. Even
so, their marriage, when it happened on September 7th, 1943,
took everyone by surprise. According to Lee Bowman, Rita
arrived on the set the day they were shooting the film's wedding
scene. 'She looked very lovely sitting there in her wedding dress while
the crew were setting up. Rita sat there with her hands in her lap, her
eyes very big and a lovely big pussy smile on her face. When any
of us asked, "What is it, Rita?" she'd just shake her head and say,

"Mmm, I've got a secret." Wouldn't say anything else. The first we knew what it was came during the lunch break when somebody brought us the papers with the headlines.'

Schwartz: 'And you know who was terribly jealous and unhappy? The director. He had fallen in love with her. He came and cried on my shoulder and didn't want to go on. He had to continue shooting every day and she was now married and looking more radiant all the time. She had a tremendous empathy, tremendous sex appeal. All those fifteen or so Cover Girls together didn't have what she had.

'Usually, you are expected to go ten per cent or even fifteen per cent over the budget, but we came in for one million six hundred thousand dollars. That was six hundred thousand dollars more than we were scheduled. Harry was very active in every detail of the film. In part I think because he had a yen for her though I don't know whether anything came from it. But I think the reason he was so happy, even singing the songs to everybody in the studio as if he were back in his song-plugging days, was that he had solved the script problem after the studio had spent so much money on screenplays.'

Cohn's enthusiasm for the film was unheard of and remarkably extensive, even when it came to spending more money. The studio wasn't geared for musicals nor were the sound stages built to encompass such complicated, expansive numbers as some of the ones Kelly devised.

Karger: 'When we were working on Gene's big solo we utilised stages eight and nine because there was only a partition between them allowing them to be opened up. That way we had a set that was two city blocks long. When Gene danced, he'd be down at the end of stage eight while I was playing the piano for him at the end of stage nine, which meant there was a time lag, like at a race track when you see the smoke come from the gun barrel before you hear the report. So they put me on a dolly and two guys with ropes over their shoulders pulled me along so I could keep up with him. That was the first time I saw Rita on the set. We were working at night then, she came in to look at it still dressed in her rehearsal clothes. The remarkable thing about her, which I still recall, even without make-up on at all, having rehearsed all day, she had that marvellous feminine look.

'She had great modesty about her own abilities but a great regard for a lot of creative people who had put things together to help her. She came to me once when I was working with my band

and she said, "People like you made it possible for me, Freddie."
Of course she had magic to start with.

'I'll tell you one thing she did that brought her way up in my
estimation. Charles Vidor was known for his outbursts of temper.
While making a film he was very harsh on a bit player to the point
where the poor guy was almost in tears. Rita walked off the set
and told Vidor if she was to go on working he would have to
change. She had a lot to do with him mellowing. I really admired
that because she used her prestige and power to get the director to
ease up on people who couldn't have done anything about it. She
cared about the way others were being treated yet she let them
walk all over her.

'Rita never realised completely what she had become or if she
did she couldn't have taken it seriously. She didn't believe she was
what people wrote about her. Anyway, Harry just treated people
as possessions, like his horses. I don't think she ever believed she
was this symbol, this thing, she just didn't think that way. Today,
she probably realises what her impact at the time on the time was,
but while she was Columbia's biggest star, and though the studio
was well aware of her value and importance to them I don't think
they conveyed this to her.'

Bowman: 'Cohn treated Hayworth like a little baby girl. . . .
And it seemed to me that everybody took their cue from him. It
was always "Come along, Rita" never "Miss Hayworth". Now
I'd come from M.G.M., and if you ever said anything like "Okay,
Norma", that man would have disappeared from the face of the
earth. It was always Miss Shearer, Miss Garbo, Miss Crawford,
and only in hushed tones. Not that Rita minded. In fact, I only
saw Rita blow her stack once, and then it was with herself. We
had a scene in the bar where she was supposed to be tiddly. She
knew her lines but somehow it wasn't going well. Anyway, Vidor
probably told her she was bad, 'cause people would say these sort
of things to Rita they wouldn't dream of telling any other star. She
dissolved into tears and walked off. Now, suddenly, everybody was
concerned about her because it affected the costs to the film. I
can't talk about her exploitation. We were all exploited to some
degree. They wanted hours out of you. Not talent. If you had talent
as well, fine. Man hours. They didn't care about you as a human
being.

'When somebody came along and told Rita she was wonderful
and marvellous, things the studio never bothered to tell her,
she'd respond. These gals were very isolated from life, like living

Between takes, Rita with *Cover Girl* co-star Lee Bowman—who recalled that girls like Rita had it tough. (Scott/Columbia)

on an island. From the outside they were so big, their position so high, that nobody had the nerve to phone them or believe that they were available. Gable could go out and women would fall all over him, and it would be all right. But a woman like Rita couldn't walk into a bar. What could these gals do? Wait for a phone call, and who'd call them? People were too scared. These gals were too important. Everybody was hypnotised by the look of this woman. The tragedy of it is that in our business so many people are under-estimated because of the sheer impact of their looks.'

One of those intimately concerned with the way Rita looked

was the head of Columbia's Photo Gallery, Bob Coburn, who for more than seventeen years took most of her studio portraits. He had become famous in the 'thirties for glamorising Sam Goldwyn's exotic discoveries. Now he was at Columbia, a key factor in the final stage of selling the studio's most saleable commodity between the time he joined in '41 and the time she left in '57. Coburn's contribution to the film went beyond the gallery on this occasion—he created and photographed the magazine covers featured in the film's big production number.

Coburn: 'The contract I signed put me in complete charge of the studio's stills department. Mind you, if I ever relaxed and let a bad picture of Hayworth or any other star out, Cohn would call me on the carpet immediately.

'In those days we had the Johnson Office, and if we had any cleavage showing the pictures would be sent back. The Code was very strict. Any sign of breasts, even the shadow between, had to disappear. A woman wasn't supposed to have any. We spent all our time touching photos up.

'Hayworth didn't need touching up. She didn't treat herself badly, she wasn't an all-night carouser, although naturally we had to watch for wrinkles under the eyes and around the neck. Of course, any skin marks, small pimples, we would take them out. I don't remember Hayworth ever looking at a picture, I don't think she ever cared how she looked in a picture. She'd come in once in a while and ask how they looked but she didn't bother checking or approving them. That's rare for women. Whereas Cohn was interested in her every minute of the day. He'd call whenever he knew from the call sheet that I was shooting her. They fought a lot. I told Cohn a million times that if he stopped picking on her I'd get what I wanted but he kept needling her and fitting in more hours.

'I'd usually talk to her all the time when I was photographing her, getting her in the mood. Then, I'd catch her at her peak. She had the famous Hayworth look, looking over the shoulder, and after doing three of those she'd had it. She'd say, "What do you want that for? Get something else." She didn't realise that she didn't have that come-and-get-me look except in that one pose.'

For its time, *Cover Girl* had a long, arduous production schedule with Rita in nearly every scene and most of the numbers working twice as hard as the rest. Everybody helped and Rita was aware of that. But, in the end, though it propelled Gene Kelly into the front ranks, the picture was sold on the Hayworth name. And the responsibility rested squarely on her shoulders to prove she could carry a picture.

Karger: 'You expected it of her. Till a take was being recorded she'd be marking time, do her steps on the sidelines, go through her routines but then when the camera was turning on she'd go! There'd be that smile, she'd light up, and everything else would light up with her. She was like a horse that trains poorly, but on the day of the meet off it goes and you can't see the rest for dust.'

The realistic attitude to the characters in the story adopted by Schwartz and Van Upp paid off. It gave the musical an un-expected bite, aided the dramatic development and effectively knitted the story numbers like 'Long Ago and Far Away' into the plot. The film was a departure from the then-current musical convention in that it told a very believable and touching love story in spite of the fact that it was all about hoofers and people in show business. Wherever possible, the songs evolved out of the personal situation of the two leading players, heightening their feelings as much as possible, as the emotionally charged romantic ballad 'Long Ago and Far Away', mentioned above, and with 'Make Way for Tomorrow'.

Schwartz: 'I knew that I wanted something small, intimate and non-Hollywood. That's what I got. But you don't know it's a hit till the public tells you.'

The Los Angeles public had their chance on March 1st, 1944.

Schwartz: 'At the first preview I was sitting next to a much married writer friend. He turned to me after the first long screen kiss between Kelly and Hayworth was over, and whispered, "That kiss lasted longer than my first marriage."'

The shooting was over, the shouting yet to begin.

On a private trip to New York, Rita had a foretaste of the celebrity madness to come. *Cover Girl* had opened to sensational reviews and heavy business at the Radio City Music Hall, where it was her fourth consecutive film to be selected for showing by that mammoth family entertainment emporium. Meanwhile, Rita had time for a delayed honeymoon. While Orson was engaged in trying to set up his future projects, Rita hoped to indulge her passion for the theatre, but her trip turned into an alarming adventure. She went as a private person only to discover what it was to be public property. Arthur Schwartz, who was at the theatre that night, recalled: 'I had called Howard Dietz and said, "I have a terrible favour to ask you. Rita called me up. I got her two tickets for the opening night and nobody to escort her." "Oh my God! I'll be ripped to pieces." "No you won't," I said. But he was right. They just about ripped him to pieces.

'After the show we were all supposed to go on to a party, but there were mobs of people, ten thick, surrounding Rita, attacking her clothing. Just out of adoration of this movie star. It was terrifying. But she was that kind of stuff at the time.'

Rita's fear of public exposure was put severely to the test again when her brother Vernon went AWOL. While her family back in Los Angeles only heard about it on the radio—Walter Winchel opening his broadcast with the news—Rita was in the thick of it in New York.

Vernon: 'I was being shipped overseas when I ran into two fellows, one an Irishman and the other a Swede. The Swede had a girlfriend in New Jersey, and the other had a girl in New York he wanted to marry before he left. We got a little tight celebrating our meeting in the Biltmore Hotel, Providence Rhode Island, where the railroad is right across the street. When we got loaded enough it seemed like a good idea to go to New York where I knew Rita was staying with Orson. By the time we got there, we were even higher. The Irishman, a man called Flanagan, was my sergeant—a real Sergeant Bilko type. He had passes for this and that, all of them illegal, and he was the one who knew when our ship was sailing. He said that we'd be sure to get back before then. So, for the next two weeks we had a bang of a time, thanks to Rita who got me a room at the Gotham Hotel, where she was staying, because I had no money. The next thing you knew there was this item about us being AWOL. Well, Rita didn't know what to do with me, because I was half-loaded all the time since I was going overseas. But the funniest thing was the business with the M.P.s.

'When we walked down a street in New York and the Military Police was coming in our direction I'd tell her to walk in front of me. When she asked why I explained that they're not going to look at me if she was in front. That's how I got past—they never even saw me. She was scared to death that they'd arrest her and me on the spot. It made her so nervous that she drew more attention to herself than ordinarily while I leisurely walked behind her like something out of a comedy. Orson was in the Hospital so Rita had time. We'd go out to eat—never very far, to Toot's Shor or something nearby, it wasn't any hike, but by the time we got there she could hardly eat she was so nervous. She was sure we'd all be stuck in jail, but she didn't know what to do with me, while I kept

Rita with her brother Vernon (home on leave), who visited her
on set of *Tonight and Every Night*. (Coburn/Columbia)

eating this Hollandaise sauce, which I'd never had before, and
loving it.

'After our two weeks, we thought we'd better get back before
our ship sailed. We're walking down this road to the camp where
two M.P.s stood at the gate. They said, "What outfit are you fellas
with?" "We're in the fourth army. You can't put us in jail, we've
gotta get on this ship." He says, "That's great. They sailed three
days ago." So then we get court-martialled of course and sent
down to prison. It was an interesting trip because the men we
were with—there were about fifty-five of us—were pretty rough;
some were in for bank robbery, statutory rape. Oh God! What a
crew there was.'

Vernon was saved from more severe consequences with the help
of his Aunt Frances in Washington who had influence with the top
brass. As Joan Haworth explained, 'Frances had an apartment

house that was so full of brass, every nook and cranny had
somebody of higher rank than the next living there. She got this
General out of bed at 2 a.m.—he'd been wanting a bigger
apartment and she told him that the price of this bigger apartment was to get her nephew back into the fold. And he did.'

Vernon: 'When I came back from the war, Rita asked me what
I was going to do. I hadn't had a formal education because the
war took up four years of my life. She loaned me the money to go
into the restaurant business. That didn't pan out because I didn't
know what I was doing. I fooled around in show business doing a
few bit parts in a couple of Rita's films, *Lady from Shanghai*, *Loves of
Carmen*; she'd help where she could. But we're a family that like to
do things for ourselves. It's best that way.

'Rita and I had a special relationship—especially after the war.
The same as between my mother and her brother, and especially
with Dad, and that's loyalty. Blood loyalty. When Rita had
reason to call me, I'd be there. We're a family.'*

Rita was back in the big stony house with the kidney-shaped
swimming pool she and Orson had rented and furnished, before
work began on her next picture. When she reported to the
wardrobe for fitting early in May, she was already two months
pregnant. Marriage and impending motherhood were evidently
agreeing with her for she was in a happy frame of mind.

After Kelly's spectacular success in *Cover Girl*, Harry hoped to
team him again with Rita. In the back of his mind there lurked
the idea of creating a dance team for the 'forties that would rival
the success of the Astaire-Rogers films of the 'thirties. He bought
the rights to the Broadway musical *Pal Joey* which had launched
Kelly on his career. Gene would re-create his role, Rita would be
the young girl the opportunistic Joey loves but leaves for Vivien
Segal, whom the studio would bring out to repeat her original
stage role as the older, richer woman. Meanwhile, Victor Saville
and writer Lesser Samuels were asked by Cohn to see what could
be done to tone the play down enough to get it past the Hays
office, but still keep to the spirit of John O'Hara's original. While
Fred Karger spent time working on arranging the score for the
film, Saville was finding it difficult keeping that bite and spirit.

In the end the project was shelved because Louis B. Mayer

*Not long after we had taped our conversation in his home, Vernon fell seriously ill.
Recovering from a major operation, the news of his brother Eddie's sudden death in March
'74, brought on his own death the same month.

Rita and co-star Janet Blair dance up a storm for Marc Platt in one of their numbers for *Tonight and Every Night*, choreographed by Jack Cole. (Gillman/Columbia)

would not countenance another loan-out for Kelly, now that his value had tripled as a result of *Cover Girl*. No financial inducements Cohn could offer, short of giving Mayer Hayworth, proved acceptable. But, eager as Cohn was to get Gene back, he could not afford to put his most valuable property on loan-out since her name was money in the bank even if he treated her like a horse in his stable. Regrettably, *Pal Joey* was never made with the perfect cast and ideal director. (By the time the script problems were solved to the censors' satisfaction, fourteen years had elapsed. Sinatra played Joey as a loveable old ring-a-ding swinger; Rita was now the stripper who had gone High Society, while Kim Novak, the studio's replacement for Hayworth, played the younger girl. And *she* got Sinatra. But that was Hollywood.)

Mayer's reluctance to loan out Kelly was perfectly understandable. Zanuck tried to obtain Rita to star in Twentieth's svelte thriller, *Laura*, but was refused. Fortunately, Zanuck had Gene Tierney who shared an air of haunting remoteness, as well as certain physical similarities, with Rita. Either actress would have been a perfect choice for the ambiguous heroine of Vera Caspary's story wherein the hero falls in love with both the illusion and the reality.

Columbia couldn't provide Rita with a part like Laura. Meanwhile, her new vehicle was to be an advance on *Cover Girl*.

Hollywood may indeed be a perfect working example of the wide gulf between declaration and result, but once again, in a year when no film would have failed anyway, *Tonight and Every Night* did indeed meet the studio's trumped-up claims. The production values were superb: Maté photographed Rita; Jean Louis dressed her for the first time and Jack Cole created the numbers. Lesser Samuels' script, based on Lesley Storm's moderately successful play *Heart of a City*, provided a sound support, and in Englishman Victor Saville, the film and Rita found a stylish director.

Story: In the heart of blitz-torn London at the small Music Box Theatre that never closes, Rosalind Bruce (Rita) and Judy (Janet Blair) are dancing stars. Into their lives comes speciality dancer Tommy Lawson (Marc Platt) and airforce pilot Paul Lundy (Lee Bowman). When her best friends, Judy and Tommy, are killed in an air raid, Rosalind rejects her personal needs, putting off her marriage to Paul to continue entertaining the battle-weary servicemen for whom the theatre provides a break from the harsher realities of the war.

One of the reasons Saville was brought in was because the Music Box was obviously based on the famous Windmill Theatre and the story needed a director who could understand the story from an authentic English viewpoint. He recalled: 'We were still in the war and the fact that I could make a contribution by projecting something English into an American film appealed to me, not the story or that it was a musical. We couldn't call the theatre the Windmill because of the copyright situation. The rights to the name would not only have been prohibitively expensive but would have restricted us to putting those numbers on a stage as small as the original theatre.'

Jack Cole, the choreographer, had a somewhat different view of what happened: 'Usually, I am very careful and do a certain amount of research before I do a number. But this thing came up very fast. Well, I came from the theatre where the director is the director and for me there can be only one person in charge. Since Saville was English and all that, I didn't do my usual research. Nobody told me that the stage at the Windmill was about as big as my bedroom. It was a lower-middle-class burlesque house. When I saw the theatre a couple of years later I went "Wooosh!" The broads stood there with their tits and ass out and didn't move. Why did Victor Saville go ahead and let me do the numbers I did? If I had known I could have done different kinds of numbers. There's always some licence in films but there was no need for what

I did. Cohn said, "Don't do the numbers like the dumb picture, so the numbers look more like Metro than they do like Columbia." '

The one potentially disastrous anomaly in the film was the virtually all-American company in what was, after all, quite clearly an English theatre. But Saville steered a safe course through the shoals via a Greek Chorus of Cockney cleaning ladies who recall the blitz and 'the American girls who entertained our boys'.

Saville: 'There were lots of American girls in places like the Windmill, just as there were lots of British girls in the Folies Bergère. Besides which, there weren't that many English girls in L.A. and none I think at Columbia, so you had to allow for that. But Harry gave me a free hand—the only thing he asked of me was that we use all the Cover Girls because they were still around and he wanted as much mileage as possible. Shelley Winters was in the film, begging me for a line, but there were so many of them, and the story was really concentrated around the principals. Lee Bowman, who was under contract to the studio and very palsy with Cohn, was put forward as our leading man, which was fine. The problem was to find a dancer who could follow in Kelly's footsteps, since we couldn't get Kelly. I had seen Marc Platt dancing in *Oklahoma*, where he had a great success, and felt he was brilliant—his solo dance to Hitler's speech on the radio was one of the best things in the film. And Jack Cole's choreography was very exciting.'

Karger: 'Cole was one of the most inspiring people I ever worked with, but was he a task master! He had his own group of dancers who he trained at the studio and Rita with them. They would be exercising from 9 a.m. till they dropped—but look where they went ... all of his people were the most fantastic dancers, Gwen Verdon, Bambi Lynn, Carol Haney, all of them went to the top. Rita realised how much he could help her and responded to him. Nothing is too much for her when she believes in somebody. She wasn't crazy about doing any more musicals—but Harry didn't give her a choice. Cole, however, managed to enthuse her. She'd been around a lot of dancers and choreographers all her life and she realised he was one of the best.'

I drove to Cole's hill-top eyrie situated above the smog that lingers permanently around Los Angeles. Hawk-nosed, flint-eyed, and ascerbic, Jack Cole, hard disciplinarian, was undoubtedly one of the most influential choreographic forces on the American scene, not just because of his own work but through the dancing troupe he trained in his years at Columbia. He first worked with Rita, tidying up a few loose steps on *Cover Girl*, then did all of them on *Tonight and Every Night*, and eventually staged the number that has become a corner stone in the mythology of the 'forties—along with Ingrid Bergman asking Sam to play it again; Bette Davis telling Henreid not to ask for the moon, and Bacall informing Bogart that a whistle would fetch her—Rita's line is a dance in a film that is not a musical but more famous than most numbers from one—'Put the Blame on Mame'.

Portraits of Cole from the 'forties would still have served for identification when we met. He spoke in fast sharp steps, but occasionally would open out into long witty runs that curved gracefully around Rita's name. 'She's a Spanish teenager really who's hardly ever grown up. Unless she got somebody around to say "Don't do this! Don't do that/Eat! Don't eat/If you're bored go to bed, get plastered," she's like a teenage girl who does whatever amuses her. I like Rita Hayworth, she's a very nice lady. One of the few nice ones in movies to work with.

'She did not have a good figure, but she has beautiful breasts, beautiful arms and the most beautiful hands in show business. Like, if you wanted to do a portrait of a Spanish lady, she was just the most extraordinarily beautiful creature to select for it. As a young woman she was always a much more beautiful person than she photographed, 'cause they did really icky Columbia make-up for star ladies, with that too hard glossy mouth.'

'She had a good body. It wasn't difficult to dress her,' said Jean Louis. 'She was very thin limbed, the legs were thin, the arms long and thin and beautiful hands. But the body was thick. She also had a belly then, but we could hide that. That's what my job was.' Jean Louis was the distinguished designer Harry Cohn had brought out from New York to head the studio's wardrobe. Like Cole, he was sympathetic to Rita and his cool, elegant wardrobe played a prominent part in defining the ultimate Hayworth image. From *Tonight and Every Night* onwards he worked on all her studio films and a working friendship developed that lasts. Preparing for a new film in 1975, Rita went back to him for her wardrobe.

Jean Louis: 'I don't know about her inside. She didn't talk much. We worked well together. If she liked the dress I was happy, but we're both Librans, too alike to talk much. She worked very hard. Often she would arrive for fittings from dance rehearsals and her feet still bleeding. But she never complained, or refused to do anything.'

Cole: 'The only thing she got worked up about was Harry Cohn. And then she could be particularly nasty, but I don't blame her for that. Harry was a very, very bright man with a very, very vulgar tongue. If you wanted to learn about making movies he'd let you down on the sets, the costumes, the editing, cleaning up the john as long as you didn't goof. That's if he liked you. But he was very nasty to actors. I'm sure Rita Hayworth must be scurrilous about him. You didn't have to be Glenn Ford or Rita. He just hated actors. He thought they were all a tub of shit and he could replace any of them in a minute.'

Jean Louis: 'Cohn tried to control Rita a lot. There was a woman at the studio who reported on every move Rita made. Rita knew what this woman was doing but she ignored it. Harry did it because he wanted to know everything that was going on in his studio. And he treated Rita as a very valuable property. We never discussed what she thought of him because Rita was always afraid her rooms were wired so Harry could listen in on her. "Be careful what you say, it's dangerous." But you have to laugh about these things because they are very silly.'

Saville: 'The difference between Mayer and Cohn was that Mayer listened. He wanted to know. He'd cross question you to find something out. Cohn never wanted to know. He was one of those people who knew everything. He worshipped Mayer, but he didn't have his understanding. Neither man had humility, but Mayer had great respect for all sorts of things while I don't think Harry respected anybody. Cohn didn't like to see things flower. No wonder Rita felt she was being held down. He had a very conventional picture mind. The only creative thing about the men in his position is their memory, like, let's do such and such a film like the one we made back when. He was a very humorless man.'

The film's lyricist was Sammy Cahn, who was under contract to the studio for a period. 'Harry Cohn was an incredible rogue. A rascal. What bothered me about our relationship is that he never understood that I was as much a rascal as he was. But whereas I'm a smiling rascal, he was a serious rascal, and the serious rascals kill you.

'Cohn used to sit in his office and all day long he used to feel he was put upon: that people were born to screw him all day long. He felt he created Rita, but the moment these Galateas came into

focus he was convinced they were dedicated to his demise,
y'know. L. B. Mayer, Goldwyn, Warner—they're all alike in this
respect. They're all Jewish gentlemen and I think that's got
something to do with it. But they're all the same man. They each
made one correct decision in their lives—and I don't know how
they made it—and that was to go into movies. Harry used to sit in
his office and everything was crisis: Rita doesn't like her dress and
it's ... "How can she do this to me!" Everything was a personal
attack on him. If he wanted something from you he could charm
the teeth out of your mouth while your mouth was closed. But if
he didn't like you, you couldn't get on the lot. A tyrant. If he was
nice to Rita it was because she was very valuable property.'

Rita, of course, was not the only star to get the special Cohn
treatment, for as Cole recalled about another contract player: 'I
was constantly being called up to Harry's office because of one
difference of opinion or another. One time this star lady showed
me her script for another of those backstage musicals and I told
her, "Dumb! Don't ask me about it, it's a piece of shit." So, the
next day Harry called up and said, "I'm gonna tell you one more
time, keep your big mouth shut." I said, "Harry, what's the
matter?" "That dumb broad is home and she won't come to
work. She said to me that you told her her new script is a piece of
shit. Did you?" "Well, yes I did, and it is." Harry said, "I know
thaaattt! But what the fuck does it matter to her. She's just a
dumb cunt with those large thighs and I'm paying her this much
money. What's she give a damn if it's a piece of shit or not if I
want her to do it. Now you phone her and get her back here."

'So I had to do a pretty terrible thing. I said I can't do it in the
office because it's too embarrassing. I'll phone her from my home.
Her maid answered the phone and asked who it was, because she
was taking it very big that she had gone on suspension, and I had
to say, "It's pussycat." Because that's what she always called me,
and I couldn't have said it while Harry was sitting in the room.'

Cole continued. 'They hired you supposedly for your "unique
and peculiar talents", told you how marvellous you were when
you arrived, and thought that in some magical way you'd arrive
at their studio and do the same things you had been doing on
Broadway, which was ten years ahead of the movies, only it would
come out differently. Inevitably you reached the point where you
found yourself saying, "Baby, if I'm going to do the same dumb
thing, it doesn't matter if my contract says I'm unique and
peculiar or not, it's going to come out the same dumb way."'

Karger: 'Harry would never hurt a picture. That came first with him. Those stories about Cohn's vindictiveness were grossly exaggerated. I heard him yell at people and I was yelled at and insulted and so forth, but when it came down to it, if you were man enough to stand up to him he would respect you for it. And he would turn around and do the nice thing. He wasn't vindictive. When it came to personal things like when my father-in-law was ill and we needed a very good expensive doctor, Harry knew about it, picked up the phone, made a long distance call, arranged for the doctor to come and took care of the bill. These ogre stories make good copy.'

Since Saville's contract prohibited Harry coming on the set the film went without a hitch, except for a potentially disastrous *contretemps* between Rita and Hollywood's acid columnist, Hedda Hopper.

Cole: 'Rita got very angry one day when she could have killed Hedda Hopper who was riding Orson Welles in her column. Hedda was walking around the studio while we were there rehearsing and Rita heard about it and said, "Just a minute. Would you excuse me for fifteen minutes." She was trying to find out what set Hedda was visiting at that moment because she wanted to go up to her and let her have one right up the nose. She was a real Spanish lady that way, and she had a real tongue when she wanted to. She was much wilder when she was protecting somebody else. Of course, I called up the public relations people and told them Rita was on the warpath, just so we wouldn't have a funny. Because they took those things very seriously! It would be a big deal if Rita Hayworth punched Hedda Hopper on the nose. I thought it would be hilarious if she caught up and let her have one. But they got Hedda out of the studio before Rita found her, and Rita is the sort of person that by night, one drink, and she'd forgotten. She was a very good natured, very, very pleasant lady.

'But you had to be careful with her. Harry Cohn or somebody in the production office might say something and she'd cry. That's when you knew she was angry. She'd really get worked up, like to the point where she was going in to see him and then, no matter what Harry Cohn said, she was going to let him have it. One good "Shove it up your arse".

'Harry would have girls around the studio as a standby if Rita should make trouble and they needed to replace her, but really to sort of cow her.* But that sort of thing, like later on with Kim

* Mary Castle, Patricia Knight and Adele Jergens were groomed to this end.

Novak, never bothered Rita. The only time we had anything funny was during a number Rita had with Janet Blair. *That* was a funny. Janet was a very bright but not very amusing lady, and this was her first really big chance. She had a fine voice and all that but she was determined to make the most of her chance—like, I can learn something quicker than Rita, only it never looked as good on the screen. But she was very pulled together, business-like, very grand as opposed to Rita.

'We had this number, "The Boy I Left Behind" where the girls do a boy going in the army, and all the examinations are by women—it was a funny number. Rita and Janet had to do a simultaneous strip in it for the physical. Well, that was really competition day when Janet Blair was going to show you that it was Janet Blair who was marvellous. What made it funny there was that they both had to wear men's long underwear with the banjo seats. Like all female people, though her figure wasn't marvellous, Rita's terribly secure of herself as a woman. She knows, and she's always been, and always will consider herself a pretty woman. She felt and looked just marvellous in the men's underwear with the crotch and the banjo seat, and her boobs looked marvellous in the button-top thing.

'Janet Blair, unfortunately, is a little girl, with no arse, no boobs particularly, a real Nellie Forbush from *South Pacific*, like a girl who didn't look too attractive in men's underwear. But she started doing the number like she was going to give herself a hernia. Neither woman made any reference to it except they both came down the middle of the stage, grinding and bumping. Rita Hayworth looked BIG! She could do all that jazz with no sweat. Janet Blair's teeth were almost falling out from all the effort—like, this is her chance to show you she was better than Rita. I didn't know what we could do, 'cause I'd say "Cut!" and look at Victor Saville, and he'd look at me with a "What are we going to do?" shrug on his face. We were building up to a kind of girl fight here. I'd say "Cut"; they'd just split. Rita would go over and do her hair, acting like nothing was happening. You'd ask "Ready?"—Rita would go "Mmm". But she went back and did it as if to say, all right baby, if you want to know how to do it, this is it. We finally had to print it before it got worse, 'cause what was going to happen in another minute was that Rita Hayworth was gonna turn around and let Janet Blair have it right in the chops. It was kind of funny.'

As a choreographer, Cole had an understanding of body

language that not everybody else shared, for others I spoke to failed to recall this subtle rivalry between the two ladies, though Saville did think that if Cole said it was so, it might be because Cole would notice those things more. There were other moments of light relief, as Fred Karger recalled.

'She was carrying Rebecca and towards the end it was beginning to show, so they had to shoot her from further on up. There is this line some character has in the film asking her if she wanted to marry the soldier. Rita and Victor got together on it and filmed two endings without telling Harry. One of them had her standing up, throwing open her coat in reply to the question, saying, "What do you think?" And there was Rita with a pillow stuffed under her dress making her look twelve months gone. They screened the film with this ending the first time Cohn saw it. He almost went through the roof. "What the hell! You people lost your minds?" Of course it was just a joke.'

Despite the strenuous schedule of dances, Rita's pregnancy created no serious problems, except for an aversion to the smell of fresh paint. The sets had to be painted and aired before she came on. As in other matters, she created no fuss. Cole recalled:

'You get some, a lot of movie ladies, who couldn't do anything but they were the star, baby, and you had to move carefully. No way you could say to them, if something wasn't right, "Well, that was a dog's dinner, let's try again." You'd always phrase it carefully, "That was marvellous, but we can really do it better, darling." With Rita you could always say, "Baby, you're stepping on your feet." She had no vanity in that way at all—no Sarah Bernhardt stuff.

'I evolved a working routine with her that I used a lot later when working with Monroe. When we'd do close-ups of certain kinds of things, like when Rita was doing the Samba, or singing, I would get within three feet of her and she would mimic me. I would wet my mouth, open it like I can't breathe, and she'd be looking at me, doing the same, like we were having each other, going on and on. She had no complex at all about somebody showing Rita Hayworth how to do her fucking eyelashes—or her sex thing for the screen. She was a wildly good-humoured lady to work with, and she worked very hard. Not that she was wildly talented, but she was wildly suited to what she was doing at the time she was doing it. She was the sum total of a group effort—the way they dressed her, made her up, wrote for her,

Where other dancers move from the hips down, Hayworth transmits excitement and rhythm from the waist up in the exotic samba number 'You Excite Me' from *Tonight and Every Night*. (St. Hilaire/Columbia)

what she did with it, it was a group job. What separates her from similar studio products is this inherent erotic thing of her own.'

The finished film possessed a smooth, sophisticated style that recalled those elegant Jessie Matthews' musicals Saville had directed in the 'thirties, but with an added dramatic element that came from the war-inspired locale. Certainly the death of two of the principals, and the uncompromising parting of the lovers, provided a surprisingly sophisticated *dénouement* for what was, after all, a musical. Indirectly this may have been the reason why none of the songs became hits. But most of the film's departures were equally subtly integrated; thus they passed without much comment or praise.

The whole thing was a striking ensemble work. The use of colour, Rudy Maté's delicately shadowed photography and the exceptionally fine décor and costumes were typical of the film's excellence, creating a realistic yet svelte world of subdued colours, a departure from the norm of glaring, garish hues that decorated most musicals. The film's dramatic line fitted with the theatrical background, gallantly conveying the wartime spirit which was as inherent in the world of entertainment as it was in the armed forces. The musical numbers fitted in realistically, while the fine-bodied songs by Jule Styne and Sammy Cahn had the strength of a book score. To these, Jack Cole set a succession of stunning routines—whether comic twosomes, exotic Sambas, grecian *pas de deux*, or a girlie finale that packed the stage—they belonged to the best dancing Rita ever did. In the Latin beat rhythms one can marvel again at Hayworth's hypnotic force as a dancer. She enters through a door, drawn by the beat of male drummers, dressed in a clinging white two-piece that accentuates her body through the provocative forward thrust of her torso—a stance that is an invitation and a promise, and has become a trademark, like her hair. Where most dancers move from the hips down Hayworth moves from the knees up, her shoulders drawn back projecting her breast cage forward in the most enticing manner only acceptable in the young and very beautiful. To see her in that moment's hesitation is to experience a sense of joy pure and simple. And all the more potent for being an invitation in the dark.

Cole: 'You couldn't treat her like a dancer—she could dance, but you couldn't put that burden on her, she didn't go to class every day. The main object in my life with a movie star of that period was not to prove my point but to make them look marvellous. Don't try to prove anything about dancing—just make them look great.

'I got to know what she could do facilely, I was always trying to make her feel confident and not do those numbers the way everybody else was doing them, where it looked like they were getting it by radar from a shortwave set. With Rita it looked like she really could do it, and more. There was the effect of "stand back I'm going to really move now". But you wouldn't know this from rehearsals. The first time I realised that, it caught me off guard but good.

'I did this number with her "What Does an English Girl Think of a Yank", a real jolly kind of bit that wasn't my type of dance at all. I had a very typical guy picked to be the sailor opposite her—a chunky, laughing boy with a lot of white teeth, dimples, all that jazz and the cap down over the head with hair curling up over; and just as we were about to shoot he sprained his ankle. It's always a big deal holding up production, specially at Columbia with the production man counting pennies. Every time there was a hold-up it would cost, so Victor Saville said, "It's your dance, you know it, you do it." Well, I'm by nature not a jolly laughing

Choreographer Jack Cole leapt into the breach to do
this nautical routine with Rita in *Tonight and Every
Night.* (St. Hilaire/Columbia)

performer so ... Victor held up a dollar. Every time I smiled he
gave me a dollar. Right? I'm grinning.

'So I rehearse with Rita a couple of times around and we're
ready to start. Well, baby, I don't know what hit me when they
turned the camera on. Monroe was the same way—when it was
for real, it was like "look out!". For the first shot I just went up six
ways from Sunday. Suddenly, this mass of red hair comes hurtling
at me, and it looked like ninety times more teeth than I ever saw
in a woman's mouth before and more eyes rolling, and ... you
know, she was the most animated object ever. I didn't know how
to deal with it, I'd never seen so much animation giving out. I just
walked away on long feet.

'Rita *always* did it for real—she always gave more than she got.

'We got along good, we liked each other. Rita knew I was very
understanding of what she could and what she couldn't do. Once
in a while I'd make a boo-boo in my effort to make her look
marvellous. She'd never object about what you told her to
do—she'd rehearse for about a week, then, when it would get
close to shooting it, we'd do this thing and she'd sit down and this

big tear would come. And I'd say, "Darling, what's the matter?" and she'd say, "I'll never be able to do it." "Why didn't you tell me a long time ago? It's not important, there's a thousand other things we could do. I don't want you to try and do something in which you'd look or feel unnatural."

'I was just trying to push her, but like I say she was very good humoured and disciplined in that way. If it was in her to do what you asked of her she'd do it very well and with energy, unlike some.

'Rita didn't waste her energies when working. None of that sex between scenes or boozing at lunch, even though things could get to be a pretty tough grind, and hooch would be the kindest thing at the end of a day. That's why a lot of them drink—you work six days a week without a break, always dieting to keep your figure, knowing the next day the camera would be three feet away from you picking up every crumb you swallowed. You get no time to develop a relationship that wasn't linked to business, while at work they'd treat you like an object—wash your hair, dye it, dry it and set it. Then make-up, gadoonk, gadoonk. Home, learn your lines, sleep and try and fit a husband in there somehow. You can't expect them to understand—so you drink.

'Rita was a lonely person, you always felt that about her. She'd sit around with the girls during rehearsals, but mostly by herself, not stand-offish, just lonely. But always a lady. Not like some of the big glamour ladies you had to be careful about. There was one. No matter how much fun you had, she always knew she was a movie star, and there'd be that moment when she'd look at you like, "I know who I am and you are dispensable, so watch it!" I was there the time the bull of the pampas was in her life. They'd be screwing their brains out the whole time, particularly at lunch. They'd come back after lunch and we couldn't get a shot of her till five o'clock she was so bleary-eyed. And you had to do your dance numbers with them in the morning because in the afternoon they'd be so weak-knee'd they'd be staggering around holding each other up. You had this huge set, hundreds of extras, all waiting while the lady would be in her make-up room, the champagne on the table, the Rhumba records playing and you'd say, "Darling, they're waiting on the set," and she'd say, "I'll come when I'm ready, honey!" And that was it. There was never any of that with Rita, and never a drink on set.

'Rita's problem was that everybody mistook her for Rita Hayworth, MOVIE STAR—when actually she was just a dancing gypsy girl who would have been very happy working in a chorus, happily married to some average-type husband who wanted a nice female lady, which she is.'

The film opened at the Radio City Music Hall—again—to excellent reviews and large audiences. Saville's American directorial debut could be considered a success and he returned to M.G.M. as a saleable director. At the time the film's real triumph seemed to be Marc Platt who, it was generally assumed, would be in fervent demand after this brilliant debut. But except for another dancing role opposite Hayworth, the public failed to find him another Gene Kelly.

More curious was the signal failure of any of the songs to catch on. Since, together and separately, Styne and Cahn were to write any number of popular hits and this score is fine, one wonders. Sammy Cahn offered one possible reason when he said, 'We worked for three hard years for Harry Cohn and wrote him all the hits he deserved—none.' He added more seriously, 'But you see, when the songs are dubbed you've got no one to promote them, no recording. I learned early in my life that all I can do is write songs as best as I can. I believe there's a destiny that looks after, promotes and protects good songs so that they emerge. Who knows, perhaps Tony Bennett will appear on television next week singing "Anywhere". That film has an elegance, Mr Saville and Jack Cole did incredible things with it. The studio didn't push the songs, I don't know why. Maybe there was a record strike in those days. Who knows.'

But the reason probably lies in Fred Karger's answer: 'I think it was because of the story. They took a very strong dramatic story with the war as background, bombs falling, somebody even died and they used this for a musical premise. Though people went to see Rita they just didn't tie all this up in their minds, it was a bit too advanced. Usually in the musicals of that period the story was slight, the star of the show breaks a leg, and the understudy comes on and becomes a star and you knew that from the beginning because the star in the story was played by a no-no lady while the understudy part was played by the star of the film. But here we had Hayworth take over and sing the title song because her best friend had just got killed in a bombing raid. It just didn't jell with the audiences of that time.'

Saville had had other things on his mind. He made the movie because he felt he could do a bit for England and the most momentous thing that happened during filming as far as he was concerned was D-Day. They heard it on the radio while shooting on the morning of June 6th, 1944. He and Rudy Maté, both Europeans to the core, broke down and cried in each other's arms. But there were no celebrations. And work continued as if nothing had happened. 'Harry didn't care,' Saville said. 'He wasn't a European. He was making pictures.'

A couple of months before the baby was due, Rita went home to rest. She read books, listened to records and acted as hostess at Orson's dinner parties, though she preferred quiet evenings with him alone or with her parents dropping in for dinner. On December 15th she entered hospital. Their daughter Rebecca was born by Caesarian operation on the 17th. Mother and child were well. Rita had worked all her life and now she looked forward to a long rest. She left hospital the day before Christmas and her parents came to dinner. Things couldn't have been better. She was surrounded by the people she loved; the child she wanted, the husband she adored, and the mother on whom she had grown more and more to depend as a close friend.

A few weeks later, without warning, Volga was dead. It happened so suddenly that friends first read about it in the papers.

Increasingly nervy and edgy, Volga developed a drinking problem, but this was not a contributive factor towards her death which resulted from generalised peritonitis. A few weeks after Christmas, Volga had complained of stomach pains; her doctor suspected flu and prescribed pain killers. Since she suffered a great deal from headaches and other nervous upsets, no one took her fears seriously at first, though Eduardo stayed home from the factory to nurse her. Over the next few days the pain intensified to the point where she could hardly stand, and had to be rushed to hospital. Now it was correctly diagnosed as a ruptured appendix, but it was already too late. She was in her forty-fifth year but looked much older when she died in January. The church was packed with students and friends from Vaudeville. She was buried in the Catholic cemetery in West Los Angeles. Eduardo took the loss hard. They had been married for almost thirty years.

Sometime later he sold the house on Sterne Drive where they had lived since first arriving in town, but which was now too full of memories. He moved in with his daughter until he found a small apartment suitable for himself on South Vermount Avenue, adjoining his new dance studio. At Rita's he slept in the library, but moved to his own place after a few weeks since Orson's habit

Rita with her six-month-old daughter Rebecca, taken by Columbia photographer Bob Coburn.

of working late nights, with friends and secretaries coming and going at all hours, gave him little rest.

The new dance school was a large hall over a hardware store. Fortunately, now that the war was over, business again boomed, keeping his mind off his loss. He ran his dancing academy philosophically, teaching ballroom, tap, ballet and Spanish according to the preferences of his customers. Although his daughter's photograph was plastered all over the walls he made no attempt to trade on his connection as the father and teacher of Rita Hayworth. Eduardo was a man of considerable dignity and integrity, and a Cansino was beholden to no one, a father least of all to his children. His school was such a success that by 1951 he could afford to buy the corner lot on Sterne Drive and Pico Boulevard where he built his own studio including living quarters with a small garden where he and his new wife could sit and sun. For Eduardo had re-married.

He met Pat, a divorcee, when she came to his school in 1946 obsessed with becoming a dancer. Eduardo taught her everything he knew. Soon she became good enough to dance professionally in clubs around the Los Angeles area. By then they had also fallen in love. Pat filled the void in his life, helping to teach classes and, like Volga, handling the business side for him. At first his children took his re-marriage hard, but with time the boys grew to accept it. Pat and Eduardo were married for twenty-two years until he died of heart failure on December 24th, 1968.

Rita's brothers, back from the Army, tried their hands at various lines of work. For a time Sonny drove a taxi, took up ballroom dancing, taught for a bit and did extra work in films before marrying and settling down. Vernon and Sonny married the same year as their father, making it a triple-header. All the marriages were extremely happy and successful. Vernon's wife, Susan, was a Yugoslav refugee who had danced in a film *Escape Me Never*, and had been one of Eduardo's students when she met Vernon and they married in 1947.

With Volga's death, Eduardo saw less and less of Rita. Whenever a new film with her opened, he would wander off by himself to see it. Like his daughter, he was proud; his second marriage had given him happiness, but what he couldn't or wouldn't say, those close to him understood. He felt the separation from Rita keenly. He was her father and he loved her.

For a long time after her mother died, Rita had difficulty retaining her social composure, barely keeping from crying when the subject arose. Lee Bowman, who had met Volga when she dropped in on the set, visited Rita soon after, bringing a bunch of red roses, and was overwhelmed by Rita's anguish: 'I told her how sorry I was. She just grabbed me and held me in her arms for some time, and cried. I don't think that deep emotion, showing it in public, was something that came easily to her. No doubt but her mother's death shook her very hard.'

Such feelings rarely surfaced in public but, privately, they would increase her phobias about loneliness and death, two factors that could only assume an increasing hold on her in the dark years ahead, when spells of inactivity in her career grew longer and longer. Moreover, she felt an emptiness in her personal life. When occasionally female friends shared her room on location or holidays they noted that she only found sleep with her head buried beneath a mountain of pillows. Later still the emptiness almost threatened to engulf her.

Rita was tired. Only twenty-six, at the top at an age when most careers would be beginning she nevertheless seriously contemplated retiring. She dreamt of a quiet life devoted to her brilliant husband and their child in which she could find the prospects of a fuller life. But Orson's many projects afforded them less time together than she wished. Barely six months later she was back rehearsing.

The modest Brentwood house without the swimming pool Rita lived in for a time between husbands. (Columbia)

CHAPTER V

MOTHER'S NIGHT IN
A TURKISH BATH

Rita Hayworth is the fourth most valuable property in the business.

Harry Cohn, 1946

Rita as Gilda. (Cronenweth Collection)

After D-Day, June 6th, 1944, the war's outcome was virtually assured as Germany retreated on every front, and the Japanese Army fell back in the Pacific. President Roosevelt died on the eve of Friday, April 13th, only a few short months before the end of the European conflict, and Harry Truman succeeded him. V-E Day was on May 8th, 1945, and with the dropping by the Americans of the A-Bomb that successfully obliterated Hiroshima, Nagasaki and 106,000 Japanese citizens, the Pacific War was over. All that was left was the signing of the treaty. On the morning of September 2nd, 1945, V-J Day, the banner headlines in newspapers around the globe declared 'PEACE!'. Fathers, brothers and sons were coming home to their families, Rationing was lifted and it seemed that the good times were set to begin again now that the world was at peace.

But, if the hot war was over, the cold war was just warming up. East-West tensions between former Allies were exacerbated by the Russians who were bent on swallowing up the conquered European countries and creating new worries for the U.S. By the end of the decade, the Americans would become paranoid about the 'Communist menace' and the U.S. Senate would conduct their notorious witch-hunts in Hollywood. The undercurrents of bitterness and disillusionment left behind by the war soon became evident. What has all this to do with Rita's Hollywood? Amazingly the movies were the first to mirror this new, disturbing undercurrent. Not overtly, for as yet there was no apparent reason to have guided them, but a wave of films, black and sour, sprang up and gained immediate popularity.

The elation of wartime musicals gave way to perverse thrillers studied with disenchantment, not all of which was attributable to the worlds of Chandler, Hammett or James M. Cain. Because of its timing and subject matter, *Gilda*, one of the first and most successful films of this new wave, was instrumental in launching the movement, defying the understanding of critics. The bulk of films released in 1945, including *Tonight and Every Night* were musicals, war heroics, or uplifting stories starring Lassie. But it was the films that went into production by the end of the year that projected the new trend. Among them was Alfred Hitchcock's masterful *Notorious*, which shared a similar setting and sub-plot with *Gilda*, and in which Ingrid Bergman consolidated her place in the heavens as one of the idols of the decade. Bergman and Hayworth polarised the public's emotional pulse—Ingrid was their Saint, Rita would be their Sinner. Both

Rita and Orson out on the town in November, 1945, a few weeks before she announced plans for her divorce.

women would exit from the decade more sinned against than sinning in a blaze of headlines bright enough to take people's minds off more serious problems.

Gilda began as scheduled on September 7th, 1945. Much to the despair of *auteur* critics now and studio production managers then, the story was pursued in a most haphazard manner, with producer/scenarist Virginia Van Upp delivering the screenplay one or two pages at a time, usually on the very day of shooting. But this unorthodox way of working had already reaped splendid rewards in Hollywood, and not exclusively at a small studio like Columbia. At Warner Brothers the brothers Epstein and Howard

Koch had hung on to their screenplay for *Casablanca* even when
shooting was half-way completed, hoping to match the latest
headline of the Allied landings in North Africa—and won an
Oscar, not to mention immortality, for their *sang froid*.

Miss Van Upp did not have the excuse of timeliness, hers being
the tried-and-true storyline of countless other movies. Only this
time the chemistry was better than usual, was in fact explosive.
During the shooting, fan magazines and gossip columns were
regaling their readers with hints of a romance between Rita and
her co-star, Glenn Ford. Finally, a formal announcement was
issued to the press: the Welles were divorcing. As it turned out,
the announcement proved less than final, and a reconciliation was
arrived at by both parties. By then, *Gilda* was in the can.

The film was another reunion of sorts. The director was Charlie
Vidor and the leading man Glenn Ford, both of whom had
worked with Hayworth in *The Lady in Question* in 1940. For Ford,
back from three years in the Navy, the picture was much more.

'When I came back from the service, I couldn't get a job
anywhere. Most of us who had been gone were forgotten and new
faces had come along and taken over. Very fortunately, I met
Bette Davis who, over Warner's objections, said, "I want this
man" and she got me the male lead in *Stolen Life* and got me
started again. I had good advance reviews on *Stolen Life*, and
Charles Vidor remembered me from *The Lady in Question* and
maybe someone at Columbia thought that Rita and I would
make a good team. I'm sure Rita must have approved by that
time, and Vidor certainly did, so that's how *Gilda* came about.

'When I went into *Gilda*, Rita was finished with Orson, and we
gave Harry Cohn a few grey hairs. We were told by the sound
department that Harry had had a microphone planted in my
dressing room. That was kind of interesting. He was worried
about my carrying on with Rita, so we gave him some marvellous
things to listen to.'

Cohn was incensed, but Rita enjoyed his discomfiture. While
she entertained Ford in her dressing room after the day's shooting
Cohn would phone down every fifteen minutes. 'What the hell
are you doing down there?' he'd shout. 'Just having a drink,'
said Ford. 'Why don't you go home,' demanded Cohn. 'I can't
keep the studio open all hours of the night. It costs money. Now
get the hell out and don't forget to shut off the lights when you
leave.' Enjoying Cohn's exasperation, the two co-stars had
another drink.

Rita with co-star Glenn Ford and producer-writer Virginia Van Upp breaking for tea.
(Cronenweth/Columbia)

'I had grown up considerably since *The Lady in Question* after
three years in the Marines and in the South Pacific. I imagine
Rita had too. We didn't know how the picture was going to turn
out. Sometimes we would be on the set in the morning and
Virginia would come in with the script and hand it to us. Rita
and I were very fond of one another, we became very close friends
and I guess it all came out on the screen. Honestly speaking, I'm
sure we all sensed something going on there, there was an excitement on the set. Mr Vidor was a very strict, demanding director
who had a streak of sadistic, Hungarian, love-hate understanding
and he sort of nurtured that aspect. His instructions before we did
a scene, on how we were to think and do it, were pretty incredible, even in today's market. I can't repeat the things he used
to tell us to think about. They are marvellous images to hold . . .'

Perhaps one should read a touch of wistfulness rather than a blunt invasion of privacy in Cohn's Watergate tactics, for nothing could have gratified more his dynastic ambitions than a romance, leading to marriage of course, between his top star and his fastest rising leading man. Even if the story of Harry's proposal to Rita were a rumour, he still must have derived some joy from the divorce announcement. Welles was yet to give Harry his greyest hairs with *The Lady From Shanghai*, but he was already sarcastically referred to as 'That Genius' by a man who instinctively mistrusted independent minds.

Two weeks after *Gilda* started shooting, it became obvious to Cohn that he was getting more and better than he had originally hoped for. The storyline devised by Marion Parsonnet had been enriched by Virginia Van Upp with new twists and fanciful dialogue. Virginia knew Rita well and was able to write lines that Hayworth could charge with meaning. Others might have been tempted into stressing double entendre but Rita knew by instinct how far she could go with a line or a gesture, and never required an occasional toning down as, for instance, Marilyn Monroe did. *Gilda* began to take shape from the rushes, good if not spectacular, then all of a sudden, as Jack Cole put it, 'it was like mother's night at a Turkish bath.'

As with so many Hollywood pictures of the Hays Office era, *Gilda* created its own sub-text, independent from a screenplay that already projected a certain sexual tension on to what was merely a standard triangle story. Most of the film's implications went way over the heads of the American reviewers, but did not escape the French who are especially clever at detecting hidden significance even when that same significance escaped the director and the performers who made the movie in the first place. This time, however, they were dead right. Glenn Ford remembers discussing all possible sexual permutations with Rita and Vidor, including a homosexual attachment between the characters of Johnny and Mundson.

In the opening shot a pair of dice roll in close-up towards the camera. A voice-over narration by Ford in the sparse Chandler style affected after *Double Indemnity*, effectively establishes him as an American gambler down on his luck in the Argentine. A crap game is in progress in a dark alley in the docks of Buenos Aires. Johnny Farrell (Ford) pockets his winnings and walks out of the game. Moments later, he has a gun in his back as he is being held up by two bad losers. A cane out of nowhere knocks the rod on the pavement and one of the thugs reaching for it almost has his hand impaled on a stiletto that shoots out of the cane. The assailants flee leaving Johnny to thank his mysterious protector, Ballin Mundson (Macready), impeccably attired in opera hat, topcoat and silk scarf, adding the right dash of Mephistophelean elegance and danger. A hint of Faust, no more, to shade the plot.

Ballin is the proprietor of a luxury gambling casino and Johnny becomes his right-hand man. A friendship develops, based partly on a shared misogyny. 'Gambling and women don't mix' appears to be Mundson's law, yet after one of his periodic disappearances—as it turns out, he is the front man for a Nazi-backed cartel in South America—he returns home with a wife. Leading the astonished Johnny to the master bedroom, he pauses outside to ask: 'Are you decent, Gilda?' 'Me? (Pause) Sure I'm decent.' We've been waiting for Hayworth's entrance for almost an hour and her appearance is prepared by the sound of her voice softly singing to herself off-camera. Then she flares on to the screen, languidly shaking back her hair and looking over her half-draped shoulder, a reprise of the famous *Life* photograph. Gilda and Johnny greet each other as if for the first time, but the audience instantly realises from their ensuing taunts and rivalry that they ache from, as much as for, each other. We are left to imagine the film that could possibly accommodate that first painful love affair. Possibly hundreds.

The dialogue between Gilda and Johnny develops into a sexual thrust and parry. 'Disaster to the wench' is Johnny's toast to the bride and groom. 'I want all of the hired help to like me,' purrs Gilda. Even Ballin joins in with his own brand of perversity: 'Hate can be a very exciting emotion. There's a heat in it you can feel. Hate is the only thing that warms me.' Johnny becomes the self-appointed guardian of Gilda's reputation. She flaunts herself at strangers for Johnny to see: 'If I'd been a ranch, they'd name me the Bar Nothing,' but Johnny is always there to keep an eye on the boss's prize possession, to take her wherever she wants to go and to bring her back, 'like the laundry'.

During the carnival, Gilda and Johnny come in for the clinch. Swept into the revelry, they dance to a lush arrangement of 'Anywhere' from *Tonight and Every Night*. This was a typical case of studio economy and should not be confused with the current craze for cribs from other films under the guise of homage. 'I have to keep talking, Johnny, as long as I have my arms about you, or else I might forget to dance. Push my hat back, Johnny.'

This photo by Coburn was approved by the Advertising Advisory Council on December 19, 1945, who have returned it with an area marked for retouching to remove traces of cleavage from final print. (Columbia)

Few actresses have had their hair used so deliberately as a sexual metaphor. It might have escaped the watchdogs on the censor board, but audiences had no such problem. They knew that hair wasn't all that Gilda let down. Back at the casino, they can't hold back any longer. Gilda: 'I hate you so much, Johnny, I think I'm going to die from it.' Inevitably, when they kiss Ballin is watching from a window.

He cannot, however, take immediate action. There are more urgent matters like getting away from the police after having killed one of his German associates from the cartel, which is now exposed. Ballin crashes his private plane into the sea and is given up for dead. Johnny then marries Gilda, but not, as she had hoped, for any romantic reason. Blaming her for Ballin's suicide, he is determined that she shall remain faithful to his memory. He weds Gilda not as she believes out of love for her but to keep her out of circulation, while refusing to lay a finger on her. This latest perverse refinement in their particular sado-masochistic affair drives Gilda to hysteria: 'You wouldn't think a woman could marry two insane men in one lifetime, would you?' She escapes to Montevideo to apply for a divorce, but is retrieved by one of Johnny's henchmen masquerading as a suitor. Desperate, she makes a spectacle of herself at the casino by performing a near-striptease. Not surprisingly, Ballin returns to avenge himself on both Gilda and Johnny, but a corny *deus ex machina* has a philosophical lavatory attendant (Steven Geray) stab Ballin with his own stiletto. Then, the audience learns what the Hays Office knew all along, that Gilda was just a tease and had always been faithful, first to Ballin, then to Johnny, a rather tall story and one to be taken with a large dose of salts.

The casual last-minute disclosure that the lady was no tramp after all made mincemeat of all character motivation. No wonder Bosley Crowther admitted to some perplexity in the *New York Times* when the picture opened at the Radio City Music Hall on March 15th, 1946 (it was the sixth Hayworth vehicle to première there):

> Despite close and earnest attention to this nigh-onto-two-hour film (*the running time was 108 minutes*), this reviewer was utterly baffled by what happened on the screen. To our average register of reasoning, it simply did not make sense.

Most of the critics agreed, except for Kate Cameron of the *Daily News*, a long-time Hayworth partisan, who gave it a good review while acknowledging that the story was just 'high-class trash'. The film went on to gross three million dollars in its first run.

The haste in which *Gilda* had been made affected only the script. The significant contributions came instead from the song-writers, the dance director, the cameraman, the costume designer, even the hairdresser. Their talents coalesced in two musical numbers, strategically placed in the story. When Gilda breaks away from Johnny, she is found in a nightclub doing 'Amado Mio', a basic Latin number by Allan Roberts and Doris Fisher; then she segues into a Rumba arrangement, the kind of graceful step that Hayworth could do in her sleep, and better than anybody awake in the world.

Roberts and Fisher also contributed 'Put the Blame on Mame'

which Gilda performs as a mild bump-and-grind burlesque routine when she takes to the floor in the casino trying to make a fool
out of Johnny and a spectacle of herself. In a long shot, we see
Gilda in the spotlight as we hear Anita Ellis singing for Hayworth:
'Put the blame on Mame, boys, put the blame on Mame. One
night she started to shim and shake, that brought on the Frisco
quake.' On 'shim and shake' there is a cut to close shot—Rita in a
strapless black satin gown, with mid-arm gloves, the inspiration
for which came to Jean Louis from John Singer Sargent's portrait
of Mrs X. As with all the best dresses made for Rita, Jean Louis
had emphasised her beautiful waist and shoulders and drawn the
attention from her legs. Motherhood gave her figure additional
ripeness which the clothes showed to advantage though firm
foundations were needed for some of the more seductive gowns.

The routine builds to a near-climax that has Hayworth strip-
ping off her long gloves, flinging them at the audience, and
requesting their help with her dress since 'I'm not very good with
zippers'. The sexual come-on put-down of Johnny implied by her
exhibition is climaxed when he hauls her off the floor with a
brutal slap. The smack figured prominently in most of the
picture's ads.

Jack Cole: 'I must say of all the things I ever did for movies,
that's one of the few I can really look at on the screen right now
and say: If you want to see a beautiful, erotic woman, this is it. It
still remains first class, it could be done right now. A lot of
old things make you go wow! And you have to remember a lot
about the period to explain why you did what you did, and make
allowances. But every time I see "Put the Blame on Mame" I feel
it's absolutely great. The funny thing about the number is that a
very famous Ziegfeld lady who had made a few movies tried to sue
me and the studio, claiming that I had stolen her routine, that
"Mame" was really hers. She was slightly nutty like very elderly
people who were once very famous sometimes get. I had to tell her
that I based the number on a stripper named Charmaine, with
whom I had once done a show, an extraordinarily beautiful broad
who looked incredible when naked. The one thing about her that
was not beautiful was her hair which was thick with polish and
which made it rather hard for her to look like a lady. I had her
wearing a very formal evening dress, like Greer Garson would
wear, and sitting very elegant with a glass of champagne in a
gloved hand, and then, very slowly, she'd undo the dress with the
other hand while all the time she kept looking at you, which is far

more erotic than looking up somebody's dress.'

Both numbers, incidentally, were planned after Rita had already begun shooting. It was another classic example of the haphazard manner in which the film was put together and how it worked. Doris Fisher and Allan Roberts were the hottest songwriting team on Tin Pan Alley when Harry Cohn's 'Gofer' brought them to his attention. Cohn had never lost his ear for a good tune and they were signed. Wanting some time to get acclimatised, they arrived three weeks early. Theoretically, *Gilda* was in the can but in fact was in the midst of re-takes to try and improve it. The night they arrived on the lot Vidor was re-shooting the 'laundry-bag' sequence, and Doris counted fifty takes before she went home to bed.

Fisher: 'Though we weren't supposed to work yet, they gave us a script the next day, told us they wanted a couple of songs and where they wanted them to come. At about 3 a.m. we went into a publisher's office on Vine Street since we had no office of our own, sat down by a piano and, I don't know, it just happened. Al came up with that title "Put the Blame on Mame" because of the script. We'd already been playing around with that feeling for a song so it just worked. We wrote that in a couple of hours. A day or two later we wrote "Amado Mio" because we had to have something with a South American flavour there. We had no idea where it was going to be, how it was going to be done or what it would look like. We only wrote those two songs. Then they had to shoot those scenes after the film was finished and inject them into the story.

'I didn't meet Rita until after we'd finished the song. I was an absolute nervous wreck then because I had to get on a stage with huge spotlights, in front of Vidor, Virginia Van Upp and everybody. I had never worked with anybody in pictures and suddenly there was this set up where I would be playing the songs for her, and I was petrified. It was about ten o'clock in the morning. Rita walked in, sat down at this little chair next to the piano and I turned to her and said, "I'm an absolute nervous wreck." And in her quiet, little girl voice she said, "So am I."

'Nobody gets close to Rita. She was terribly aloof as far as I was concerned, almost untouchable in so many places. I always analysed it as insecurity. I don't remember the initial reaction to the song, but it wouldn't have mattered to me anyhow because I knew it was great. About two weeks later we started to dub the songs. Before then, Nan Wynn had been dubbing all Rita's

pictures, but we couldn't find her or she was somewhere else at
the time. We got Anita Ellis. She sang like Nan, elf-like, breathy
voice. When you look at that number and analyse it there are the
broad strippy gestures that Cole gave her to do. But the voice
when you separate it is a little voice because that's the way Rita
was. I never had time to go and watch them shoot the *Gilda*
numbers, because no sooner had we finished writing those songs
than we were put on writing numbers for about twelve "B"
pictures one after the other.'

'Amado Mio' is practically a throw-away, but since the steps
were second nature to Rita she wasn't worried. There was no time
to set up rehearsals for 'Put the Blame on Mame' and this
bothered her. Fred Karger and Jack Cole set up shop in the
adjoining sound stage, Karger playing piano, Cole thinking up
steps, breaking it all down, all in between shots. If Hayworth was
not needed for one particular shot, she was given fifteen minutes
to prepare for the next, and she would then come and work with
them.

Vidor was partial to Rita, sympathetic to her and having
worked with her twice before, understood her working method
better than anybody else. In an interview he gave several years
later he recalled the tough conditions in which they worked.

We didn't have a finished script, we never knew what was
coming next and we even started the picture without a leading
man. Every night as we quit we got the next day's scenes. Rita
had to study at night, so did I, so did Jean Louis the dress
designer, but somehow he kept one leap ahead of us all. So that
particular 'Mame' morning, none of us knew how Rita was
going to look. She sauntered on the stage holding her head up
high, in that magnificent way she does, stepping along like a
sleek young tiger cub and the whistles that sounded would have
shamed a canary's convention. She enjoyed every second of it.
Then she did that elaborate difficult 'Mame' number in two
takes. I always tried to give Rita her big dramatic scenes during
the morning and shoot around her in the afternoon, because by
then she's usually been up since six in the morning, and even if
it doesn't show in her face you know she's worn out. Her best
take is usually the second, sometimes the third. If you don't get
it after that you're in trouble, for she's all emotional and arrives
at everything emotionally. After the third take she's emotionally exhausted.

There was only one scene that gave us a problem and that was where she struck Glenn in the face, because this was counter to her own impulses. She wouldn't do that in real life any more than she'd commit murder. She's much too gentle, much too feminine. Besides, that's not the way she gets her objectives. In that particular she reminds me of Gandhi. She knows exactly what she wants. She will stick indefinitely to an ideal or an ambition—but she doesn't fight for it. She waits—quietly, passively, a perfect example of composed non-co-operation. By her very stillness she gets what she wants.

It's my peculiar fortune to make my pictures with Rita at a time of some personal crises in her life. When we began *The Lady in Question*, she was getting her divorce from Ed Judson. When we started *Cover Girl*, she was just about to marry Orson Welles. During the shooting of *Gilda* she separated from him. One morning on *Gilda* she did not report for work. We were briefly told it was impossible for her to get to the studio. That night, their parting was announced. She turned up the next morning, her face without colour, her eyes without tears, her voice empty, but she kept her mind on her scenes and did them perfectly. I don't know why they separated. She never talked to me about it. I doubt that she has talked to anyone and unlike most women stars, she has no 'chum', no 'best friend'; she keeps her own council. But she is my favourite star, even though it sounds very indiscreet of me to say it.

Any trepidation that Columbia may have felt about changing the Hayworth image was swept away by the film's phenomenal success. To be on the safe side, however, it had been decided that a typical Hayworth musical, if such an animal existed, should be in the works before *Gilda* was released. And so, while all the advertising material for *Gilda* exploited the shady lady image to the hilt by having Rita in the 'Mame' gown trailing a fur piece behind her proclaiming to the world 'I was true to a man once and look what happened', the studio officially announced that the next Hayworth vehicle would restore her to musical comedy and Technicolor. (*Gilda*'s well-upholstered *demi-monde* was photographed by Rudy Maté in appropriate blacks and whites.) As it turned out, *Down to Earth* was the last of the 'typical' Hayworth musicals. In it she played a goddess no less, the muse Terpsichore, patroness of the dance, and what's more, a virgin. In subsequent musicals like *The Loves of Carmen*, which was more of a drama with

The caption on the back said that 'Rita Hayworth, soon to be seen in the Columbia picture *Gilda,* takes a minute to talk shop with Columbia's president, Harry Cohn, during a party given by Miss Hayworth to honor Frank P. Rosenberg, studio publicity director. Anita Louise listens in.' (February, 1946).

music, *Miss Sadie Thompson* and *Pal Joey*, it was Gilda rather than the Cover Girl who sang and danced and drove men away from their sweethearts and wives.

Even with the phoney Hays Office postscript, Gilda was one of a new breed of heroine, the deadly female mantis of mid-'forties Hollywood, the woman with a past who had already cropped up in the novels of Hammett, Chandler and James M. Cain, and the films made therefrom: Mary Astor in *The Maltese Falcon*, Claire Trevor in *Farewell My Lovely*, Barbara Stanwyck in *Double Indemnity*, Lana Turner in *The Postman Always Rings Twice*.

No sooner had Columbia felt that the new, tarnished Hayworth had in fact obliterated her established image than a dark, moody *pastiche* of the above titles entitled *Dead Reckoning* was made ready for her. The role of Coral Chandler was tailored for the Gilda Hayworth complete with Jean Louis wardrobe and torch song by Roberts and Fisher, but there was more to the part than a rag, a bone and a hank of hair. Coral was a killer who meets her doom in a car smash after unsuccessfully trying to bump off the hero.

Orson Welles beat the studio to it by launching *The Lady from Shanghai* in which Hayworth was to carry the archetype to cool perfection, and Coral was eventually played by Lizabeth Scott who was not under contract to the studio. Blonde, emaciated and husky-voiced, Scott, a butch Veronica Lake, seems now the antithesis of the Hayworth image, but it's quite probable that Columbia considered her as a possible replacement, or at any rate a threat, for their biggest star. As for *Dead Reckoning* it now seems a shame that Rita could not accept, for it would have provided her with a very good, if under-rated director, John Cromwell, and cast her against Hollywood's mightiest myth, Humphrey Bogart.

As it happened, *Down to Earth* did considerably more for Rita than was expected. The musical started shooting on March 25th, 1946, exactly one month after the release of *Gilda*, with Alexander Hall an expert at whimsy directing and Jack Cole in charge of the choreography. Shortly after, Hayworth, whose reputation as a punctual hard-worker was unblemished, began to miss rehearsals and exert an unheard-of resistance to studio schedules. She had been getting good advice and was now acting on it—all part of a well-planned campaign to re-negotiate her contract with Columbia.

Jack Cole: 'They didn't treat Rita the way other studios treated a star. She never had anything to say about the script or when she was going to work. Harry Cohn could say: "This is the script, be there Monday 10 a.m. to have your costume fitted." And that was it. He never asked her if she wanted to do it or whether she liked the script or how she felt about the part. Just do it! As if you were some kind of a horse. Harry Cohn had a right to do it, he ran the studio, it's just that he did it so badly. His whole thing was that he just didn't treat her as if she was a star at all but just some broad who worked for the studio and if she didn't like it, fuck her. "What she need a chintz in her goddam dressing room for?" They didn't do all those dumb things that keep a star happy. Zanuck was that way with Monroe. Instead of putting a car at her disposal every day to take her to and from the studio, or doing up her dressing room which would have cost them nothing, they'd say, "Why should we?" Baby, they should have because it makes the girls feel they are marvellous and that you adore them. It creates a different attitude, and she likes the studio. Instead, they treat you like shit and you learn the ropes. She starts to film but two weeks later she's off, and what are you going to do with the footage now! There'd be seven hundred and fifty thousand dollars down the drain and all the bright ladies learned that. They'd always do two and a half weeks and stop—"I'm dizzy tomorrow, I think I'm getting pregnant." And all this could have been avoided if they'd been treated with some consideration in the first place. Harry could have saved himself a lot of trouble later if he'd treated Rita a bit nicer.'

To handle the operation, the William Morris Agency advised her to start her own company, and so the Beckworth Company, (a combination of syllables from Rebecca and Hayworth) was formed. A new contract was drawn up in which Beckworth would receive twenty-five per cent of the profits of every Hayworth picture, while she continued to collect her usual salary, which in the fiscal year 1947 was estimated as $375,000, or $17,756 a week.*

The new contract would go into effect after Rita had completed *Down to Earth* and one additional picture still to be decided. Eventually, Hayworth sold her participation back to the studio and the Beckworth Company merely appeared in the credits of *Affair in Trinidad* and *Miss Sadie Thompson*.

A decade after the historic agreement, Harry Cohn granted *Time* magazine an interview for their cover story on Kim Novak, whom Cohn had chosen and groomed as Rita's successor at Columbia, and he still had something to say about it:

> Hayworth might be worth ten million dollars today easily! She owned 25% of the profits with her own company and had hit after hit and she had to get married and had to get out of the business and took a suspension because she fell in love again! In five years, at two pictures a year, at 25%! Think of what she could have made! But she didn't make pictures! She took two or three suspensions! She got mixed up with different characters! Unpredictable!

Behind the exclamation points and the absence of commas there is the businessman's eternal exasperation at the whims and frailties of the manufactured object.

There was no doubt about Rita's nationwide impact. The most

---

*Other stipulations were that:

1 She must always be portrayed sympathetically on screen.
2 Her role in any picture must always be the leading one.
3 That the picture must be made in Technicolor.
4 And that the budget for it must be at least one million dollars.

unexpected tribute—and, in retrospect, the most debatable—
came from the forty thousand men involved in Operation Crossroads, (the first atomic test of the post-war era). A pin-up of the
star was used to decorate an atomic bomb equal to twenty
million tons of TNT that was then dropped on Bikini Atoll in
the Marshall Islands on July 1st, 1946. Newsreel coverage of the
event featured Rita's picture as well as the most awesome blast
the world had seen to date, the kind of publicity that Hollywood
deemed invaluable. Rita found it deplorable.

Down to Earth was in production the rest of 1946. At a loss for a
story that could accommodate the talents of Hayworth and Larry
Parks, who had impersonated Al Jolson in *The Jolson Story* that
same year, a sequel was concocted to *Here Comes Mr Jordan*, a
successful Columbia fantasy of 1941 which had featured Claude
Rains as a sort of executive advisor to the Almighty coming down
to earth to straighten out some celestial mix-up. *Down to Earth* was
to retain the Mr Jordan character (played this time by Roland
Culver), two of the original cast, (Edward Everett Horton and
James Gleason), and the original director, Alexander Hall. The
Hayworth team included Jack Cole, Jean Louis, Rudy Maté, her
by-now-official songwriters Roberts and Fisher, even George
Macready as a Broadway gangster faintly reminiscent of *Gilda*'s
Mundson. *Down to Earth* turned out, to put it charitably, patchy.

Like all patchwork it required much cutting and stitching
which, added to the elaborate production numbers, made it one
of the costliest pictures ever undertaken at Columbia. Cohn would
fret whenever the shooting fell behind schedule, then withheld the
film's release for a good eight months, giving time for *The Jolson
Story* to saturate the American public and make Larry Parks a
star. The production was somewhat hazardous. Once, during the
shooting of the grand finale, a gilded elevator cage bearing the
nine muses was being hoisted in the air for a lighting set-up when
a cable snapped and sent it crashing to the floor ten feet below.
Fortunately, Rita was not present at this particular rehearsal for
she was supposed to have been hanging outside the cage, waving
her arms in mid-air. The chorus girls were hysterically screaming
for help, unable to extricate themselves from the debris while the
assistants rushed to summon a photographer who busied himself
taking pictures for the insurance company. Five minutes later,
Cohn was on the set wanting to know what had happened. He
accepted what was merely an unforeseeable accident, then in-
structed Cole to devise a new finale that would not require Rita to

As is often the case, when the film is bad, the stills have to be even prettier: Rita as the Goddess Terpsichore doing her bit for the publicity department and her favorite portrait photographer, Bob Coburn.

be up in the air. The original number had necessitated the building of an expensive monorail; it was totally discarded and is nowhere to be seen in the release print.

The film exploited the idea of having Terpsichore incensed at the notion that a Broadway musical is about to portray her as a modern, jiving sexpot, and her arranging, through the suave Mr Jordan, to come on earth and tone up the production. Posing as a dancer, she has no problem in replacing the blonde chorine (Adele Jergens, dubbed by Kay Starr) cast to impersonate her and she convinces the director (Parks) that swing is wrong and that what the show really needs is pure neo-classical dancing. Smitten with the muse, the director gives in and the production becomes a highbrow ballet that flops out of town. Aware that times have changed, Terpsichore realises that the show must go back to its original concept. It becomes a Broadway hit, not the least because of her own participation as leading lady. She must, however, return to Mount Parnassus where Mr Jordan unveils a bit of the future so that she may see herself hand in hand with the merely mortal director she loves.

From the above synopsis it's clear that *Down to Earth* is hardly the witty demystification of Broadway artiness and pretention that, for instance, Vincente Minnelli's *Bandwagon* was. Among several miscalculations, the highbrow-versus-lowbrow theme backfires: the Greek ballet, of which we see only a tantalising excerpt in the film, is by far the best musical number in it, not at all the constipated culture of previous, and even later, movie excursions into the ballet, with an intriguing score by a serious composer, the Italian Mario Castelnuovo-Tedesco.

Jack Cole: 'There was a problem: to do a number that would be Terpsichore's idea of a number, and it had to ruin the show; it's very difficult to do what is supposed to be a boring number and still not be boring. I must say we solved it very well, and Rita is so beautiful in it she's not to be believed. That shot of her in close-up with gold sand drifting through her fingers...! There's some serious dancing in it by Marc Platt, and Rita *does* dance; all the things I wanted her to do, she did. She worked like a Trojan throughout the picture which took a long time to make. She knew I loved her and trusted me absolutely.'

Cole worked her potential to the limit. She was, of course, no modern dancer like Carol Haney (who can be glimpsed in the Greek number), but for sheer movement she was unbeatable and probably Rita was well aware of this for she insisted in retaining a somewhat hazardous run down a curving ramp even when Cole and Fred Karger decided against it. Hayworth persisted and the original choreography remained even if it entailed running barefoot down the ramp until her feet blistered.

After over a dozen scores for 'B' musicals since they began on *Gilda*, Fisher and Roberts had been excited to be involved in what promised to be a big one.

Fisher: 'The producer on that was Don Hartman. He'd just come over from R.K.O. and was the top "class" producer in the country at that time. A very intelligent, cultured man, he didn't want just songs that would be commercial, he wanted the whole thing integrated into the picture so that it would flow with the script. We worked a year on that picture, getting together with

Jack Cole where he would express what he wanted, the kind of costumes for the numbers, all that.

'Originally Hartman had wanted Jerome Kern or somebody very big, which was natural since it was his first (and as it turned out, his last) picture on the lot and he wanted everything to be big. Harry wanted us to do it since we were already under contract and he wouldn't have to pay a huge sum to outside writers, and he and Jonie Taps really believed that we could do it. They sort of insinuated that I had to do a big sell job to Hartman. I played about six songs we'd done—and when I sold, believe me, nobody could leave the room. I sold so strong. And he bought it. After listening for two and a half hours we were in. That was quite a feat, because he could have had anybody in the world—there was no limit to the budget. It was the most expensive film the studio had made to date, costing something in the region of five million.

'The opening song was a huge piece of material called "The Nine Muses"—a fast marvellous piece that went on and on. Then there was "People Have More Fun Than Anyone", and "You Can't Convince Me", "This Can't Be Legal" [a number for Larry Parks, Rita and Marc Platt] and "Let's Stay Young Forever". It's rare to have so much special material in a movie. Usually it's just a string of pop songs, but these were all integrated with the story line.

'Larry Parks had just finished *The Jolson Story*, which was the biggest thing that ever happened at the studio, and all the time that we were on the stage scoring *Down To Earth*, their music people would come running in screaming, "Just a minute. We've got to do a chord. We lost a chord on *The Jolson Story*." And we'd have to stop in the middle of a whole production number, and the orchestra would have to go "Toot te too". That went on and on—it was maddening. Those were the two biggest things going. There weren't any after them or we would have done them.'

The score apart, the picture suffered from a critical case of mismatching. Whereas Glenn Ford always looked as if he had just made love or was about to, and could sustain a scene with Hayworth by simply staring at her and being stared back, Larry Parks lacked a sense of humour and looked as if he were sulking all the time. Ironically, he used his own voice in "They Can't Convince Me", the one song in the film to attain a modicum of popularity. The score as a whole failed to take off. But Cohn's high hopes for a new male star collapsed when audiences kept expecting to hear the voice of Al Jolson whenever Parks opened his mouth to sing. Shrewdly, he put together a sequel to the Jolson picture entitled *Jolson Sings Again*, released in 1949. It proved to be that rarest of birds in Hollywood, a sequel almost as successful as the original. A third instalment, however, would have been out of the question and, anyway, Jolson died the following year leaving Parks voiceless. The House un-American Activities Committee then cut short Parks's career, but from *Down to Earth* the impression is that it would have died of natural causes, at least at Columbia.

Rita's popularity continued to soar. Critics and public were quite aware of the film's shortcomings, yet they concurred that Hayworth never looked lovelier and it was only fitting that the Love Goddess of the twentieth century should be playing a goddess in a film. In that respect there were no quibbles.

By the time *Down to Earth* was premièred—at the faithful Music Hall on September 12th, 1947, eighteen months after the first day of shooting—her private life had moved on a pace. She had officially separated from Welles in March and taken up residence with Rebecca in a rented Brentwood house which did not even have a swimming pool. But Rita was still very much in love with her mercurial husband. She had even effected a reconciliation after their previous separation to work with him on the film that can be read as the final touch on their marriage, but which survives as a monument to their respective careers. *The Lady from Shanghai* had been completed early in 1947 and was awaiting release pending cuts and retakes that Welles had agreed to perform after screening his first cut for Harry Cohn. But the strains on Rita during filming had been noticeable; at one point she had had to be carried from the set with 103° fever, and their working partnership did not augur a return to a marital one, once the film was completed. Welles' subsequent trip abroad, and his rumoured affair with the Italian actress Lea Padovani, didn't improve matters.

Rita was granted custody of Rebecca, which was all she asked for, and with the Cansinos dropping in for more frequent visits, dates with Hollywood's eligible bachelors, and a proposed trip to England for the opening of *Down to Earth* in the offing, the atmosphere around the Brentwood house became homely and relaxed. It was there that music critic Winthrop Sargeant came to call on behalf of *Life* magazine which had commissioned him to do a now classic cover story on Rita.

The Sargeant piece, entitled 'The Cult of the Love Goddess in America', displays a mock scholarly approach and a mild macho admiration for the latest product of the Hollywood treadmill, but is in reality a snide put-down of both Hollywood and Rita. The author flashes the usual credentials as a member of the Eastern cultural establishment, deplores California's isolation and lack of interest in current trends of thought, and, disappointed at finding neither a sphynx nor an authority on sex but 'a rather likeable, simple and completely unaffected human being', makes Hayworth out to be a shy placid Trilby moulded by the hands of several Svengalis, the latest in line being Orson Welles, who, it must be admitted, looked the part. Sargeant also reported that Rita seemed always ready to stand up for her husband.

Before its release, *The Lady from Shanghai* was already rumoured to be a turgid fiasco, a thriller without rhyme or reason that, according to the legend, Welles had agreed to make for Columbia in exchange for $50,000 Cohn had invested in his stage production of *Around the World in 80 Days*. A less flamboyant version held that Welles had merely borrowed the money from Cohn at the time of his marriage to Hayworth, but such a pedestrian explanation would not hold against the fabulous tale of how Welles had finagled the sum on the phone from New York. Improvising an absurd storyline, he was supposed to have been trying to think of a title for the film, until he accidentally glanced at a cheap paperback the wardrobe mistress happened to be reading that day. It was *Lady from Shanghai*, a title that must have held all manner of exotic resonances for Cohn since he came through with the money.

The play was being produced in the princely manner befitting an impresario like Mike Todd, but despite a rare Cole Porter score (rare in that it failed to produce one hit song), and Welles taking over the role of detective Dick Fix and playing it in a variety of disguises while performing all sorts of parlour tricks, *Around the World* died after seventy-four performances on Broadway. Welles had another flop to his record, albeit a less prestigious one than *The Magnificent Ambersons*, but Cohn and Columbia had reasons to rejoice, although it wouldn't seem so until much later and by then, Harry was no longer alive.

At the time, for the studio as much as for the majority of Hayworth fans, *The Lady from Shanghai* was most memorable for the dark day when Rita was shorn of her voluptuous red mane to become a short-cropped glacial blonde. But for cinephiles all over the world, *The Lady from Shanghai* is today the one Hayworth film to withstand absolutely the test of time and go down in film history. These two different appraisals have been counterposed almost since the day the film was released, when the *Los Angeles Examiner* summed up the general feeling:

> There ought to be a law against the kind of murder and mayhem Orson Welles, genius at large, committed in making a picture called *The Lady from Shanghai*. I rather imagine Harry Cohn, Mr Boss of Columbia, feels the same way, for in eighty-six minutes Willie Wonder Welles completely destroyed the beauty, glamour and feminine appeal of Rita Hayworth (to say nothing of the illusion of being an actress) which Mr Cohn had spent expensive and careful years in building.

The past twenty years have seen Welles vindicated by film critics and historians who now rank *The Lady from Shanghai* only a few notches below *Citizen Kane*. As for Hayworth, she never exhibited any but the most total confidence in her husband's abilities as a film-maker, nowadays taking all the belated praise in stride: 'Honey, I knew it was a classic while we were making it. Harry didn't think so though.'

As a matter of record, Harry turned apoplectic after the first screening, offering one thousand dollars to the first person who could explain the plot to him. Perhaps Welles was not so sure of himself either. After the rough cut was screened for Cohn and Virginia Van Upp, he agreed to re-write and re-shoot the more confusing sections of the picture. Up to then, Cohn had given Welles free rein at the studio. Welles had even cast the roles, signing Everett Sloane, Gus Schilling, Erskine Sanford, Harry Shannon and Richard Wilson, all of whom had worked with him before, at more than their usual fees, a largesse that didn't sit too well with people at the studio. (The actors, Sloane in particular, repaid Welles with intense, high-pitched performances unique for the Hollywood of the period.)

A running feud with production manager Jack Fier had ensued by then. As recounted by Bob Thomas in *King Cohn*, it came to the point where Welles posted a sign reading 'We have nothing to fear but Fier himself', to which Fier retorted with one inscribed 'All's well that ends Welles'. The picture went well over budget

Historic Hayworth hair cut by Helen Hunt, supervised by Orson Welles (off camera) and attended by the world's press.

and schedule: allotted $1,250,000 and sixty days of shooting, it came in at two million, and ninety days. Some of the footage shot on location in San Francisco and Acapulco had later to be matched with close-ups taken at the studio, and while the film was officially the work of cameraman Charles Lawton Jnr, the Hayworth close-ups were rumoured to have been done back at the studio by the dependable Rudy Maté. All of which was in flagrant violation of studio policy and seemed unjustified expenditure.

As for the widely contested haircut, it may have irked Cohn to see his prize star divested of her most distinctive feature, not to say a most effective means of expression, but even then he refrained from intervening. The momentous operation was performed by Helen Hunt summoned from her honeymoon in New York and supervised by Welles, who personally selected the dye and, after Rita had been turned into a 'topaz blonde', urged the hairdresser to cut ruthlessly. It was later reported, or invented, that fans and fetishists all over the nation had besieged the studio, unsuccessfully, with requests for a lock of hair. It was also bruited that Columbia had offered the hair to Madame Tussaud's in London, but since no wax effigy of Rita Hayworth ever materialised, the ultimate fate of the fiery tresses long remained a mystery. Actually, they met a perfectly prosaic fate. Helen Hunt, who presided over the sacrificial shearing cleared it up:

> When I met Rita to do the job Orson and sixteen photographers were there in my department. Orson stood over me and the Press stood on chairs all along the back. I think Orson wanted to take credit for a new Rita, but it didn't take—the public wanted Rita as she was. Rita was always being told what to do by her husbands and she did it willingly.
>
> Many people wrote for a lock; even a minister from Canada who wrote and said it was against the teachings of the bible to cut hair, gave me a quote and ended up saying it was the most beautiful hair he had ever seen and could he have some. The hair was finally tossed in the basket. Rita didn't have enough hair left to look lush because I cut her hair by degrees until Orson was satisfied. The pictures which show Rita holding her hair are made up. This hair belonged to a little seamstress in the Wardrobe Department, but that's another long story. Rita was very lucky with her hair—it grew so fast she never needed to wear a wig. After the film was finished she went to Florida for a few months and when she returned it had grown out black—I tinted it again and she was back to her old self.

If the cut and topaz colouring failed to catch on across the country it did have its humorous consequences at the studio, whose employees' minds weren't always their own. Cohn ordered and everybody obeyed. Even the strong-willed Doris Fisher had to go through the transformation and do her hair the Hayworth way.

'I got a call from Harry to come right up. He said, "We're going to do something smashing. We're going to revolutionise the movie industry. We're going to cut Rita's hair. She's going to be a blonde. Every woman will go out and cut her hair and be a blonde." Then he looked at me and said, "You are going to go to Helen Hunt and get yours done now." '

In *The Lady from Shanghai*, Welles plays an Irish sailor and adventurer named Michael O'Hara, and Hayworth is Elsa Bannister, a blonde in distress he rescues from some muggers one

evening in Central Park. She admits to being born somewhere off
the China Coast, in 'The second wickedest city anywhere', the
first being Shanghai where she lived for some time under the
Japanese occupation. Elsa is somewhat enigmatic about the rest;
she doesn't smoke but accepts a cigarette from O'Hara as a
memento of their meeting; she carries a gun in her purse although
she claims that she wouldn't know how to use it; and she tries to
seduce O'Hara into joining her and her husband on a cruise to
California via Panama and the Mexican coast. O'Hara muses (in
Welles's richest brogue): 'I don't like a girlfriend who has a
husband. If she'll fool him, there's a good chance she'll fool me.'

The next morning, Elsa's husband turns up at O'Hara's hang-
out in a waterfront café. He is Arthur Bannister (Everett
Sloane), a reptilian cripple and 'the world's greatest criminal
lawyer', who talks as if he were forever cross-questioning a suspect
on the stand. Bannister offers to enroll O'Hara as his wife's
bodyguard, and Michael accepts only because, as he visits the
yacht, Elsa's maid hints that her mistress might be in real danger.
In Caribbean waters, Elsa and Michael exchange hungry looks
and aphorisms:

Elsa: I was taught to think about love in Chinese.
Michael: The way Frenchmen think about laughter in French?
Elsa: The Chinese say that it's difficult for love to last long.
Therefore, to love passionately is to be cured of love. There's
more to the proverb. Human nature is determined. Therefore,
one who follows his nature, keeps his original nature in the end.

The boat, appropriately named the *Circe*, touches port to
collect George Grisby (Glenn Anders), Bannister's partner in the
law firm and almost his match in perverse game-playing. In a
typical Welles sequence, dialogue overlaps as tension mounts:

Bannister: Michael, Mr Grisby just told me something I'm very
sorry to hear. [*To Elsa*] Lover, this really concerns you more
than anyone else.
Grisby: [Singing in an off-key reprise of Elsa's song at the piano]
Don't take your arms away ...
Bannister: According to George here, Michael is anxious to quit.
Grisby: [Singing] Comes a change in weather ...
Bannister: Did you know that, lover?
Elsa: [A wisp of a voice] No, I didn't.

Grisby: [Still singing] Comes a change of heart …
Bannister: Shut up, George. What's the matter, Michael? Are the hours too long?
O'Hara: No, sir.
Bannister: How about the money?
O'Hara: I don't care about that, sir.
Bannister: So money doesn't interest you, Michael. Are you independently wealthy?
O'Hara: I'm independent.
Bannister: Of money? Before you start that novel Elsa says you're going to write, you better learn something. You've been travelling around the world too much to find out anything about it.
Grisby: That's good, Arthur.

Throughout the above exchange, Elsa remains almost silent, but is nevertheless still the centre of attention, sunning herself on deck, aloof and fathomless. Later, during a jungle picnic organised by her husband, she is the only one to appear undisturbed by what Bannister refers to as 'a beautiful, guilty world'. While O'Hara comments on the soundtrack, 'It was no more like a picnic than Bannister was like a man', the film cross-cuts from the actors to a world of predators aroused by their intrusion: Elsa/bird, Bannister/crocodile, Grisby/snake. Welles sustains the animal imagery throughout; for example, when O'Hara describes a school of sharks fighting to the death among themselves, and later by having Elsa meet O'Hara at the San Francisco Aquarium, where moray eels and octopus are gruesome witnesses to their rendezvous.

To earn the money needed to rescue Elsa from Bannister and escape his inevitable persecution, Michael agrees to a crazy scheme whereby he will sign a bogus confession of having murdered Grisby. Obsessed with the idea that civilisation is doomed by atomic warfare, Grisby wants to stage his own death and disappear quietly into the South Pacific. Even admitting to murder, Michael is told that he cannot be prosecuted unless a body is produced. In exchange for $5,000, O'Hara signs the document, only to find himself framed on a murder charge when Grisby is killed that evening. (The staccato technique that Welles carried over from his radio days almost makes such a twist plausible and in true thriller fashion he allows the audience no time for thought. What makes this exchange so especially masterful is his shooting

Rita and Orson Welles (1947), co-stars of Columbia's *The Lady from Shanghai*, discuss their next scene as the crew prepares for a set-up. (Cronenweth/Columbia)

of it on a high hill in broad daylight against a romantically beautiful backdrop of ocean and sky, instead of the usual conventional dark shadows.)

Bannister offers his services as a defence lawyer, calculatingly speeding O'Hara's way to the death house. As sentence is about to be passed, O'Hara escapes from the courtroom by feigning to take poison. From there on, the story races to a bizarre finale staged in a maze of mirrors at a deserted fun house, where Elsa, Bannister and O'Hara converge for the final showdown. Elsa is exposed as the mastermind of another plot in which Michael would have been the fall guy, an elaborate plan to murder Bannister and share the insurance money with Grisby. Somewhere along the way, Grisby lost his nerve and shot a Bannister bodyguard. Elsa then killed Grisby. As their images are reflected hundredfold, Elsa and her husband shoot it out. When the last mirror is shattered, the lawyer is dead and Elsa lies mortally wounded. 'Come back, I'm afraid, I don't want to die,' she screams pathetically after O'Hara, who offers a parting pearl of Wellesian wisdom: 'Every-

End of a film, end of a marriage. (Cronenweth/Columbia)

body is somebody's fool. The only way to stay out of trouble is to grow old, so maybe I'll concentrate on that. Maybe I'll live long enough to forget her. Maybe I'll die trying.'

The Welleses seemed outwardly on good terms while making the film. The Acapulco locations had been shot in a relaxed mood, away from surveillance, with Errol Flynn's yacht, the *Zaza*, doubling for Bannister's boat. On weekends, Rita and Orson would fly to Mexico City to attend the bullfights; it was a case of nature imitating art, if one remembers her Dona Sol in *Blood and Sand*, shouting *olés* at some Mexican stock footage.

A little known side line to the main event was that while on location in Acapulco, Hayworth supposedly played a cameo in a Mexican picture directed by Norman Foster, a friend of Orson, whom she also knew from the old Fox days and who was to have directed her in *Lorna Hansen*, the film to be made after *Down to Earth* if Rita hadn't decided to work with Welles instead. It was a comedy in which the sailor hero looks for a mermaid; Rita appeared as herself and had one line (in English): 'Looking for me?' Whether the scene really appeared in the release print or whether Columbia exercised pressure to have it deleted, has never been determined, and neither has the name of the movie.

When the unit moved back to the studio, the Brazilian poet Vinicius de Moraes, author of the play *Orfeu da Conceicao* later filmed as *Black Orpheus* was at Columbia to study production techniques. He and Welles, who had lived in Brazil while making the aborted *It's All True* six years before, found a lot to talk about. De Moraes was allowed to follow the shooting.

De Moraes: 'There was a scene in *The Lady from Shanghai* where Rita Hayworth was lying on a boat, in a bathing suit. One of the lamps exploded and a man on the set leapt like a cat to cover her body with his, so she wouldn't get hurt. But she didn't seem at all frightened. Orson shouted a bit, that was all. She had a quality of languor, a stillness filled with voluptuousness. They called each other "Momma" and "Poppa". It sounded very artificial. With Orson she was just able to put a word in here and there because he would hold the reins of the conversation. She seemed to be impressed by him. He would direct her very little, he was mainly concerned with other people on the set. When you saw them together, on the set or socially, you had the impression that she was effacing herself for him. Orson wasn't very delicate about women, you know. He once told me that women were things that you had to use. I saw her many times afterwards, in the clubs, after the separation. I remember her dancing with Victor Mature at Ciro's, strikingly beautiful, very much the star. I think she was showing off a little, wanting people to know that she wasn't unhappy. She was a woman who liked to dance and to be loved.'

The film, made in the winter of 1946-47, gathered dust and opprobium in the Columbia vaults until April 1948. Even with additions and corrections, it would have been permanently shelved had Columbia not been determined to recoup their investment. For what was the public to think of their Love Goddess meeting such an ignominious ending, dying, and dying alone at that, while her leading man (not to mention director and real-life husband) walks out on her? Consciously or not, Welles had delivered the *coup de grâce* to the image of the buoyantly sexy woman. Rita would return, but never quite as before: as Carmen, as a pale carbon copy of Gilda in *Affair in Trinidad*, as a life-bruised camp-follower in *Miss Sadie Thompson* and *Fire Down Below*. It is all the more insidious since Welles sets up in the early part of the film the established image with a spectacular shot of Elsa/Rita sunbathing on a rock under the lustful gaze of the men aboard the *Circe*—Aphrodite but also a siren—and again, soon after, aboard the boat lying at anchor in the sultry night air, when she hums what could be an old Gilda tune ('Please Don't Kiss Me', which Cohn had apparently insisted on).*

The song serves to create another beguiling false front for Elsa, romanticising her motives, which in truth are all pretence. Elsa is a lady of ice masquerading as fire. She slips emotions on and off like rings, adept at playing with feelings because she has none of her own till she is exposed as a spider lady trapped in her own net all sticky with lies. It's intriguing to speculate on how much Welles the artist draws from Welles the husband for the use he makes of Hayworth. Does the secret of Rita's introversion rest in this cold, comfortless, frigid goddess? Does the artist understand where the husband failed or is this a husband's vengeance—or just what the part demanded? There is also Welles's self-declared misogyny (despite his several marriages!) to bear in mind when watching this double game he plays with the Elsa/O'Hara characters.

Writing about Welles, Bessy, the French film critic, quotes Orson telling him: 'Women are stupid; I've known some who are less stupid than others, but they're all stupid.' The author concludes from this that the film is a settling of accounts with Rita. If true—and it seems a bit fanciful—it would be an astonishingly ungenerous last gesture to the wife who had borne his child, and whose name on the contract made this film possible. At any rate, whatever the real motives might be, the film, as all of Welles's work, is full of games, none more so than this marvellous Chinese puzzle. As the darker image sets in, Elsa attains dream-like dimensions of power and deception. As of this moment Elsa is no longer the helpless victim of an intrigue. In the Chinatown sequence that follows Michael's escape from the courthouse, she is seen imparting mysterious orders to some Chinese cohorts, a blonde, tautly commanding Dragon Lady. Finally, she appears at the centre of the web, icy, all-knowing, holding in her hand the

* Because of danger of attack by crocodiles and snakes on land and barracuda fish in the water, two bodyguards were taken on to protect Rita. For the sunbathing scene, thirty Mexican beach boys were hired to scrape poisonous barnacles from Morro Rock.

fate of every character. The image is repeated *ad infinitum* in the mirrors before it's obliterated.

With this film Welles took his leave of Hollywood, where he was no longer allowed to make films (only to act in them) for Europe, where he was to start a new career as errant genius and outcast. He was to film *Othello* in Morocco, stage Melville's *Moby Dick* in London, remake *Citizen Kane* as a thriller in Spain. A decade later, he returned to Hollywood to direct *Touch of Evil* which shares some of the brilliance of *The Lady from Shanghai* as well as the same undercurrent of disenchantment. Then, he departed once more. In the divorce hearing (November 10th, 1947), Hayworth testified: 'Mr Welles showed no interest in establishing a home. Mr Welles told me he never should have married in the first place, as it interfered with his freedom in his way of life.' It was a simple enough statement that fan magazines embroidered with complaints about how Welles stayed up all night writing, and about how difficult it was to live with a genius.

Rita's reticence about discussing the break-up did not deter Louella Parsons who had a grudge of long standing against Welles that even her fondness for Hayworth failed to curb. As was her custom, the ruling sob sister asked Rita to see her for tea and a chat after the Welles's second separation. These 'chats' were a star's commitment few could afford to ignore, for Louella's vengeance was mightier than her praise. But like most people who grew up under the spell of Hollywood, Rita had read and enjoyed Parsons' column or heard her on the radio, first as a child, then as a star and even while married to Orson. It was a source of minor irritation between husband and wife, for he could not stomach what he called the columnist's illiteracy and narrow-mindedness. He was also possibly irritated by Louella's continuous jibes at the man who had made *Citizen Kane*—the film she and most of Hollywood assumed to have libelled her boss, W. R. Hearst.

By the time the cosy chat appeared in print several months later 'It's like this Louella . . .', Rita had started work on the first film for her own company. What bitterness she had expressed during the interview had gone for she was still very much in love with her wandering husband. But in the article she came in on cue:

Orson's a genius and never forgets it. But I don't want to say too much against him because he's the father of my daughter. And I think if you loved a man enough to marry him, the least you can do, if you must part, is to say nothing against him.

So Louella, suffering under no such restriction, says it all for her. She expresses her hopes, those of Rita's myriad fans, that Rita would henceforth steer away from geniuses and start living her own life, seeing more of Hollywood, perhaps marrying a nice movie star like David Niven whom Rita had been dating (among other bachelors) while waiting for her divorce to become final. The article ends on a hopeful note: Rita was sailing for Europe, her first trip abroad, and Louella, remembering that once before there had been a reconciliation, breathes a sigh of relief at the thought that there will be an ocean between her and Welles. (She obviously ignored the fact that Welles was on his way to Rome to play Cagliostro, the magician, in *Black Magic*. Rita was to leave little Rebecca in care of her aunt, Frances, and would be accompanied by her friend and secretary Evelyn Lane. Miss Lane was Cohn's executive assistant and to describe her as Rita's friend was a droll piece of journalistic euphemism.

Columbia had agreed to pick up the bill, arranging for Rita to be present at the Gala World première of *Down to Earth* in London. She sailed from New York on April 16th on the small Dutch boat, the *Veendam*, on a two-month goodwill trip that included being mobbed and cheered by crowds in Amsterdam (Dutch bulb growers voted her 'The Most Wholesome Girl In The World'), Belgium, France and Switzerland; entertaining American troops in Nuremberg for the July 4th celebrations, and capping it all with her first ever visit to London on July 16th.

It was the beginning of her love affair with England even though the British press made the title of that vapid musical she had arrived to promote more literal than ever. She had descended to feverish expectations that were quickly squelched. They were expecting another Barbara Stanwyck who, a few weeks before, had captivated everyone with her poised and outgoing personality. But they were confronted (and then only rarely) with a quietly dressed, retiring young mother who stayed in her suite in the Savoy Hotel until five in the afternoon, and ventured out accompanied by bodyguards. The journalists were like a pack of hungry dogs snapping for morsels to relieve the post-war gloom and latching on to Hollywood celebrities to provide the excitement. If the stars failed to comply, stories would be made up. The style of vicious personal gossip typical in the English press had long made trips to London a traumatic experience even for more extrovert celebrities than Rita. She had been mobbed before because of her popularity, but this was the first time that she was attacked for not living up to the image that had given her this fame. But it was only a mild foretaste of what she would experience on her trip a year later, when her public image and private life became one on the front pages. On this present visit, as Margarita Cansino, Rita found few enthusiasts among the fourth estate.

It wasn't all her fault either for the London Columbia office went to extraordinary lengths to keep her from her public, and the reception they arranged for her was described by *Film Weekly* as 'the biggest joke in London'.

At the première, four thousand fans were denied the sight of her arrival. She was sneaked in through the stage entrance of the Gaumont Theatre in Haymarket, and left by the same route once the performance was over. That evening, she really looked the part of the glamour queen, gowned in silver and cream, wearing a short ermine cape, and her hair, red and back to shoulder-length. (A waggish columnist was to insinuate on the speed with which Rita's hair had grown back.) She had been introduced to the exclusive first-night audience by Group Captain Douglas Bader, a popular flying ace, and the film's reception had been polite enough. To her, sitting in the company of Anthony Eden and the Duchess of Gloucester, it had seemed sillier and more embarrassing than ever, and her self-confidence was badly shattered. She wanted to make sure that she wouldn't have to return to that type of film, and Cohn had given her hope.

Columbia had recently acquired the film rights to the Garson Kanin Broadway hit *Born Yesterday* and Rita was set to play the role of Billie Dawn, the 'dumb broad' heroine for one of her upcoming projects. But first there was a more conventional project in the pipeline. By the time that was completed, personal events of a more resounding nature would have overtaken her, putting paid to her appearance in the comedy that might have given her career the impetus to help her break the typecasting that so dogged her. It would have provided the opportunity she had hoped for. 'I never really thought of myself as a sex goddess,' she said, 'I felt I was more a comedian who could dance.'

There may have been some deeper less easily perceived cause dooming the project. Had Rita played Billie Dawn, mistress of the aggressively boorish junk dealer Harry Brock (a recognisable caricature by Kanin of his former boss Harry Cohn) she would have stepped into a role specially created for Jean Arthur, who had of course been Rita's predecessor at Columbia. Miss Arthur withdrew from the play during the out of town try-outs. Perhaps it was the similarity to their own situation at the studio in relation to Cohn that jinxed the play for both actresses?

On July 24th, after a less than ecstatic week in London Rita set sail for New York on the *Queen Elizabeth*. The fact that David Niven had just arrived to make a film, thus starting up in the English press the old Hollywood gossip of a romance, was another spur to her departure.

Interviewed on the ship dock, Rita said that she was hoping to go back to England after her next film because she had not enough time to see half the things she had planned. All she knew about the film (*Lorna Hansen*) was that it would be a Technicolor costume picture set in New Orleans with Bill Holden, Randolph Scott and several thousand cows. But she refused to be cornered by personal questions about her marriage and Niven, leaving a studio spokesman to explain: 'After all she's a married woman. She is not even divorced. They are good friends.' And concluding diplomatically, 'She likes him as much as any Hollywood star.'

Back in Hollywood Rita and her advisers decided that the first film under her new contract had to be a sure-fire success. So *Lorna Hansen* was shelved while the Gilda type was revived as none other than fiction's classic vamp Carmen. *Down to Earth* had enjoyed full houses despite thud reviews, but the public had shown their preference for Rita as a red-maned *femme fatale* and what more appropriate role could there be than Prosper Mérimée's vixen who had successfully driven men to murder in more than twenty films. As a part for Rita the role was inspired typecasting—she was part Spanish, a dancer, and despite two failed marriages and one child, her image was linked in the public's mind with the sirens of old.

To further insure the film's success, the studio spent over two and a half million dollars and reunited as many of the *Gilda* team as were available. But things were not the same. Charles Vidor, still bitter with the studio from having lost his court case against Cohn, was set to direct; Glenn Ford, an unlikely choice for a Spaniard with his apple-pie American face, was cast as the sexually enslaved Don José; only Jean Louis proved as skilled in creating Rita's alluring early nineteenth-century costumes as he had been with her modern wardrobe. The rest of the production staff were people she knew, though Helen Deutsch's screenplay

The Loves of Carmen. (Cronenweth/Columbia)

could have done with Virginia Van Upp's guidance, but she
was unavailable. And Jack Cole had left as well. Since Rita's
dances were Spanish-based it was common sense rather than
belated nepotism that prompted a recommendation of her father
as choreographer.

Rehearsals for the numbers were already under way when the
film started shooting on November 15th; it took eighty-one days
to complete. While the auguries had been good, and the expense
involved was reflected in the finished product, the results never
succeeded in fuelling the fire that had been anticipated. The
causes for the film's artistic failure were several: for one thing,

here was a subject that would have benefited by being shot among the actual Andalusian locations—instead, they had to be simulated in the forest wilderness ringing Mount Whitney, where the temperatures at night were so low that the crew had to live in heated, portable dressing rooms. It got even colder when they shot special sequences at the timberline, eight thousand feet up. Another criticism was the screenplay that, although keeping closely to Mérimée's outline, could not come near to his hard, sharp prose; scriptwriters' competence apart, the strict Hays Office would not have countenanced a literal translation of the book's amoral, independent heroine who took love and death so casually. An air of compromise can be sensed in other areas. This was Hollywood's, not Mérimée's, Carmen. Glenn Ford felt terribly miscast in his role though the chemistry between Rita and himself had not diminished in the move from Buenos Aires to Seville.

Ford: 'That film should have been scrapped. It was just dreadful. If you can imagine me a Don José: I mean ... that was ridiculous casting. But of course it was with Rita and she wanted me to do it and I thought, well, with Charlie Vidor directing, in colour and everything, I'd give it a try. And, oh my God! If I came across as bewildered, wounded, and naïve it's because I felt that way. I learned one lesson from that performance—never do a costume picture. The critics tore me to pieces and they were absolutely right.'

Rita had still not given up on the idea of a reconciliation with Welles. There was no other man seriously involved in her life, but while this left her in a state of emotional languor, professionally her maturity and capability as a sensitive, thoughtful actress was evidenced by her performance. She is the *auteur* of her film, and its attraction and success rests on her presence. While make-up, hair and costume had to conform to Hollywood's idea of a gypsy so that physical grub and sweat were not allowed to show on her face, and her beautifully manicured hands suffered no broken nails, the intensity of her performance created a credible characterisation in which the passion, fire and flamboyance that were part of Hayworth's cinematic stock-in-trade found an appropriate receptacle. Whatever the other players may have felt about their roles, Rita brought compassion to the roving hearted gypsy's proud and restless nature. All of Carmen's coquetry, her passions, her superstitions and sudden angers were made incarnate in the film. Critics, studying the latest effort of the much-discussed Rita

Hayworth accused her of posing, albeit beautifully. But it was more than a beautiful pose an audience responded to, as when, rather than sacrifice her freedom in José's arms, she tosses her life on to his knife without a trace of doubt, taking his blade like a liberating draught. That moment, more from Racine's pen than Mérimée's, brings with it memories of other roles and some she should have played.

There were no major hitches on the film, and if Mérimée turned in his grave, well, Rita's public turned up in droves.

Rita's only personal problems occurred because of her father, though no one outside the family or close circle of friends would have been aware of any discomfort she might feel from working with her father again after a lapse of so many years. Only this time the roles were reversed. She was no longer the obedient pupil but the star and Eduardo's employer. Matters were not eased by the studio's hiring of a Flamenco specialist who was, nominally, there to assist Eduardo, but actually to advise Rita. It was especially difficult since the woman hired for the job, Antonia Morales, had been one of his students.

Antonia: 'I was brought in to audition for Vidor because they needed someone who knew Flamenco and understood that period. I had not seen Rita since we were students, but she remembered me and asked me to work with her because she wanted someone who was fresh in their outlook, but she told me she would have to work it out with her father first because she did not want him to feel she was going over his head. She hates hurting people, but it still made things difficult because here I was in the middle of a family situation. So I would have to teach the Flamenco steps to Eduardo and he would then teach them to Rita, like those breaks when José comes down the bridge and Carmen's doing some kind of dance. First I'd tell Eduardo and then I'd get Rita on the side to tell her. Of course Eduardo was bitter, after all he'd been my teacher, but there was never any row on the set.

'But it was really a horrible film. The trouble was it wasn't Spanish at all. The designer did not know anything about Spanish villages or tavernas; while the composer was producing Mexican music which was just wrong. And of course if you tried to tell them so, they hated you for knowing it was all wrong. Then I was sent to check out the costumes. Jean Louis was the designer and he was all for me, but the technical advisor who should have known these things was very unhappy because I was stepping on his toes. Rita tried to get them to do things right but she doesn't like to interfere so she concentrated more on her performance which was the only Spanish thing about the film.'

Exhausted from the gruelling work schedule, Rita needed a holiday. Work on the next film wasn't scheduled till the fall, so Rita planned to be absent for several months. Since Cohn wouldn't spare his assistant Evelyn Lane for such a long period, Rita left, accompanied only by her secretary and a woman friend, Leigh Leighter. With very little luggage, hardly any of her glamorous wardrobe, since this was meant to be a busman's holiday, she left for New York early in May, to see some of the new plays before taking the boat to Paris. Rita had a chance to catch up with the comedy hit of the season *Born Yesterday*, Judith Anderson's superb performance as *Medea*, Wendy Hiller in *The Heiress*, and her friend from *Cover Girl*, Phil Silvers, starring in a new musical comedy *High Button Shoes*. Perhaps also to take in some of the new European films, especially the Italian ones whose post-war, neo-realistic school had created a storm of excitement in New York's cultural circles. Compared to the highly publicised Hollywood productions Rita and her contemporaries were making, these early works by Rossellini, de Sica and Visconti, though seen by only a few, nevertheless spearheaded an attack on the once impregnable Hollywood fortress where it would hurt.

The real box-office threat to the American monopoly posed by the European cinema was some years away. But culturally it would be felt sooner, and one of the American public's hallowed idols cracked almost immediately because of them. Ingrid Bergman, whose rise and fame paralleled Rita's, was at the pinnacle of her career. The previous season she had crowned a unique position as the nation's virgin Goddess when even Broadway's acid critics succumbed to her as Joan of Arc in Maxwell Anderson's play. When it was announced that she would film it, the powerful women's leagues who saw Bergman as an inspirational symbol of the home and the hearth, proposed raising a statue of the French Saint in the star's likeness. Miss Bergman, who was neither Saint nor Sinner—and certainly no fool—let it be known that this would not be a good idea. What she couldn't prevent was the reaction to events sparked off after she had seen Rossellini's *Open City*. She was so impressed by what she saw that she wrote to the Italian director on May 8th, offering him her services for a suitable project. What followed is history.

Now a whole series of intriguing speculations arise:

What if Ingrid Bergman had not gone to the movies and if Rita

Hayworth had missed her boat and returned to Hollywood?

Did the intense furore soon to break over their heads, causing their names to be bandied about, to be censored in print and on Capitol Hill as lurid examples of Hollywood immorality, help contribute to that incipient air of post-war hysteria, and thus, by the graphic illustration of the attraction of Hollywood as a limitless bounty for front page publicity, did they focus the attention of the witch-hunting Senate Congressional Investigation Committee on the movie capital?

Did they ever meet years later, with their European adventures behind them, and compare notes?

While the two women's paths ran their course in New York that tranquil month of May, back in Hollywood another woman, Norma Jean Mortenson, took her first step on a screen career that would lead to her apotheosis as Love Goddess and Child-Woman in the last gasp of the Hollywood all three had known. As Marilyn Monroe, she played in *Scudda Hoo, Scudda Hay*.

Rita's boat left on cue with her on board. Who could have foreseen that *The Loves of Carmen*, which opened that September would be her last film for four years. There was no gypsy fortune-teller to read the tea leaves. And had there been, it's doubtful that Rita would have heeded her anymore than Carmen did. Although she returned from her holiday for re-takes and pre-production work on the long-suffering *Lorna Hansen*, she didn't stay to make it. When at last Rita took up her career again, she had changed. Hollywood had changed. But for a few brief years in between she experienced the great romance of her life. And she provided the world with a ringside seat to an event more spectacular than any film she could have made.

CHAPTER VI

THEY ALL MARRIED GILDA

It's nice to be included in people's fantasies but you also like to be accepted for your own sake.

Marilyn Monroe

Inevitably, stars' personal lives figure in any biography written about them. Their popularity is linked to their personalities, though they work in a medium that necessarily selects and magnifies some parts to the exclusion of others. Understanding them and their way of life serves somewhat to explain their appeal before the camera. This applies to most people in the public eye but to movie stars more than others. Their on-screen gestures, thoughts and actions are deliberately intended to be taken for an extension of their selves. And to some degree this is valid. Some actually are what they are made out to be. Others may *become* in reality what they appear to be.

But there are those, like Rita, who are the *reverse* of their image. True, Margarita Cansino and Rita Hayworth meet in the cheekbones; their movement is one in the dancing. Rita Hayworth's dignity is wholly Margarita's. The showier side of her screen persona, too, is an extension of the real thing—the studio's idea of the public's demand. But it is Margarita Cansino who falls in love, gets married and has children—not Rita Hayworth. And it is Margarita who has to cope with the image when it goes sour.

Margarita fell in love with Aly Khan in the summer of 1948. In a way it happened through *Rita Hayworth*, world celebrity, one of her generation's idols. How else could she have entered Aly's circle? Fame is a passport, but it's no *carte blanche*; it's certainly no protection. And it is *Margarita* who would suffer the experience.

When a star first starts out on his or her career, it's easy to think of the press as a friendly ally. The recognition that comes from their mention is rewarding, but quite misleading. The reason for their attention? Nothing less than the key element in a star's success—the air of fantasy that captures the public's imagination and sells tickets, also helps to sell papers. A star's fans respond in a basic, primitive way. They love their chosen idols much as they might a pet dog or a canary or a dress—someone or something about which it is safe to fantasise. They accept private emotional outpourings, but only those that make no uncontrolled claims on one. The same phenomenon is at work today, of course, for all our supposedly increased awareness. Whether it's the Beatles or Bowie or Janis Joplin we still have stars, and for the same reason—though those who aim for symbolic status in the 'seventies claim to do so with eyes open wide.

Long before Rita went to Europe, she had been on the covers of *Life*, *Time* and countless other magazines. It was no longer a accolade—merely part of the studio's promotion to sell films based on her popularity. But the headlines Rita was to receive because of her romance and marriage with Aly Khan were a deliberate and calculated attempt to exploit her to sell newspapers. Today their affair would still attract a hue and cry, but it would not be a scandal, able to wreck careers and lives. Rita was copy in the way that Jean Harlow had been 'copy' when her husband killed himself; just as Marilyn Monroe was copy when the pressures broke her down and she fled into hospitals, and eventually to her death. The way Liz Taylor, Mrs Onassis or the Jaggers are. As food for the gods.

Marilyn had movingly expressed their dilemma in one of her last interviews:

When you're famous you kind of run into human nature in a raw kind of way. It stirs up envy, fame does. People you run into feel that, well, who is she—who does she think she is? They feel fame gives them some kind of privilege to walk up to you and say anything to you, you know, and it won't hurt your feelings—like it's happening to your clothing.... They kind of look towards you for something that's away from their everyday life, I guess you call that entertainment, a world to escape into, a fantasy. Sometimes it makes you a little bit sad because you'd like to meet somebody kind of on face value.

Monroe had tried to come to terms with her success and its restrictions; she understood that her commodity value overrode considerations of the personal suffering it might cause her. She had to watch helpless while her private affairs were offered up for headlines. In the end, the burden became more than Monroe could bear.

Margarita, however, though perhaps unable to verbalise her situation as well, was stronger. She survives.

From the time they first met until their last parting every move she and Aly made was photographed, written up, dissected, held up to ridicule and censure, not a scrap left unturned. Neighbourhood cinemas were blatantly advertising newsreels showing the latest development in the Hayworth/Khan romance—and used her name on the hoardings to attract the public in. When at last the press moved on, they left Rita's reputation looking like the landscape an army of warrior ants had crossed.

Yet, amazingly, she has come through this passage of her life with dignity and pride bruised but intact. Even as cameras and microphones jabbed the air perilously close to her face, her dignity protected her. The press, especially the English, has apparently never forgiven her—they still exploit any opportunity to splash Hayworth mercilessly across their pages.

What has Rita Hayworth's marrying Aly Khan to do with the films she made? Or with why people flocked to see her in them? For what reason did I choose to write about her? Of all her bouts with the headlines, her marriages and romances, this is the one that cannot be ignored. In the end, when all is said and done, the whole fantastic circus was like a movie. It still retains all the ingredients for a box-office smash—a true-life fairy-tale romance with two great stars, exotic locations, drama, thrills, terrifying chases, narrow escapes and ... a happy ending. Only it wasn't a film. And in the end there was no happy ending.

THE BEGINNING

'His whole life was so different. It was too difficult for me. I wasn't prepared for it, and, who knows, he probably wasn't prepared for me.'

Rita Hayworth

EXTERIOR. LUXURY LINER ON THE HIGH SEAS.
VOICE OVER SOUNDTRACK.

Since childhood Rita had a wanderlust. Before she left Hollywood she had told a reporter that when still a little girl she had wanted to be a boy so that 'I could grow up to become a sailor or an explorer and travel. I have just one wish, to take a trip around the world, just to roam, to live for a year like the natives of each country.'

DISSOLVE TO:
INTERIOR SHIP'S CABIN. CLOTHES ON BED; ROOM EMPTY; DOOR TO ADJOINING ROOM OPEN.

Rita's compulsive shyness kept her below deck for most of the ocean voyage. She could not bear the avid stares that greeted her appearance in the dining room, and so had her meals sent to her cabin.

DISSOLVE TO:
AERIAL SHOT OF PARIS TAKING IN FAMOUS MONUMENTS IN QUICK SUCCESSION. CAMERA MOVES DOWN TO HOTEL. PICKS OUT PROMINENT NAME: GEORGE V.

DISSOLVE TO:
CAMERA AT GROUND LEVEL OUTSIDE HOTEL ENTRANCE: BACKS
OF COATS; PORTERS STRUGGLE WITH LUGGAGE; RITA, FACE
TURNED AWAY FROM CAMERA, DISAPPEARS BEHIND REVOLVING
DOOR.

Her first stop on her arrival was at the hotel for a pre-arranged
meeting with Orson in yet one more attempt at reconciling their
differences. It failed. A few days later Rita was rushed to the
American Military Hospital with a severe virus infection. The
combination of exhaustion, emotion and tension had sapped her
strength. She had to be given blood transfusions for over a week
before her condition improved enough to be sent to recuperate in
the south of France.

DISSOLVE TO:
EXTERIOR, THE CÔTE D'AZUR. BRILLIANT SUNSHINE. CAMERA
PANS FROM YACHT TO HARBOUR, THROUGH TOWN TO HOTEL,
LANGUIDLY, PICKING OUT THE OCCASIONAL FACE IN THE
CROWD. THE RICH ON PARADE. MUSIC UP.

Viewed from the yachts at anchor on the sparkling blue Mediterranean, or from her suite in the luxury Hotel du Cap
d'Antibes, the Côte d'Azur presented a glamorous, sun-bronzed
paradise virtually unscathed by the recent ravages of war. Its
millionaire denizens, free of the economic restrictions imposed on
a less fortunate world, treated it as a private preserve for their
games. Monte Carlo, in the glittering pin-head principality of
Monaco, was only a few miles away. Cannes with its casinos had
again begun to make a splash with the start of its annual International Film Festivals. Saint Tropez was, then as now, haven
of fishermen, painters and the young set. Because of its splendid
views, its climate and restaurants, the area had always been a
playground for princes, playboys and prostitutes of both sexes, as
well as haven to artists, emigrés, social climbers and most of the
ex-kings who now sat in the shade dreaming of their time in the sun.

After a spell of comparative quiet, when the only ones able to
enjoy the sights or afford its amenities were the conquering
German army on leave, the Riviera was again enjoying a boom.
Shopkeepers and hoteliers were doing a roaring trade, reminding
croupiers and portiers of the resort's golden age at the turn of the century. If the local inhabitants felt any resentment over their spoilt,

rich guests, they were too busy raking in the profits to betray it.

That summer, everyone with money and time was there; the Shah of Persia, the Duke of Windsor and his Duchess; ex-King Umberto of Italy and his daughter, the Princess; Onassis and Niarchos, their fleets, and their wives; Cole Porter and Elsa Maxwell; South American sugar kings, Texas oil moguls and the usual gaggle of Emirs, Sheiks, Rajahs and miscellaneous potentates—everyone except King Farouk of Egypt, soon to be deposed, and the Aga Khan. But the latter was well represented. At the heart of the social whirl prowled the Aga's eldest son, restless and commanding, the most talked about, written up, envied and adored playboy of his generation—Prince Aly Khan.

Into this world where wealth and beauty abounded, where illusions were staked on the spin of a wheel, and few turned out to be what they had seemed in their smart clothes and couturier gowns, stepped Gilda. No, not Gilda. There never was a woman like Gilda. Not even Rita, but Margarita. Her descent still passed for the ultimate illusion that moment. She was an American, young, beautiful, alone and one of the most glamorous women of the day. She was also rich. Unbeknown to her, out of sight in her darkened hotel room, she became the number one topic at dinners, and goal of every would-be Casanova and fortune hunter on the long and winding beach.

DISSOLVE TO:

CAMERA OUTSIDE HOTEL WINDOW LOOKING IN. A SUITE OF ROOMS IS HINTED AT BY DOORS ON THREE SIDES OF WALLS. ROOM SEEN IS DRAWING ROOM. THE RADIO IS ON MUSIC PLAYS; AN EMPTY WINE GLASS STANDS ON A SMALL TABLE BY COUCH; DOOR TO ADJOINING ROOM IS OPEN. CAMERA MOVES ROUND ROOM PICKING OUT ITEMS: A SCARF, A PAIR OF GLOVES ON FLOOR; PHOTOS OF RITA, ORSON AND REBECCA IN FRAMES; FRENCH PAPERS WITH PHOTOS OF HER ON FRONT PAGE. THE ROOM IS EMPTY BUT WOMEN'S VOICES CAN BE HEARD FROM ADJOINING ROOM. ONE LOUD, THE OTHER SOFT. A TELEPHONE RINGS. DARK-HAIRED WOMAN, MID-TWENTIES, ENTERS, ANSWERS AND HANGS UP. CAMERA MOVES IN FOR CLOSE UP. DOOR CLOSES.

Rita Hayworth was not available. The young good-looking Shah of Persia sent her flowers; the South American millionaire tried bribing her secretary to get to Rita; the Greek shipping fleet owner sent baskets of food, champagne and costly tokens of his esteem. Rita put the flowers in a vase, ate the caviar, drank the champagne, sent back the bracelets and remained incommunicado. When she went window shopping or for a walk along the beach, few recognised the quiet American in baggy shirts and slacks as the rich and exciting Hollywood movie star. Feeling physically weak and emotionally bruised, Rita planned to terminate her stay as soon as she was well enough to leave. There seemed nothing and no one to hold her.

DISSOLVE TO:

OVERLAPPING STILL PHOTOS OF ALY KHAN AT RACES, AT PARTIES WITH FRIENDS AND HORSES. MUSIC: HIS THEME.

Aly—the less than spiritual son and potential heir of the Aga Khan, spiritual leader of the Ismailis and reputedly the richest man in the world—was also planning a change of scene by flying to Ireland for the races. His latest acquisition, none other than future Derby winner 'My Love', was running. At thirty-eight, Aly, married but separated, possessed of a charm that would have made him a success without his wealth, was a glittering prize. Many women knew him, few caught him and none held him. He had been doing up the villa he had bought on impulse a few months earlier. Now he wanted a break. Of course he knew that Rita was around. Not only was Aly a connoisseur of beautiful women but an enthusiastic movie buff as well. But where was the point in competing for a woman who refused to show herself when a steady flow of others were willing to throw themselves at him. He could afford to bide his time.

DISSOLVE TO:

INTERIOR OF LIVING ROOM. MORNING. SUNSHINE DEFLECTED BY HALF DRAWN LOUVRE BLINDS. CAMERA CLOSE UP ON:

Elsa Maxwell, the plumpish, middle-aged unlikely Scheherezade to ex-kings, playwrights and any social climber who could afford her talent to amuse. She had hoisted her reputation on achieving the supposedly impossible: preventing the rich from getting bored and showing them how to spend their money. She wanted Aly, whom she adored, to dress up a soirée she was hosting at the swank Palm Beach Casino for a Texan oil farmer crashing society with his oozing millions. Elsa already had one admiral, plus the

Marquess of Milford Haven, but Aly Khan was a star attraction. To get him to delay his departure it became Elsa's job to invite someone who would pique his curiosity. The evening, Saturday, July 3rd was a few days off.

CAMERA STARTS TO PULL BACK, SHOWING ELSA SITTING AT DESK LITTERED WITH PAPERS, TYPEWRITER AND PHONES. PICKS UP PHONE AND DIALS.

She had her work cut out. Elsa knew Rita from her war-benefit days in Hollywood's *Charlot Revue*. She would get her. Reaching Rita was no problem. Elsa Maxwell got on well with kings because she got on well with the people who made an ex-king feel like a king—the maître d's, doormen, chambermaids and telephone operators who could get things done when every other means failed. It was easy for La Maxwell to contact Rita by phone; convincing her was more difficult. Rita refused politely. 'Don't speak to me about dinner or anything else; my heart is rather broken. I'm in all this trouble about Orson, and I can't think about parties.' She doesn't add that, following a lightning visit from Welles for discussions on their daughter's future, she was still feeling upset. Politely she adds, 'Besides, I haven't got anything to wear.' Elsa needed no more than that. She described the sort of evening it would be, convivial company, good food and ... a real, very charming prince. She gave Rita the names of a smart dress shop and a stylish hair salon, then clinched her case. 'Dinner is at nine-thirty. Come in white and come in late. Make a grand entrance. It will be good for your morale.'

CUT TO RITA'S ROOM. CAMERA ANGLED TOWARDS SUNLIT WINDOW CATCHING SILHOUETTED FIGURE REPLACING RECEIVER ON HOOK.

CUT TO:

CLOSE SHOT BLACK SEDAN; LONG ANGLE TO TAKE IN CAR DRIVING UP TO CASINO. SKY DARK BUT STREETS AND HOTELS BLAZE WITH LIGHTS. A WOMAN IN BOUFFANT WHITE SKIRT IS HELPED OUT OF BACK SEAT BY CHAUFFEUR. PEOPLE PASSING BY STOP TO LOOK. CAMERA TRACKS WITH HER INTO THE CASINO, DOWN LONG CORRIDOR TO LARGE IMPOSING DOOR. SHE STOPS. CUTS TO INSIDE ROOM WITH CAMERA ANGLE ON DOOR. MUSIC: LUSH ARRANGEMENT OF THEIR THEME.

Rita flanked by her hostess Elsa Maxwell and
another guest, Lily Pons, at the Casino Palm
Beach, Cannes, the night she and Aly met.

Rita's entry to the party was sheer Hollywood. Even those who
knew her films were unprepared for what they saw. One moment
they had been drinking, chatting and speculating over Elsa's
mystery guest, the next moment the doors opened as if by magic.
There stood the fourth most valuable property in Hollywood,
looking steadily at a group of people who were names to her and
nothing more. The rich might grow blasé more quickly, but on
first impact they're no different from poorer folk. They were, let it
be under-stated, impressed.

Aly was talking with Elsa when, suddenly, he jerked upright
and pointed like a bird dog: 'Who *is* it?' he demanded. 'That's
your dinner partner,' Elsa answered. 'I asked her especially for
you.' Then she bustled to Rita, took her hand and led her to a
place beside Aly.

Any previous qualms Rita may have had about attending a
social outing with a roomful of strangers were smoothly solved.

Aly, never taking his eyes off her, talked. He was at his most charming, intelligent, and lively. And Rita made a good listener. The rest of the party might as well have been somewhere else.

DISSOLVE TO:

INSERT. MAN TALKING INTO MIKE. CLOSE SHOT. INTERIOR.

Emrys Williams, Aly's chauffeur, bodyguard and friend for nineteen years: 'The Prince had been chased for all his life by beautiful women. But Miss Hayworth was different. He had to chase her. From the moment he set eyes on her he wanted her, and what Prince Aly wanted ... he got.'

DISSOLVE TO:

EXTERIOR. LONG SHOT OF BLACK SEDAN DRIVING UP INTO THE HILLS OVERLOOKING CANNES. HAYWORTH AND ALY IN BACK. CAR STOPS AT NIGHTCLUB. MUSIC: CRESCENDO.

*   *   *

They danced past midnight.

The whole evening went like a film script. If anything, Rita's reticence with strangers—what often looked like aloofness—only stimulated him the more. He had to see her again. Would she come to tea the next day? Never mind that there was no food, or much of anything else in the house. That could be solved. Never mind that he had booked his flight to Ireland for the race. There would be another race. His chauffeur would collect her from the hotel.

Exposed to the full force of Aly's persuasive charm, Rita gave in. To Elsa Maxwell she only said, 'A nice little fellow.' But those who knew Aly were more impressed. It took a lot to make Aly forget his horses.

The renowned Casanova behaved like a romantic schoolboy on his first date. Carefully he dropped Rita off at her hotel, then raced back, roused his sleeping friend, shouting, 'Daff! I want you to go out now, buy a radiogram and the latest records so we can dance. She's coming to tea today.' The bleary-eyed Emrys had no idea who Aly was so excited about. 'He was leaping around my room, slapping me on the back, pulling off my bed covers, telling me to get it right away. I had to tell him that I couldn't get one anywhere at 6 a.m. But he was galvanised by meeting Rita. Now he wanted to get the château ready so it would look all right when

Miss Hayworth came to tea, after I and everybody had been trying without much success to get him organised.'

Unlike his boss, Emrys wasn't dazzled by his first sight of Rita Hayworth when he drove to collect her. For one thing, Rita had forgotten that she had agreed to go to tea, and kept him waiting while she finished a very long lunch with the persistent South American millionaire. For another, she was dressed for a casual visit, not for a glamorous party.

Emrys: 'I had seen her in films, but that day she wasn't very striking. No make-up, pretty casual, just dressed in ordinary slacks and a white shirt. Of course, she has a striking face. I was nervous to be in my little Simca five-horse-power car with a woman like that, but she didn't seem to mind. Mostly she asked me questions about Aly: 'What's this boss of yours like? I understand he's one of the biggest playboys in the world.' I never liked to let the Prince down, so I told her all about his serious side; his duties in Pakistan as leader of his Muslim followers; his work in Europe as one of the leading horsebreeders, and what a clever, generous man he was. By the time we got to the château, I think I'd converted her.

'Aly had many girlfriends, and whether it was because she was Rita Hayworth that he fell for her I don't know, but he was film mad: a real cut-up. Long before he had met Rita he had loved her in *Gilda*, and went to see it three times when it was playing in the Haymarket, and later on as well, after he met her. Of course he was a real playboy in some ways and he really adored women. But his infatuation with Miss Hayworth was something special. With the others all he wanted to do was to get them in bed. That was no problem. They'd fly in from London for the afternoon if he wanted them to. But with Rita he laid on the dancing and entertainment in a way that I never saw him do with anyone else.'

The setting for their first private meeting was ideal. If anything, almost too much so. Rita Hayworth had spent her film career walking through some spectacular sets. But Margarita Cansino had remained relatively untouched by the tinsel that surrounded her. Ostentation had always failed to impress her. But she was not immune to beauty, and the Château l'Horizon, overlooking the Mediterranean, was a superb sight, by day or by night. It had originally been created for a woman of taste by men of refinement and skill. Aly, awaiting Rita in the freshly painted doorway, his shirt loose at the neck, sleeves rolled up, the blue sea sparkling behind him, with eyes only for her, was a romantic sight. How much more so to a woman in need of romance. He would not

have been unaware of how effective a proper setting could be as a
first step to a romantic tête-à-tête.

Everything about it was on the grand scale, the tree-lined
driveway up from the hill, the salon on the ground floor—large
enough to garage a hundred cars—which looked out on a broad
terrace bounded by a stone ballustrade. At either end of the
terrace a flag of steps curved down towards the large swimming
pool with a shute straight out into the sea. The exquisitely
designed lawns stretched to the shore, guarded from unwelcome
approachers by a wall of rock rising out of the water. Under the
terrace, facing the pool, was an immense cocktail bar; a long,
eighteenth-century, marble-topped table stood in the hall. A
statue of Hercules was placed protectively in the driveway. There
were still a few loose odds and ends to be completed, for Aly had
only just moved in and had not yet finished doing it up. But these
would prove incidentals once it found a châtelaine. Aly's custom in
that respect had been to choose his hostess for dinner parties and
social occasions from his far-ranging selection of eligible mistresses. A room was always kept ready for the particular lady, in
all his houses. It was a civilised, continental arrangement that had
worked rather well till now, ever since he had started to live on his
own. His profligate generosity soothed most feelings should ladies
meet or husbands intervene. If any lady stayed long enough to get
other ideas, well ... Aly was already married.

When Aly saw Rita drive up, his impatience was forgotten. He
was a romantic. And here was Rita Hayworth, hair made resent-
ful by the wind, cheeks flushed, walking with that tall, proud
bearing, smiling, radiant, looking as if the house had been awaiting her.

Aly was a man who for most of his thirty-eight years had been
restlessly searching for a change, new experience, fresh sources of
excitement. A beautiful woman was a challenge he could never
resist and he was infatuated with the look of this woman as he had
never been before. Rita's initial hesitation made her all the more
exciting, and the knowledge that Rizi Pahlevis, Shah of Persia,
was waiting to have dinner with Rita later that evening while she
elected to stay for an improvised meal with him, made Aly as
ecstatic as if he'd won the Derby. That evening they drank only
champagne with their meal and danced on the terrace to music
from the hastily bought records. Slowly he drew Rita out of her
shell, watching her reserve give way to laughter, to warmth.
When Williams drove her back at 2 a.m. he was struck by her

extraordinary high spirits. Returning to the château he found Aly in the same state. 'Now I have two "My Loves",' he said, happy as a sand boy.

Here was the beginning of a fine romance. But marriage?

His wife, mother of his two sons, one of whom is the present Aga, had been a former London society beauty, Mrs Joan Guiness. She and Aly were married in 1936, but since the war they had lived apart. The separation was amicable. For the sake of their sons, and to help restrain Aly from any hasty matrimonial move, they agreed to stay married. Should he seriously wish to re-marry, then she agreed not to stand in his way. In return Aly had settled £3 million on her, and tried not to embarrass her. (Since his private life, though hyper-active, drew mostly on their circle of friends for his love-affairs—the wives and daughters of the best houses of England—it remained discreet.) His system seemed flawless. Etiquette governed adultery. An oblique comment in the social columns was rarely allowed to become a scandal on the front pages. There was a way of doing these things. Aly's world was a bachelor's dream that he seemed unlikely to sacrifice. For, as he told Elsa Maxwell (who told the world), he didn't think he was the marrying kind.

For that matter, though Rita's divorce was going through and would be final in November, she hadn't come on holiday with the thought of finding a husband. Besides, she'd heard enough about Aly to be wary of getting involved. And there were other, stronger reasons for pausing. They both loved to dance, true; but while their similar interests were few their differences were many. She was a Catholic, Aly a Muslim, son of a religious leader whose family claimed direct descent from the Prophet Mohammed. She shied away from social intercourse and never felt completely at ease in a crowd or with strangers, whereas Aly thrived on meeting and entertaining people. Rita was a homebody who looked on marriage as a peaceful haven; Aly an extroverted rover who thought nothing of going off on a safari one day, or flying off to a party wherever it happened to be. She was simple; he sophisticated. She monogamous; he notoriously polygamous. . . . Someone close to them at the time thought that the only two things they had in common were when they would get married, and when they would get divorced. Be that as it may, it was not inconceivable that, if allowed time to discover more about each other, their romance might still have ended in wedlock. But the choice wasn't theirs.

In the past, Aly's relations with the press had been amicable, and he may have thought that the old-boy network would help to keep Rita's name out of the papers, as it had been able to do with earlier affairs. At the outset their romance wasn't serious enough for them to give the problem much thought, or they may simply have underestimated their news value. But Rita Hayworth belonged to the media. Her life was public fantasy. A love affair between a movie star and a prince was the stuff of fairytales. The whole world wanted nay, demanded a share in it. Aly Khan was a public figure in his own right, next thing to God for millions of devout Muslims who named babies in his honour and came to his door as pilgrims for his blessing. Rita Hayworth was one of the most famous women of the day, Goddess of Love to millions of devout movie-goers who attended her shrines, copied her clothes, her hairstyles and named their daughters after her.

All of the Aga's wealth couldn't have kept this affair a secret. Had they both been single, everything would have been all right. There was another even more important reason why Aly had to be extremely circumspect. As potential religious leader of the millions of Ismailis who looked up to his family for religious counselling and as an example he had to avoid a scandal of this nature reaching them and he was frightened of his father disinheriting him. Thus it was imperative that, above all, there be no photographs. Even while people knew about it and talked about it, that was in the realm of rumour. Photographs would have been proof.

Rita was to discover once and for all that a star on earth had no hope in heaven of being left alone. As the Spanish proverb said: take what you want from life, but pay for it. The time to pay had begun. The months ahead turned into a cat and mouse game: Rita and Aly on the one side, the press on the other. Under the ceaseless pressure of their pursuit across half of Europe and America, what had begun as a summer romance ended up as a three-ring circus, inevitably culminating in a marriage that— except in the world of movies—never stood a chance.

But regardless of whether she met with approval or disapproval, when in love Rita was all woman, and she let the rest of the world go by.

Unlike most of the men she had known in Hollywood, Aly was fun; he knew how to take life with ease and offered it to her with a smile. A welcome balm to a woman who had just come through an emotional wringer and badly needed reassuring affection. In addition to everything else, Aly possessed a quality few could resist—any woman he talked to felt she was the only one in the world for him. Rita's nature was complementary—she listened as if there was no one else in the world for her. A perfect match, except that the charm was part of Aly's stock-in-trade, the bait to hook the fish, whereas Rita's response was wholly ingenuous, arising out of her desire for the man who would take care of her.

That Monday morning Emrys drove his boss to Paris to find a chef. This was Emrys's first indication that Aly's feelings for Rita had affected his whole attitude. 'Now everything had to be perfect to impress her. The new chef was then rushed to the Maison Lafiette, one of the Aga's houses outside Paris, and told, "Select the finest china, pots and pans you can find. We are going to set up a wonderful kitchen in Cannes." He even bought extra table linen.'

After that Sunday the two spent every available day together. If family business took him away, he would make sure to phone several times a day; but whether he went or stayed, every morning, rain or shine, Rita would wake to find three dozen roses in her hotel sent from Aly—with love.

He did everything to make her happy. Quick to understand, he realised that she had a very gentle, sensitive nature, and since she was still going through a painful emotional period he took care that she would not be upset. He thought constantly of new ways to keep her excited: secluded restaurants safe from preying eyes where they could dine and talk, and dance, for Rita loved to dance. As soon as the villa was ready to receive its guest, Rita moved in. By now the press had also found out and hid behind trees near the estate in the hope of catching the two together. Suddenly it was getting impossible to find a restaurant where journalists wouldn't already be waiting. The hint of a scandal only sharpened their detective instincts.

It became Emrys's task to prevent the press from getting their photos; he was offered over £1,000 in bribes by them, and when those failed, they tried blackmail. One of the enterprising French *papparazzi* got the bright idea of posing a prostitute in a red wig against the gates of the château kissing a man looking like Aly. He threatened to print this photo with Rita and Aly's names underneath it if he wasn't given an exclusive. He wasn't, and the fuzzy photo was published.

They decided it would be best to get away, hoping to escape

detection by holidaying in Spain. While there she could meet her relatives, many for the first time, but especially Padre who had retired there, and Aly could capitalise on the trip to visit Spanish breeders to discuss new stock for his stud farm. They envisaged a relaxed, pleasant drive through the Pyrenees, down to Madrid, Seville, and on to Portugal. Three weeks together and away from it all, with Emrys who had been given no advance warning along as chauffeur, chaperone, chief cook and bottle washer—just in case.

Emrys: 'At first it all went very smoothly. They flew to Biarritz in Aly's private plane where I was waiting with the car. We crossed the frontier at Irún without any problem. It was because the Prince decided to drive himself that the accident arose that made our whereabouts known. He drove into a donkey cart. Nobody was hurt and we paid the driver off but he recognised "Senorita Gilda" and talked.

'At the hotel in Madrid we walked into a nearly deserted lobby, then suddenly found ourselves surrounded by photographers who popped from behind armchairs, pillars and palm trees. It became like a scene from the Marx Brothers; Aly threw his coat over Rita's head and held her down till we got to our suite, in which we boarded ourselves. They were prisoners in their hotel rooms while I guarded the door. This poor woman. You couldn't even let a waiter into her room because it might be a press man with a camera. When she needed to do some washing we couldn't trust the maids, so I had to wash her knickers and stockings for her. When we tried to go out and dine we were followed by no fewer than nine cars packed to capacity with Spanish reporters and photographers.'

Though they managed to make their escape from the hotel they still found it impossible to evade further discovery as Emrys recounts:

'Aly managed to meet his friend the Duke of Alba, a fellow horse breeder who arranged for us to see a bullfight a little way out of Madrid in Toledo where he thought nobody would follow us. When we arrived there the fight was on. We were just sitting there when all of a sudden people started whispering "Gilda, Gilda". Then the whole crowd took up the chant. We hadn't been there an hour; the crowd forgot all about the bullfight and the bull, all they wanted was to get close to her, and Rita was beginning to panic. It took a whole crowd of Spanish policemen and myself, all pushing and shoving through the mobs to make our escape. After that there was no point in staying in Madrid—so we decided to try and make it to Seville.

'We managed to get out of Madrid without being followed but on the way we stopped off at a hotel for a bite to eat, and the head porter looking at Rita whispered to me, "Senorita Gilda?" They recognised her everywhere, then they'd phone the news around. We were driving with the radio on and heard it broadcasting our route, so that people listening could watch out their window as we drove by. But despite the problems, this was a very happy time for the two of them—you see, there were no other women around, and though they had to be careful not to be photographed together, they were together, just the two of them.

'In Seville they managed to enjoy a night away from strangers and journalists. Rita even threw a party for her relatives—a real family get-together, about fifty of them with her grandfather the most stylish of the lot. We had taken over a hotel outside of town. To stop the taxis bringing press out I bought up all the taxis. That night cost a fortune but it was worth it. He loved her relatives. They were very simple, lovely people. Nearly all of the Cansinos were dancers and Flamenco guitarists. Everybody got up to play and dance. Then Rita danced with her grandfather who simply adored her; then they played gypsy music and Rita did a solo. The prince looked at her as if he had never seen her before—she was so alive and radiantly happy.

'I have a hunch that up till then he hadn't really been serious but now he wanted to marry her. He kept saying to me, "Daff, isn't she beautiful, isn't she beautiful." When we drove home they turned to me and said, "This was the best evening ever. We've never enjoyed ourselves so much before."

'We left for Portugal a few days later but it was the same thing all over again. Everywhere we went there were crowds. We would drive into a small town, and they'd want to give her the key to the city, and expect her to open bazaars and things like that—so we just kept on going.'

By the time Aly's pilot flew his plane down to take them back to Biarritz, the whole world knew that Prince Aly had been on holiday with Rita. In Cannes the press had set up a round-the-clock vigil on the Number 1 romance in the world, with time clocks and telescopic lenses, planes circling overhead and boats prowling off the shore. This affair, rich in glamorous triviality, was exactly what people craved to counteract the chill of the endless Cold War news from the front pages of their papers.

Emrys Williams (in hat) keeps reporters and photographers from
Rita and Aly, while they were hiding out in Aly's château in Cannes.
(Emrys Williams)

Here was fun and glamour, something that happened on another
planet, to people not of this world.

Back at Columbia, Cohn was fuming at the unsavoury publicity his star was getting. It jeopardised the studio's investment in
her as-yet-unreleased films. There were hints that the powerful
women's organisations and religious leaders were looking askance
at the publicity surrounding a married mother in Europe with a
married man. No talk yet of boycotting her films, but....
Perhaps, if Rita could be made to change her mind, and leave
Aly....

Rita returned to Hollywood in the first week of September,
ostensibly to start work on her next film under her new contract,
but hoping to find some privacy in her home town. The journalists, photographers and newsreel cameramen were already at
the airport in a repeat of her European experience. If Rita was
ruffled she didn't show it. The time-honoured cliché that had

become a Hollywood euphemism—'We're just good friends'—was
trotted out as questioners zeroed in. She smiled for the photographers. Then a studio spokesman whisked her away. Nobody
found out if her 'friend' was to join her or when, or what the nature
of their relationship was.

Apparently, as Rita told a friend, 'Aly's asked me if I'll marry
him when he is free. We talked a great deal about his family,
especially about his wife and sons. Aly wants me to meet his
wife—but I don't want to do it.'

As everyone knows, absence makes the heart grow fonder. Her
Aunt Joan who also saw her then was left in no doubt about
Rita's emotional state: 'This girl couldn't talk about him without
her eyes filling up with tears. She was so enchanted with him, she
couldn't bear it. Every time she opened her mouth and mentioned
his name she was choked up and her eyes spilled. She didn't cry,
but they glistened with tears. She couldn't think of him without
her heart throbbing. I don't think she ever thought about the fact
that his whole philosophy on life was so different from hers. But
these girls don't have time to think about things like that. They
are emotional creatures or else they couldn't be actresses.'

Then Aly arrived. The assembled newsmen found out that the
purpose of his visit was to buy some horses for his father's stable,
attend the races and visit some friends. He had a lot of friends in
the United States and hoped to see them. Asked about 'the friend'
he smiled: 'Miss Hayworth and I are just good friends. There
exists a wonderful and healthy relationship between us.' Then he
rented a Spanish-style bungalow across from Rita's house on
Hanover Street. While she reported to the studio for publicity on
Carmen and fittings for her next film, Aly attended the races. Most
evenings however the two could be seen dancing in popular
nightspots off Sunset Boulevard. Though Hollywood's parochial
atmosphere—led by Hedda Hopper's clucking that neither was
free to marry—did not impress Aly, he enjoyed seeing Rita in her
element. Dining out with a few friends like Mary Pickford and her
husband as chaperones, Rita's radiant happiness and Aly's rapt
concentration on her lent a new meaning to being 'just good
friends'. Any lingering doubts Rita might have had about Aly as
husband and father faded when he played with Rebecca. He
adored children and even the serious little four-year-old responded to his warmth and mad-cap humour.

But Cohn, despite sharing Khan's passion for horses and
women, remained uncharmed. There was too much at stake. He

resented a prince interfering with his plans; disapproved strongly
of Rita's association with Aly and warned her of the potentially
damaging publicity her romance could have on her box-office
drawing power. His reasoning left Rita cold. Before Harry could
talk to Aly, the Prince had left town and Rita with him. On the
eve of November 1st, 1948, Rita, Aly and her secretary, Miss
Haran, took the midnight plane to Mexico City.*

Next to the United Nations, Hollywood with four hundred and
fifty correspondents had more accredited foreign and national
journalists than anywhere else in the world. If the two had
seriously hoped to find privacy in Hollywood they were mistaken.
It was a classic case of 'out of the frying pan, into the fire'. When
the press caught up with them they moved to Acapulco.

Cohn decided to send an emissary to Rita to convince her of
her folly and the wisdom of returning to her career. Virginia Van
Upp was posted to undertake the delicate mission. She arrived to
find the famous couple prisoners in their hotel, the air tense from
arguments, both complaining bitterly.

'It's your fault, you wanted to be a movie star,' Virginia told
Rita. And to Aly, 'It's your fault, too; you're not exactly John
Doe.'

'Who is John Doe?' Aly demanded, staring at Rita. Miss Van
Upp tried to explain the expression to him but he remained
unconvinced that John Doe had not been one of Rita's lovers.

When Rita asked to speak to her privately about her relationship with Aly, Van Upp, tactful and ever a friend to Rita,
realised her mission was abortive. Yet Rita voiced unease:

'I love him but I'm worried.'

'What about?'

'It's your fault.'

'Why?'

'Because you wrote *Gilda*. And every man I've known has fallen
in love with Gilda—and wakened with me.'

Virginia did what she could to help Rita handle the press.
Rumour and scandal were so rife, Aly dropped out of sight while
Rita returned to Mexico City with Virginia and, on her studio's
advice, held a press conference. The journalists listened politely to
her future film plans then zoomed in on her private ones. But she
was prepared.

'Would she marry Aly Khan while they were both in Mexico?'

*A meeting that had been set up for her and C. B. de Mille to discuss her
playing of Delilah in his upcoming epic was cancelled by her departure.

'I'm not divorced yet.'

'Where was Prince Aly?'

'I don't know.'

Something had to happen, even though there was little time to think about it rationally.

A fortnight later they flew to Havana. In Baptista's strictly controlled Cuba they found a bit of privacy, and actually had a marvellous time. Then back to Hollywood where she had to pick up her final divorce decree and inform Cohn that she would not be reporting for work. He promptly took her off her $248,000 salary. The *Hollywood Reporter* quipped: 'FROM COHN TO CANNES TO KHAN TO CANNED!' Rita put her Hollywood home up for rent, packed sixty bags and, accompanied by her secretary and her four-year-old daughter, left for Europe on the liner *Britannic*, sailing from New York on December 16th. But there was no escaping.

Each new item about them grew more mocking and acid-tinged. Even the respectable papers took swipes at them: 'THEY'RE OFF! RITA, ALY SAIL' was the headline in one, which then proceeded to ridicule:

Rita Hayworth, looking as pale and haggard as though she had walked all the way from Hollywood, her four-year-old daughter Rebecca Welles, and His Extremely Royal Highness Aly Khan, Rita's gold-plated boyfriend from mystic India, sailed for England yesterday aboard the luxury liner *Britannic*.

First, Rita and Aly sneaked out of the Hotel Plaza at 59th St. and Fifth Ave. Aly made it because all the ladies and gentlemen from the newspapers had their lamps lighted for La Rita. And they caught her, too, as she and the baby and her secretary, Schiffra Haran, were being hustled into a hired limousine. But did the reporter ever get a brush off! Asked why she had not consented to an interview, the glamorous gal replied: I want privacy, but that seems to be impossible with the American press!'

And with the Hayworth chin, sans make-up lifted loftily, the actress stepped into the car and was whisked to Pier 54 at 14th St. and the North River.

There, more hocus-pocus took place. Rita, little Rebecca and Miss Haran, followed by several baggage handlers and cheered to the roofs of the wharf-house by some 200-odd long-shoremen, were hustled to a special gangway—the one ordinarily used, dock workers said, to take bodies aboard or to carry off the ship's refuse.

But that made no difference to Rita. She sailed right up the plank and disappeared into the cavernous belly of the *Britannic*, hurried through the galley, where a gang of pot-wollopers got a look at her, and proceeded to suite A.51, which of course is on A Deck. [*Rebecca and Miss Haran occupied Cabin 55.*]

The reporters were right on her heels, but a fat lot of good it did them. They braced the Hollywood beauty with questions, but she gave no audible replies. A steamship official tried to arrange a brief interview, but Rita wearily answered: 'The reporters got me at the hotel. There is no comment I could possibly make.'

While all this was going on, Aly slipped up the regular gangway and, gaining top deck, mingled with the crowd, which kept him safe from detection. After a while, he descended to A Deck where suite A.61, on the opposite side of the ship from the actress he presumably had been romancing, was ready for him. One reporter tried opening the door but had it slammed in his face. Miss Haran did see reporters for the benefit of posterity but all she would say was that, as far as she knew, Aly might or might not be sailing on the *Britannic*. She added that Rita didn't know either. And that was that.

Thus did the Hayworth depart these shores, maybe to marry Aly, old boy, when his divorce becomes final in about four months, as some say, or maybe just to make a couple of pictures in England to pad out the old bankroll. But one thing is sure: she really did sail aboard the *Britannic* at 4 p.m. yesterday—so did Aly.

THE SCANDAL AND THE PAIN

No one saw them on the ship; they disembarked separately when the liner anchored a little before midnight on December 23rd, near Cobh off the southern coast of Ireland. To ever ready shoreside reporters Rita said, 'I am very fond of him—no wonder our names are linked.' Then, with Rebecca and her secretary, she drove from the quayside without Aly. Not far along, at a side road, an estate car was waiting, driving behind them to block the road against pursuit. Aly leapt from the car and together they drove to Kilcullen, his Gil-Town stud farm, for a quiet family Christmas.

From there he gave his statement to the journalists in an effort to calm his father back in Cairo who was growing increasingly upset over the stories that slandered his family's good name. The old differences between father and son that flared up so easily clouded Aly's happiness. The old Aga had been a notorious playboy in his youth but had not taken kindly to his son stepping into those shoes now that he was getting older. He was capable of enforcing his displeasure with his son—for he controlled not only the purse strings but also Aly's future. But anyway, nothing Aly said altered the situation or calmed the storm that broke over them.

The English mass circulation papers, while exploiting the affair to the hilt, took violent exception to the sight of a grim-faced Rita carrying a sleepy-eyed child as she raced from ship to shore, cars to hotels, and on through the nights, in an effort to escape the reporters and photographers who made the deception necessary.

After Christmas, Aly had to go to London on business before they could continue their holiday, and Rita came with him. They flew in to London greeted by headlines denouncing Rita as an unfit mother for having brought her daughter along. Some articles, like those in the widely circulated *The People*, revealed a blatant racist bias in the guise of moral outrage. 'This affair is an insult to all decent women,' they claimed in an article that betrayed the fact that their self-righteous hostility was due less to a duty to uphold public morality and more to sour grapes that the couple in question simply didn't seem to give a damn about the press. How else can one explain:

> This is the last time that this newspaper will report in its columns details of the squalid love affair of this ridiculous film star Rita Hayworth and Prince Aly Khan. We have taken this decision on the grounds of public decency because we believe that the extravagant expeditions of this coloured Indian Prince and his 'friend' have become an insult to decent minded women the world over.

And they continued in that vein for ten column inches and on innumerable occasions over the succeeding months.

Till Aly could legalise their position and stop talk by marrying her, elaborate precautions were still needed to maintain the pretence of their living apart. Thus, when they flew into London, Rita and Aly entered the Ritz by different doors and left the same way the next morning.

Emrys Williams: 'That was another epic escape from London—though it was the same wherever we went. That morning I put my little station wagon at the back of Berkeley Street and had another car near St James's Palace. Rita and Rebecca came in the Hillman to St James's Park; I transferred them into the Prince's Lincoln and drove them into a hangar at Croydon Airport. The Prince's plane came to the hangar, they opened the door, put the steps out and we all ran like hell into the plane. You can see it all on the newsreels. Rita is a very serious person and although I suppose she had quite a dramatic life before she met Aly, I don't think she saw the funny side of all this. Little Rebecca was really afraid of the press, always popping flashbulbs into her face, and would cling to her mother or hide behind me in public.'

From London to Paris. From Paris to Gstaad. And on to Murren, the Swiss winter resort and another right royal mess. They booked in at the Palace Hotel where unbeknownst Aly's wife and his two sons were staying. They were so busy running that neither had stopped to think where it was leading them. Although Aly had a long-standing agreement with his wife to enable their children to spend Christmas with their mother and the New Year with him, her departure had been delayed. Somehow she left the hotel just prior to her husband and Rita's arrival.

The press maliciously chose to distort the truth the better to portray Joan Khan as the humiliated and ridiculed wife. To further the image of the spoilt star flaunting propriety at every opportunity, totally unsubstantiated rumours of Rita's pregnancy began to appear in print. The *Sunday Pictorial* described their trip as 'a very sordid business'. Back in the United States Rita's name was raised by a member of the House of Congress; the powerful women's club organisations advised their members to boycott her films. The *Hollywood Reporter* published an editorial urging the film industry to wash their hands of Miss Hayworth. *The Loves of Carmen* played to sensational business.

Meanwhile, a prisoner wherever she went, Rita was growing depressed. She had begun to worry a great deal not only because of the effect all this tumult had on her daughter, but also because of her own future with Aly. He had asked her to marry him several times, but he had yet to start divorce proceedings.

Aly's problem was that, though in love with Rita, his need for other women had not abated and Rita was aware of this. All she had ever wanted was one man for her own—it didn't matter whether he was a prince or a truck driver as long as he was hers. Of course she knew of Aly's background but failed to understand that for all his European upbringing and Italian mother, Aly was very much a Muslim in his attitude towards women which, with all the good will in the world, he wouldn't change. Theoretically, his religion allowed him to have four wives and as many mistresses as he could afford. He was European enough not to have four wives, but he tolerated no such restrictions on the rest. It was not at all uncommon for Aly to bed six women a day, literally seeing one out one door while Emrys kept another waiting in the next room.

It takes a very sophisticated, cynical or opportunist woman to settle down to marriage to such a man for what his position could offer her in return. Rita was none of these. She was in love. And she believed him when he told her he would change. And she, too, tried to adjust to him, but that was hopeless. Referring once to her years with Aly and the other women, Rita said, 'I paid no attention because, well, what was I supposed to do?' Besides, at that moment, she had no alternatives. These were not the liberated 'seventies, and Rita was a woman, not a feminist. Unlike a man, when things become strained, a woman could not go out and escape for a few moments on the town. Besides, she knew no one there, had her daughter to look after and since they could not be seen together and she could not go out alone, had no alternative but to stay in her hotel room until they could plot another move. All she was left with when things got tense was a drink to muster her spirits even though this led to more arguments for Aly was a strict Muslim when it came to alcohol, and disapproved of her drinking.

Still, they were close to each other in these months in a way few couples ever are. Their relationship was undergoing a baptism of fire that would act as a link until his death. It was something they could share—two against the world.

There were those around them at this time who overheard their rows and seriously doubted that they would stay together, much less that they might eventually get married. At one point Rita considered leaving Aly and taking Rebecca back to the States, but such thoughts were short-lived. Any lingering doubts Aly might have had faded as he saw the name of the woman he very much loved dragged even further down for loving him. Discussing their future, they decided to marry as soon as possible. It became Emrys's job again to devise a plan that would get them out of

Château de l'Horizon—Rita's home in Europe. (Acme Photo)

Switzerland and back to Cannes, back to the villa. There their affair began. There they could think. In a letter to his wife, written from the château on January 14th, 1949, Emrys told her,

> We were chased out of Switzerland by the newspapermen, but managed to dodge them in Lucerne, down a small street, where we lost them for forty-eight hours. They looked all over France and Switzerland for us before they caught up with us. As if they (Rita and Aly) hadn't enough problems already, they picked up lice on the train.

When the press caught up with them again they were furious. Emrys described their abortive invasion of the château in the guise of a rescue mission. 'That Friday three hundred journalists in fifty motorboats, a cavalcade of taxis and an aeroplane attempted an assault on the villa shouting, "We've come to liberate Rita." ' Since they were the cause of her 'imprisonment', the villa's inhabitants failed to appreciate the irony in that promise. Emrys kept them from landing on the shore, while the gardener and butler patrolled the gates, but press reports, exaggerating their failure to get through the barricades, spoke about the huge police force hired to prevent them. 'I was the whole of the police force there,' said Emrys, 'and the things they called me for not letting them have a photograph or a statement were the only things they daren't print!'

Before Aly left Switzerland, his father had sent his fourth wife (a former Miss France before she became the Begum Yvette) to tell Aly that his father was ill from being so upset and wished to see him. Now that they had made up their minds to get married, Aly wanted to reach his father to gain his blessing and introduce him to Rita. Daffy Williams had been the first person Aly told of his decision; as always Daffy got them from the château to the Aga's villa at Yakimour without being caught.

Williams: 'That wasn't easy. I got the idea of disguising René and Susan, our butler and maid, as the Prince and Rita and to drive them away from the château at high speed. At an arranged signal, the car sped up to the front door, and the butler and maid, with their hands over their faces and collars turned up, raced down the steps and jumped into the car. It worked. The press followed in hot pursuit. Then, just to make sure in case any were left, Rita and Aly lay down in the back seat of another car, and we drove to his father.'

The meeting served to melt the ice between father and son. In his autobiography the Aga wrote: 'They came to see me at Cannes, and I asked them if they were really devoted to each other. They both said that they were, so I advised them to get married as soon as possible.' Later, when the press realised their mistake and arrived, he told them, 'I very much disliked the idea at first, but then I met Miss Hayworth. She is charming. So modest and sweet. I know of no one more quiet and ladylike. American women are the most charming in the world.' Meanwhile, Rita and Aly had already driven, undetected, back to the château. Aly was very pleased that his father approved of Rita and liked her. For a time, his marriage to Rita served to smooth over the recurring bitterness between him and his father.

Divorce proceedings were completed and in a press conference

held at the villa on January 18th, Aly announced, 'I'm going to
marry Rita ... as soon as I'm free to do so.' To the journalists
searching in vain for his fiancée, he explained that her absence
was due to a touch of 'flu. In fact he had had no intention of
subjecting Rita to them so soon. Besides, he wasn't divorced yet.
Then he handed round two typewritten, unsigned statements
from both of them. Aly continued to answer their questions with
relaxed good humour, in French and English, telling them that
the marriage 'will be as soon as possible', and that 'it will not be
necessary for Rita to become a Muslim'.Emrys caught two photographers creeping around the side of the house trying to get a shot
of Rita.

With the news official the press eased off. Now the couple could
go out together without fear, for the moment, of being photographed together. The announcement apparently assuaged public
outrage—until the next scandal broke. But then the scene shifted
to Italy and Ingrid Bergman. From now till their wedding day,
life was a continuous social round—a permanent lunch buffet.
They drove to visit the Aga for an official family grouping to
which the press was invited. The photos showed Rita radiant in
black sweater and bouffant plaid skirt, and Aly, his father and the
Begum Yvette smiling happily. Privately, the Aga believed
rumours of Rita's pregnancy and kept urging them to marry as
soon as possible. Wherever they went now, they were mobbed by
well-wishers. At Epsom racecourse they had to have the help of
over a hundred mounted policemen in order to escape in one
piece. At the Paris Opéra, attended by the President of the
Republic, the audience had eyes only for Rita. Outwardly, she
now smiled confidently. Inwardly, she still wanted to run.

Their new freedom to accept dinner engagements enabled Rita
to observe her future husband among his circle of friends. They
were a different crowd from any she knew: colder, superior,
mocking. To them she seemed shy, unglamorous and unworldly.
In turn, she was baffled and discomfited by the international set.
Most of them spoke French, a language she couldn't speak but set
out to learn. It was a clear indication of what life as the wife of an
international society playboy might be like. There were also his
duties as his father's representative to their religious followers
which she would have to learn to share. Wherever Aly went,
whether Paris, London, even on the Riviera, there were always
certain to be some who came for an audience and a blessing.

Meanwhile, plans for their wedding went ahead without certainty of a date. They hoped to have the civil marriage performed at L'Horizon so that it could remain a private affair.

Item: April 1st, Rita said she expected they would be married in four weeks, and travelled to Paris to choose her trousseau from Jacques Fath's salon—the details were kept a closely guarded secret.

Item: Aly's divorce had gone through in Paris in April. Rita's name was not mentioned; the two boys were confided to the father, with the mother's consent.

Item: May 14th, Aly announced the great day would be May 27th, 1949. The invitation cards were printed up but the date left blank, to be filled in by hand in case of any further delays.

Aly probably believed it when he said, 'It will be a very simple wedding, very intimate, only close friends of Miss Hayworth and myself will be present.' But after all the hoopla leading up to it there was little hope of that, and plans were adjusted accordingly. As the day approached, arrangements for the wedding and reception rivalled the Aga's Diamond Jubilee, when his considerable weight was measured in diamonds at a public ceremony witnessed by tens of thousands of the faithful.

To make sure things would go smoothly, Rita's long-time manager and a family friend of many years, Lee Ellroy was flown in from Hollywood to manage the 'quiet' wedding. Aly also hired the Riviera's top professionals to see to the catering.

Item: Over 600 bottles of champagne were laid in; 40 huge lobsters; 110 lbs of cold meats; 10 lbs of caviar; 25 lbs of salad; 500 biscuits, 40 lbs petits-fours and the wedding cake weighed 120 lbs.

Item: The luncheon at the château after the wedding would be supervised by Jacques Duclos, director of the Cannes Casino; the chief consultant was M. André, proprietor of the Casino; the chef for the occasion was Gondolfo—his creations, titled by Aly, included the coupe 'Cover Girl', and the bombe 'Gilda' and 'Strawberry Blonde'. Jules, bar manager of the Carlton supervised drinks—his most successful cocktail was the 'Ritaly': two thirds Canadian Club, one third Italian Vermouth, two drops bitters, a dash of Angostura, a dash of yellow chartreuse, poured over crushed ice, expertly shaken and topped with a cherry.

The few 'intimate' friends of the bride and groom grew into an international *Who's Who* of Aly's acquaintances. (Over three hundred were asked, eighty-three specially printed invitations being sent out by hand.) These included the Aga, the Aga's ex-wife Princess Andrée and his current Begum, as well as titled

Indians, European royalty, wartime friends, Paris society, family intimates. Among the crowd only half a dozen were guests Rita could call her own. These included Lee Ellroy, Charles Vidor and his wife and Hollywood columnist Louella Parsons who had arrived under her own steam but exercised her *droît de seigneur* to become a guest. Rita's relatives could not afford to come, but telegrammed their love. Harry Cohn, who could, refused in a fit of pique but was persuaded to send a terse telegram: 'Our sincerest congratulations and best wishes. Joan and Harry Cohn.' In fact, few of Rita's Hollywood friends could make it since the wedding date was not definite until the very last moment. One notable exception, for this reason was Elsa Maxwell, without whom all this might never have happened. She sent a telegram explaining, 'You promised to let me know three weeks before and as I did not hear from you made other plans too late to cancel. All my love and best wishes to the sweetest people I know. Elsa.'

The names of guests, preparations for the occasion, speculation about wedding gifts, snippets of gossip that seeped out of the château from staff hired for the occasion, were daily news items. It allowed humorists like Giles of the *Daily Express* to extract fun from the fuss for one of his cartoons. Below a drawing of grimy miners lining up by a bus stop, he wrote: 'Miners get everything these days, pit-head baths, race horses for pit ponies, bulletins on Rita Hayworth down at coal face....'

Bar talk described the engagement ring Aly had given Rita as a diamond the size of a belt buckle and worth a king's ransom.

Item: The 12-carat diamond was valued at £18,000 cost. His wedding present to Rita was a £6,000 Alpha Romeo—which he took back after the wedding and replaced with a little two-seater made for her by Pigoni.

Item: The morning of the wedding the Aga's gift to the bride arrived—two diamond earrings. Aly observed, 'Is that all? I expect he will get her something else as well.'

Item: Among the expected shower of gold and silver presents were some with a special meaning. Orson sent her a spaniel puppy named 'Poogles'.

Item: An Indian artist cast an exquisite marble sculpture depicting two hands joined in space, hers and Aly's, to symbolise their union. It was one of the few personal things she took with her when she moved out.

In the midst of the rush there was time for personal moments. One such was a luncheon to meet the artist Utrillo. He was an old friend of Aly and adored Rita. 'We went to his hotel suite and he [Utrillo] greeted me at the door saying, "I am so sorry, I did not have time to go out and pick you some fresh flowers so I painted you some," and he handed me a still wet painting of flowers, which was signed "To Margarita (my real name), Utrillo". I will always treasure that painting.'

Others were also busy making their arrangements for the great day. Towns along the Côte d'Azur vied for this tourist attraction event when it became clear that it could not be held at the château. The French Government got into the act, ruling that the ceremony, like any other, would have to be run off at neighbouring Vallauris' small shabby *Mairie*. A press conference called by slender, affable Communist Mayor, Paul Derigon—who seemed to have forgotten his party line as he appeared as deeply impressed as anybody by what he referred to as 'this very great occasion'—quickly degenerated into a battle royal, with swarms of journalists making out their own passes to the wedding, then shoving them under the dazed Mayor's nose for signature and stamping. As a result of the numerous forgeries another method of admittance to the château had to be devised.

Item: The Mayor declared that the day of the wedding would be a holiday.

Item: The town council approved the planting of temporary trees to line the roads to town, and agreed to reinforce their modest police force with one hundred special gendarmes as well as plain clothes men hired by Aly, to maintain security and keep unwanted visitors out.

The Mayor's biggest problem was how to squeeze two hundred international press representatives, described by *Time* 'like a plague of love-starved locusts', not to mention leading citizens of Vallauris, into the *salle municipale*—scene of the ceremony—which could barely hold a hundred. When he suggested that only photographers should be allowed into the *salle*, pandemonium almost broke out. Finally he calmed them down, and after a stormy hour, compromise was reached: the cameramen would be admitted in the space reserved for the public, and every section of the French and foreign press would be represented.

Item: Earlier in the day Rita received a shock. Rehearsing for the wedding on the château lawn, she saw a dead man washed up on the rocks below. The rest of the rehearsal was cancelled but by evening she had recovered sufficiently to accompany Aly, who had hired the Casino Cinema in Cannes for a private screening of

The day before the wedding, outside the Casino Cinema in Cannes where they attended a private screening of her latest film, Aly begs people to leave them alone. (Emrys Williams Collection)

The Loves of Carmen, a print of which was sent as a present from Columbia. He invited sixty guests including the staff. Afterwards he took them to the hilltown restaurant Les Terrasses at Mougine for a specially selected dinner. Leaving the cinema they were nearly mobbed. While Rita, wearing an elegant white Dior suit jacket with incongruous rolled-up blue jeans stood looking on, Aly exasperatedly pleaded with the people to leave them alone for a bit. But later, when a reporter managed to get near her for a statement, she said, 'I'm so excited, I can hardly think. I'm sort of lost in a dream world. When someone asks me a question, I bring myself to and grunt.'

Item: The Mayor was a vegetarian and only drank water.

Item: Rita took French lessons so she could say the traditional 'yes' in French.

Item: Rita wore two hairdos—the one in the morning her American style; the one in the afternoon was with a chignon held at the back with a comb.

Item: Her dresses by Jacques Fath were called: Balancine (a two-piece outfit in wool); Astragal (made of an absorbent pink cloth); and Life (an evening dress in white ottoman). She had selected her trousseau at Fath's Paris salon, where the dresses were modelled by his top mannequin, Bettina.

Friday May 27th, 1949. The little community was in a holiday mood. The schools, the potteries and practically everything except the cafés had shut down. Girls from the factories where they prepare orange blossom essence for perfumes waited four hours in the blazing sun to catch sight of the couple. The gendarmes wore white gloves. Jeeps from the Nice police patrolled the streets giving orders by loud speakers, and Mayor Derigon couldn't hide his emotions. This was the day of his life! Several years ago he had received the President of the Republic, but what was that compared to being *vis à vis* with an international star and an Aga Khan who was worth his weight in diamonds!

Item: Police lined the route from the Prince's château beside the Mediterranean to the Town Hall on top of the hill.

Item: The first procession of cars brought fifty guests, most of them women wearing saris. The second flotilla, entering the town square to stop before the Town Hall, contained the Aga Khan who had returned from Switzerland the night before, and the Begum. The crowd shouted *Vivats* to him—he acknowledged them by blowing kisses.

The excitement grew and the shouts rose even louder when it became clear that another procession of cars sighted coming up the hill was the one with Aly and Rita. An Alfa Romeo, driven by Aly's brother, Prince Sadri, stopped in a cloud of dust and the future husband dressed in striped trousers, a black double-breasted jacket, stiff collar and cravat of grey satin, leapt from the car and entered the little room where his father, the Begum, General and Mme Catroux, Louella Parsons, Mme Jacques Fath, ravishing in black with a little hat, the Princess of Bourbon, the Prince of Orleans and Bragance, and a gaggle of Emirs and Hindu princes were already waiting.

They turned their heads to the door as the crowd massed in the square let out a renewed roar. Rita Hayworth, wearing her 'secret' dress of ice blue crêpe and picture hat to match, had arrived. Police struggled to keep back the crowd as the Mayor, wearing his tri-coloured sash, moved forward to greet Rita as she stepped from the car.

She appeared very nervous as she was asked to say a few words into the radio microphones and she clutched a lace handkerchief

Rita and Aly wed, May 27, 1949. (Emrys Williams Collection)

and a bunch of white roses with orange blossoms in her black-gloved hands.

Aly and Rita sat in armchairs of red velvet, directly opposite the Mayor before a round table, ornamented by a rich cloth loaned by the Aga, under the statuette of Marianne, national symbol of France.

Item: 11.16 a.m.—Aly Solomen Khan, age thirty-eight agreed to take Margarita Carmen Cansino, age thirty, for his wife. After the reading of the civil code, Rita whispered '*Oui*'. The register was signed. The Prince of Orleans and Bragance brought out the rings. Rita helped Aly. Aly helped Rita. They kissed. Photographs were taken. Then the Mayor, now addressing Rita as 'Your Highness', made his speech. There had been fears that it might contain some party line homilies, but, in the event, none were forthcoming. He thanked Prince Aly for a gift of 540,000 French francs (£492) to be given to the local poor and gave him a *livret de famille* or official family record book with space for twelve children. The whole ceremony had taken half an hour.

In the square, the police cordons were broken as the couple came out into the sun, and cheering crowds throwing rice prevented Rita and Aly from making their way to their open car, driven by Emrys, for several minutes. At last, the car-cortège proceeded back to the château, followed by the members of the press. There the reception was already in progress. Yves Montand's throaty voice (Edith Piaf had been first choice but was unavailable) came faintly over the public address system. Servants were still giving last-minute touches to the food as the hungry Aga, at a centre table, began to eat on his own. The newly-weds walked hand in hand down to the sea, to the serenading of a six-piece orchestra while they were having their pictures taken ... again, and again, and again.

Item: In the pool of the château, where 200 gallons of eau de cologne scented the air, floated an arrangement of little white flowers in the initials of the couple M & A.

Item: Food was served on little tables set for two to four people on the terrace. More than 1,200 dishes, 1,500 glasses and as many knives and forks were used.

The maître d's began to serve the caviar, the salmon, the lobster *à la Parisienne*, the fowl from Grasse, the spring vegetables and the pineapple ice-cream.

Item: 'The guests consumed 25 litres of orange juice; 40 bottles of gin; 150 bottles of champagne; 60 bottles of liqueurs, 100 bottles of Italian Vermouth, as many again of French Vermouth, and 50 bottles of Cognac,' wrote one of the maître d's, Paul A. Buisine, for *Cinémonde*. 'And this was before lunch was served.'

Item: The wedding cake, weighing 55 kilos and made in Paris, was mounted in Cannes and had its final flourishes added by the patisserie-makers at the château.

The couple were vague when pressed about their future plans. A honeymoon? Well, Aly volunteered that he hoped to attend the

Derby at Epsom Downs on June 4th.* Rita planned to start work
on a new film. Back at the party, she sank down next to her
father-in-law. 'Too much caviar, Rita,' he murmured, 'too much
caviar.' Starry-eyed Louella Parsons heaved the final sigh in her
report to her readers. The groom, she reported, 'wearying but still
buoyant, dropped on one knee and, with old-world gallantry,
kissed Rita's slipper.'

The night was spent at the château, and the next day the
Muslim marriage ceremony performed at the château by two
Ismaili priests. It was very simple and rapid. To fulfil the require-
ments of the Khan, Rita had to take an Ismaili name—Rehmat
Khanum—which means Lady of Blessings from the Almighty.
There were only about ten people present. 'They included my
friends, my brother, and the Princess's daughter, Rebecca,' Aly
told the press. And he hoped now there would be no more
publicity.

Item: Within a few minutes of the wedding, the Vatican sent
out the following comment: 'The Church will completely ignore
this marriage. As a Catholic, Miss Hayworth should know that
her civil marriage has no value in the eyes of the Church.'

Even though the Côte d'Azur prided itself on its blasé attitude
to most goings on, the detachment of its inhabitants was seriously
ruffled by the events that had taken place. And just below the
brightly-lit château stood the little run down railway station, a
poignant reminder of the post-war slump and bleakness that
shrouded much of the rest of the world. Of course, there had been
carping from some locals who had resented this display of luxury
as if there had been no war, no starvation, as if champagne could
drown out memories of recent sufferings. But it was almost
1950—and memories are only so long. For most people who sat
down with their evening papers to read about the happenings
over the past year, Rita marrying her Prince was far more
attractive to contemplate than recalling a past that was already
fading into history. And to most of the people there that day,
people in the town and guests at the party, there was no thought
of railway stations and poverty. For Rita Hayworth's wedding
was really like something out of the Arabian Nights.

Back in Hollywood, newsmen descended on Eduardo's house.
It was around 1 a.m. when they roused her father from his bed,
got him dressed, dragged a desk into the huge dancing room on
the floor below and took his picture. The next day, the front pages

*He watched his other 'My Love' win that year.

of some of the Los Angeles papers carried this photo with the caption, 'The Lonely Father'. Dorothy Valdespino came over and found Eduardo and his wife still upset by what happened. 'They pushed him around. He didn't know what was going on. There were so many of them there, wanting to know why he wasn't invited, things like that. Eduardo never realised what they were doing to him until it was all over. It was a really mean thing to do.'

Item: A few days after the nuptials, copies of Rita's Jacques Fath wedding dress were available at Macy's and department stores across the United States. The version by Roseweb Frocks also had the V-neck top, the belt, the pleated skirt, and the flounce. The only thing missing, sighed the adverts, was Aly Khan. It was available in brown, black, or 'bride's blue' for a mere eighteen dollars and seventy-four cents.

*   *   *

DISSOLVE TO:
INTERIOR OF PRIVATE HOSPITAL ROOM. FLOWERS IN VASES; FLOWERS IN POTS; FLOWERS EVERYWHERE. IN CORNER DOCTOR AND NURSES. CAMERA MOVES TO CLOSE SHOT OF THREE FIGURES: RITA SMILING IN BED, BESIDE HER A SLEEPING BABY AND HER HUSBAND LEANING OVER THE CHILD. SUPERIMPOSE CAPTION: LAUSANNE, SWITZERLAND. DECEMBER 27TH. 9.45 A.M. THEIR DAUGHTER YASMIN WAS BORN.

Two years after the wedding the fairytale was over.

DISSOLVE TO:
EXTERIOR SCENE. WINTRY, DARK. LONG SHOT FROM ON HIGH LOOKING AT A HARBOUR. CAMERA MOVES IN. SOUND UP. LIGHTS AND LAUGHTER FROM PASSENGER LINER PREPARING TO SET SAIL. WHISTLE BLOWS. SUPERIMPOSE CAPTION: LE HAVRE. MARCH 25TH, 1951. CAMERA FROM DOCKSIDE ANGLE FOCUSED ON THE *De Grasse*. CAMERA STARTS TO PULL BACK AS SHIP FADES INTO A BRIGHT DOT ON HORIZON. THEN DISAPPEARS. DARKNESS. OVER THIS BACKGROUND 'THE END' TITLE SUPERIMPOSED. MUSIC UP.

CHAPTER VII

'BACK AGAIN!'

She sat loosely in the slip, regarding the body in the slip with a kind of angry, detached impatience—the body perpetually pummelled, massaged, costumed, rigged out and displayed. . . . Nothing about her gave her peace; she had reached the point where, if it had anything to do with her, she was at once displeased and wearied. She railed at the dieting and reducing she had to do. The fits of nibbling that would overtake her for days on end.

Daniel Fuchs *West of the Rockies*

Rita had left Aly in the middle of the African safari they had begun as a second honeymoon to close the spreading rift between them. It was certainly no secret that the marriage was shaky. Still as much in love with her charming husband as ever, Rita was finding the strain of his hyperactive life more than she could take or adjust to. His continuous round of social functions gave her no more opportunity to set up the home that she dreamed of than with Orson. Inevitably, with two such newsworthy figures, their public spats attracted headlines. Their private rows had the servants taking sides while almost from the outset Aly's cynical cronies were laying wagers on the duration of the marriage.

Emotional, vulnerable and overly sensitive, Rita would usually end their rows by storming out of the restaurant or casino they visited, while Aly remained to play or go on the town with his ever present, indulging friends. They were *his* friends; the women he knew resented her, and the men he hung out with knew too well that while Aly saw nothing unusual in his own flirtations, he would brook no such behaviour in his wife or tolerate another man making a play for her. With Rita back alone in their large house, the servants could hear her cry herself to sleep on more

Rita and Aly aboard Errol Flynn's yacht, the *Zaza*, rented for a cruise in the Mediterranean during happier days. The same yacht Rita had been on before, when she and Orson rented it for *The Lady from Shanghai* (1950). (Emrys Williams Collection)

than one occasion. Ironically, it was when she had enough and flared up at him, throwing books or jugs of water, that she was most *like* the woman he adored her for. Besides, when Rita was in love, she was like a little girl, and wanted nor needed anybody else around. She felt cut off from her friends, her only confidante, her secretary. She wanted to be alone with her husband and their children and resented being shown off as the prize goldfish in his bowl. It was a situation that had roused her Aunt Frances into a fury over Aly, the time she had come to stay with them. But Rita would hear no complaints against him—not even from the relative she loved like a mother, and who she knew loved her. Things could not go on this way. Rita's heart was for her husband, but not for the life that went with him.

Though Rita possessed all the attributes to assure a fine place in this world, it did not attract her. She was too serious to enjoy the sham, too romantic to accept happiness as the world saw it if she knew it wasn't real, too withdrawn to enjoy its pleasures, and, one must add, too selfish and wilful to change or adapt her personality to new interests when these ran counter to her own inclinations. She was no more the Princess Margarita Khan than she had been Gilda, but her husband didn't understand this.

The marriage had reached an impasse. In an effort to break it, Aly had the clever idea of combining a tour to include his religious duties with a champagne safari that would take them away from his European friends and give him and his wife time to be together. From the outset Rita had doubts. The second honeymoon included four Moslem millionaires who came along to play bridge with Aly, two cooks, one valet, two pilots, three secretaries and two aides. One trunk held the champagne; another the refrigerators. Aly had friends everywhere. Wherever he landed there was bound to be a party. He also invited two of her friends along, Leigh and Jackson Leighter, in an effort to please her and keep her company. Certainly Aly meant well. That, of course, wasn't the problem. They hadn't been long afoot before the familiar pattern of the life he had promised to leave behind re-emerged.

1951 began with a sorry bang. At a New Year's Eve party in Cairo attended by King Farouk, Aly had a whale of a time. Rita sat by looking increasingly grim. Tired of the fat Farouk's fawning attentions, upset by the free language of the men, angered by her husband's lack of concern, she was growing restless. When on top of everything else she believed that Aly was paying more attention to a woman at another table than to her, she stormed out. Aly liked Rita excited but it wouldn't do to have a scene in the club amidst the noise and gaiety. He rushed after her but came back alone. Of course people talked. Once again Rita returned unaccompanied to the hotel.

The woman suffered from neglect. But not the star. She may have wished to bury herself in her husband's life but she could never shake off her own fame. Wherever Margarita went, Rita Hayworth still had her fans. A young admirer had gone so far as to save his money to pay for a three-day stay in the same expensive luxury hotel when he heard she and Aly would be in Cairo. For the sake of an autograph he kept a continuous watch for a glimpse of his idol. That New Year's Eve like all the other nights he stood chatting to the hotel porter.

'It was like a marvellous dream. One moment I was talking to this fat doorman who was telling me all about the movie stars who had stayed there, and I was thinking that I must go home tomorrow and explain to my parents where I have been, then suddenly, there is Miss Gilda. It was a warm night but she was wearing a beautiful fur coat, looking marvellous, you know. Her face was flushed, very dramatic, and all that wonderful red hair. She was wearing only one earring. The other one was in her hand. She dropped it on the steps and I ran to pick it up for her. She hadn't seemed to notice at all. When I gave it to her she gave me this wonderful smile—very *Gilda* you see—but she looked far away. I don't know what I said. I don't think I said anything, I was so thrilled. She looked like I had expected, very glamorous. Then she was gone inside the door. It was all so fast. I think she must have been walking because her face was flushed—it made her look so beautiful, so dramatic. When I got back home I had a big row with my parents who didn't believe me and were angry that I spent all that money. But I didn't care.'

The recurring fights bore out her fears. Then also impinging on her were Aly's duties and her responsibilities as his wife. She found that she was expected to be on public display as the future Begum, which involved a round of duties to take her among the wives and families of the Ismaili communities. As in the early days of her career when, as a starlet, she was sent out by the studio to garner publicity, so now, as a princess, she found herself opening fêtes, judging baby contests and awarding prizes at schools. In her role as future Begum, Rita was left alone among strangers. She who had found the semi-formal Hollywood dinner parties with people she knew uncomfortable, now found herself heading an endless round of teas with the wives of other Ismaili leaders who, she could see, were studying her minutely as the woman who would one day become their Begum and, as such, would serve as an example to the women of the sect. She suffered from the close scrutiny but could do no more than smile.

With the exception of the Leighters, she had no one to whom she could talk, no people of her own race with whom she could relax. A further irony was that the white British communities in Nairobi shunned her, not because she was an American film star, but because she was married to someone whom they regarded as a 'coloured'. Rita raged at the injustice and hypocrisy and found Aly's dismissal of their petty racial prejudices hard to accept. She couldn't understand, or perhaps was unaware of Aly's own, unique

revenge against the white man's prejudice, which he had when he
slept with their wives and daughters. When, at last, Aly flew
ahead to Telek to continue with the safari party, Rita pleaded
illness but promised to follow him as soon as she was recovered.
Instead, it was the Leighters who arrived at Aly's camp a few days
later with a note from his wife to say that she was leaving for
Europe. Contrary to the stories that later sprung up, Aly flew
back to Cairo in an effort to change her mind. Husband and wife
talked, but nothing was resolved. The next day an official smoke
screen was given to the press explaining that she was tired and
missed the children. Aly continued his tour of duty alone.

By coincidence, Rita arrived back at the château on the same
day as her father-in-law returned to Cannes from Pakistan. What
happened next was foolish and irrational and can only be explained by the strain of the past few months. She had already
planned to return for a holiday to the States, taking Rebecca with
her, but now, with the presence of the Aga nearby, she suddenly
feared that she would lose Yasmin if she left without her. She
knew that the old Aga adored his only granddaughter and her
first-hand experience of the far-reaching power and influence of
his wealth and position, suddenly caused Rita to behave not
reasonably but as a mother might, instinctively and uncaring
whether her actions would be understood or hurt others beside
herself. Assisted by the Leighters and Susan, the children's nurse
who was loyal to her, Rita felt she had to flee and embarked on a
midnight dash to Paris, then on to Le Havre where they boarded
the liner *De Grasse* leaving for New York. When the news reached
Aly in Cairo he did not try to follow her.

In her haste to be gone there had been no time to pack more
than a few basic things for herself and the children, nor even to
arrange about money for tickets, which the Leighters loaned to
her. She returned to New York broke. The money she had saved
while working had dwindled away while she was married. Admittedly, Aly's generosity was legendary but, as only those close to
him knew, Aly was not wealthy in his own right. As Rita explained when asked, though her husband had been extremely
generous with her, buying her expensive clothes and jewellery,
'He is dependent on what he is given by his father, and his
allowance does not always cover his tastes.' But the bills for these
would still have to be settled, and though Rita would never say so,
her attitude to what she had has always been: 'What is mine is my
husband's.' Aly would have thought of it as no more than a

temporary loan but somehow she never got it back. She had had
other expenses in the years before and during her marriage to Aly:
her house in Hollywood to keep up; secretaries to pay; the
expenses incurred when she and Aly were travelling around
Europe before her marriage.

The upshot of it was that she now had to be advanced money
by her agents to settle bills that were coming due, and to cover
upcoming needs. Many came—the boat fare, a new wardrobe,
her suite at the Plaza, wages for secretary and nurse, press agent
to shield her from the press, lawyers—bills mounted up and would
have to be met. Till she had decided on her next step she had to
find a way to keep herself. She had not made up her mind for
certain when she fled if the rift with Aly was to be permanent, but
events moved on and with them the pressure to decide. Rather
than turn to her husband, which would be a *de facto* admission
that she had been in the wrong, something her pride would not
admit, she hastily agreed to sign a new contract with her old
studio that gave her back the trappings of her fame but not her
former power. For one thing she did not have script approval.

The studio's explanation for exacting humiliating conditions
was the fear that she would be a box-office risk after a three-years'
absence from the screen. Then after they signed her they turned
around and set about exploiting her for all she was worth, as if she
were nothing more than the latest ten-day wonder. The publicity
department's job was made easy by the millions of dollars' worth
of free publicity provided by the press, who were busy plotting her
next move. Eager as the front office was to get Rita on film,
however, the studio found that they had no suitable Hayworth
property ready to go on the floor.

The only film of any importance with a role for Rita was the
upcoming version of the best-seller *From Here to Eternity*. The
studio was preparing this to be a multi-million dollar blockbuster. The key feminine role of Karen, the adulterous army wife was
ideal for Hayworth. It would have given her a class production
and a key role in the most talked about property of the decade.
But apparently not for her comeback, since Deborah Kerr got the
part eventually. There were several reasons given. For one thing,
it was not scheduled to begin shooting until 1952; for another,
since it was planned as an all-star production, it was felt to be a
waste of Hayworth's box-office. The reasoning was that Rita
could sell a film, any film, strictly on the strength of her name
above a title, so why wait and waste it. She might be able to fit

Karen in later. There was an undeniably indecent haste to get her before the cameras.

What they came up with at last would have served as a 'B' melodrama at the bottom half of a double bill. Even at that it was little more than an idea, one that the original author was having trouble making head or tail out of. It resulted from one of Cohn's charitable gestures. To help Virginia Van Upp at a time when she was also undergoing personal problems and needed some money, he bought an idea she had. And that idea was now chosen to celebrate the end of Rita's marriage and her much publicised comeback.

Ironically, considering the haste involved, nine months elapsed before filming could begin, on December 17th—enough time to have found something better. She had left New York for Reno, taking her daughters, to sit out the necessary six weeks in the desert, preparatory to filing a suit for divorce.

Meanwhile, Aly was also under considerable pressure from his family to avoid further scandal and patch up the marriage. The day after he read of Rita's decision to sue for divorce, he wrote to her, pleading with her to hold off any final action till he could see her and they had time to talk things out. His charm still worked on her hopes for a happy end. Though unhappy, she was still more than a little in love with him. She postponed divorce proceedings in order, as her lawyers said, 'to give Aly six months' grace to re-woo her', but she continued with her application for a trust fund for Yasmin. The weeks in the desert were long, hot and boring, for Rita was certainly not in the mood to mix with other lonely divorcees who would be curious to see how she took it. Her time was taken up with her restless daughters, and the waiting. But there was space to simmer down—for the ignominies of the past to be shaken off. She could go back to Los Angeles, not as a refugee from another broken marriage, but to the dignity of her work.

It is the custom of Hollywood stars arriving in town by train but wishing to avoid the usual mob and the journalists at the Los Angeles Grand Central Railway Terminal, to disembark at Glendale. There, someone from the studio would be on hand to greet them, help with luggage and get them into a car and home. So Rita returned, but when her train pulled into the station, there was no one there from the studio. Alone on the platform she struggled with the children and luggage. A press agent from another studio, who had come to meet Tony Curtis, spotted Rita and left his assistant to deal with Curtis while he went to help her. But there was no one from Columbia—yet Cohn could hardly have failed to know she was coming back, and where and when.

When she reported to the studio there was still no script to show her, but the publicity department was busy banging the drums. Her face, hands, feet and body once again became studio property to be used to sell toilet articles: nylons, headlamps, face creams, three different brands of cigarettes and other affiliated Columbia investments. '*Sultry Rita Hayworth—more beautiful, more electric, more impassioned and vibrant—is back! And it was only when her glowing presence first lighted the screen in Columbia Pictures exciting ... did we realise just how vitally she had been missed!*' Hooray for the Exhibitors Campaign Book!

It seemed as if nothing she could do could please Cohn. There would be any number of reasons for him to pick on her, to upset her. She was handed orders to attend fittings when there was still no script, just a vague story outline. '*Sultry Rita Hayworth—more beautiful, more electric, more impassioned and vibrant than ever—is back!*'

Cohn would insist Rita report to the studio like any other employee, though there was nothing there to occupy her. Nobody could understand Cohn's attitude towards her. An experienced professional top-ranking star and mature woman, she was being treated as a rank beginner. If she decided to balk at the rush or question the project, there was the immediate threat of suspension that would take her off salary and add new law-suits to her other problems.

Professionally as well as emotionally, her life revolved in a familiar vicious circle. The stars' tried and trusted way of dealing with similar situations and getting their own back, feigning illness or pregnancy, could not help her here. The delays would only be temporary and bound to stir up more trouble which, in the present situation, she was hardly equipped to handle. Even so, it became obvious that something had to be done soon, for it wasn't Rita's recalcitrance that was holding up production. They hadn't even assigned the film a director yet. Rita's own favourite, Charles Vidor, with whom at least she would have felt comfortable, was no longer with the studio—he, too, had had one row too many with his boss and was now working successfully elsewhere. With Vidor's departure, Columbia's roster of contract directors with a knack for making women's pictures was nil.

Fortunately Vincent Sherman, who had been responsible for many of the best known Warner Brothers films of the 'for-

With make-up artist Bob Schiffer getting a last touch-up before a take. (Lippman/Columbia)

ties—including *Mr Skeffington* with Bette Davis, *The Hard Way* with Ida Lupino, *Nora Prentiss* and *The Unfaithful*, two superior vehicles starring Ann Sheridan, and several of Crawford's better films—was on loan to Columbia. It was because of Joan Crawford that Sherman found himself at Columbia, just when they needed him most. Having successfully worked with Joan on two films at Warners, she asked for him to direct her when she went to Columbia to star in a re-make of *Harriet Craig*. Despite his admiration for Crawford, Sherman hadn't been excited about re-making what was already a re-make, but found that his studio had already agreed the loan-out, leaving him with few options unless he wanted to break a very good contract. While Sherman didn't think much of it, the critics liked it, Crawford liked it, it more than made its money back so Cohn liked it too. When Sherman read that Columbia had the rights to *From Here to Eternity*, like most directors in town, he wanted to do it and phoned Cohn: 'I did that crap for you, *Harriet Craig*, why not give me a crack at this in return?'

'Well, he stalled. There was trouble about censorship and there were some doubts whether or not they would ever be able to make it and keep to the book's flavour and spirit. But he asked me to come over and see him about something else. He was a wily old bird. I guess along with a few other writers and directors I was one of those who got on great with him. When I saw him he told me, "Listen, we'll talk about *From Here to Eternity* some other time, but I've got something better for you." That should have put me on my guard from the start. "How would you like to do Rita Hayworth's comeback picture?"

'Well, who wouldn't. Before she left films to marry Aly, Rita had been one of the hottest box-office properties in town. Now she was back. I was a bit surprised to be offered the film because there were other, bigger directors in town who would have given their teeth to make a film with her. I knew Harry was clever and there was going to be a catch, so I asked him if he had a script for me to see. Well, he says, "Got a great story. Great. Would you like to do it?" "Well, I wanna know what it is." "Listen," he said, "you're a good guy, Vince, I'll give it to you straight. I'll give you the whole thing—twenty pages of screenplay. You go into the outer office, read it and then we'll talk again."

'It took me fifteen minutes. What it was was a springboard, that's all. A man who returned to Trinidad to discover his brother murdered and the brother's wife is suspected of the crime.

' "What happens from here?" I asked Harry.

' "You like that much?"

'I said, "Well, yes. It's all right as a springboard. Trinidad is a good colourful location." Cohn asked, "Is it a deal? I'll pay you your salary."

'I had just made *Lone Star* at M.G.M. as a freelance director and my salary was pretty high just then. He said, "Let's shake on it. You do it." With Harry, a shake was good enough. Then he told me to go downstairs where Bert Granet and Virginia Van Upp were. "Virginia is writing the screenplay and Bert is going to produce. Talk to them. Tell them to tell you the rest of the story and that you're going to direct the picture."

'Bert introduced me to Virginia, and then I told them Cohn had asked me to do the Hayworth picture and that I was looking forward to hearing the rest of the story from them. That resulted in a long silence. Virginia said, "Gee, Bert, I'm so tired trying to lick this one scene, why don't you tell Vince the story." Bert said, "Virginia, it's your picture, your script, I really think you should

tell the story." My heart sank while they were hesitating over
who should tell it. Finally they compromised. Bert said, "Look
Virginia, you start, and when you get tired I'll take over." She
didn't look excited.

'Two hours later, having listened to both of them, I realised
that they had five stories if they had one. I asked if there was
anything I could read. There were pages and pages, about fifteen
hundred of them—notes, unfinished screenplays. When I left to
start work on it, Bert walked out with me. Cohn had sent Bert in
to get the Hayworth picture moving. Now I find out that he's
been sweating over the script for sixteen weeks and was so
miserable he was going to get off the project; he suggested I do the
same. Bert said, "I know Harry, if this doesn't come off he'll look
around for somebody to blame and I don't want to be there when
it happens, because I can't see it coming to anything." I asked
him not to get off yet when I only just got on, but to give me a
few days to feel my way around. But he wanted to make a move
and I couldn't stop him.

'The next day I'm in my office going through the material
when Cohn called me up and immediately started: "I don't like a
quitter! Granet just told me he wanted off the production. I don't
like that." I said, "You can't blame him, Harry. He doesn't feel
it's getting anywhere and doesn't want to be responsible for
something he doesn't like." And I told him that he didn't have a
story. Harry said, "Don't you think the hell I know that? I know
what the problem is as well as Granet does, but I need help right
now." Then he says to me, "The dame came back unexpectedly.
New York's been screaming for a picture with her as fast as
possible, and I've been looking for something for her to do with no
luck. Finally I went to Virginia who told me she had a story that
would be great for Rita. So I bought the goddamn thing, paid her
fifty thousand dollars for it, and we've been struggling here for
sixteen weeks trying to do something, while we've been paying
Hayworth her salary the whole time with nothing to show for it.
Vince, I need help."

'I appreciated his honesty, even though he initially tricked me
into agreeing. And there was the excitement of doing a picture
with Hayworth. I was also intrigued by the challenge of trying to
make something out of nothing. Harry said, "Do the best you can,
Vince, but get me a picture, because the investment is building up
and I've got nothing to show for it. Don't offer her too much
dialogue. Cut to her face and have her say, 'Who me?' Play to her

reaction—she's a great reactor. Give me ten to twelve reels of film, a couple of dance numbers, some conflict between her and the man, and some exotic backgrounds. If you do that, I'll give you a deal for another picture." He thought that we oughta get Virginia off the picture because she was having private problems at the time that were upsetting her and not helping her work any. Now Cohn couldn't fire Virginia himself—they had been, and were, friends—so he got Bert to talk to her as his last act as a producer. Now I had to get somebody fast and called in James Gunn, a guy I'd worked with several times at Warners. To be honest, I stole things from several other films—something from *Notorious*, something else from *Gilda*. And the newspapers then were writing how the Communists were going to utilise the Caribbean for submarine bases. That gave me the idea for injecting some political intrigue. It was flimsily put together, just a piece of crap, but I didn't have time to do anything else. But I knew what we were doing. My eyes weren't closed.'

With a shooting date in sight, the campaign for the film was stepped up. Cohn laid on a big spread to announce the start of filming, first inviting Louella Parsons to a private do in his office and ordering Rita to be there. It was to be Hayworth's first meeting with a member of the Hollywood press since her rupture with Aly. Till now she had refused all attempts at interviews—an act that of course had not endeared her to the columnists. Sherman was to be there as well.

'Harry briefed me on the routine. He was going to invite Louella down to the office, then Rita would come in ... "and we'll have some drinks, and it'll be a big hello between the two of them, and yourself. You tell Louella a little, not too much, about the picture. The main thing is to have Rita talk to Louella."'

[*Modern Screen*; June 1952. EXTRA! RITA HAYWORTH TELLS ALL TO LOUELLA PARSONS!]

'It was very amusing to see Cohn setting this up. There were flowers in the office, liquor, sandwiches and so forth. Louella was there all dolled up waiting when Rita came in wearing just a pair of blue jeans, a simple shirt and moccasins. I could see Cohn was furious. He said nothing to Rita, but he called me back after it was over and said, "How d'you like that! I set this thing up for her and she comes in dressed like some bum off the streets. Why the fucking hell doesn't she dress like a princess or something." At

this point I still didn't know about the long backlog of animosity
between Cohn and Rita, that they were always getting at each
other. This I discovered later. Personally, I loved her for her
simplicity. She didn't give a damn about the thing. I don't think
she ever had much love for any of the newspaper people and
columnists. I found myself very impressed by the way she carried
it off.'

Since it had already been decided that the story would allow
for a couple of dance numbers to be interpolated at some stage,
rehearsals for these began while the script was still being worked
on. Few of the Hayworth stalwarts were left at the studio—her
cameraman Rudy Maté had become a director in his own right,
Virginia Van Upp coping with her own problems was off the film
for the duration, and choreographer Jack Cole had left the studio
long ago. Only Jean Louis and Helen Hunt were still around
from the original coterie that had contributed to her security and
success. But the Hayworth dances were obviously going to be one
of the key selling ingredients of the film, and to ensure that these
would not disappoint, Cohn imported Valerie Bettis, a dynamic
dancer from New York, to choreograph them. Rehearsals were to
take several weeks for Rita's muscles, as happens with dancers,
had become flabby during her married years. Cohn came down
one day to watch her in her practice leotard and thought she
would need a lot of work to get back into shape, for her muscles to
tone. Valerie thought three to four weeks would do it and this was
a godsend to Sherman, who was still trying to lick the story. It
would also give him an opportunity to get to know Rita on a more
informal basis before filming began.

About three weeks later, he told me, 'Gunn and I had been
working late at the studio. Rita had finished her practice and was
looking in great form when she dropped by at the office to ask
how things were going with the script. We had only seen each
other casually till then. She stayed with us for about forty-five
minutes; we had a couple of drinks, and I asked her if she had any
engagements for dinner because Jimmy and I were going out for a
bite to eat and we'd be very pleased to have her join us if she felt
like it. The three of us went over to Lucy's to have dinner. I was
surprised that a woman as attractive as she was would be alone,
but I figured she must still be upset about Aly. She wasn't too
communicative at first, but after we had a couple of cocktails she
told us something about the trip she'd taken to Africa with Aly
Khan and so forth. About an hour later Jimmy said he wanted to

get back to work on a couple of scenes we had to finish that night. I planned to join him after Rita and I had coffee.

'We talked a bit about the film—I think she felt I was trying to be as honest with her as I could about the situation. I told her it wasn't a great script or anything like that but I hoped that we'd be able to make something that'd be saleable. I don't believe in lying to actors. At any rate, we got to talking and she indicated that she was very lonely. I felt that here was a girl who was very insecure and still very upset about the break-up. There was a basic sadness about her which I guess sort of seeped into the film.

'I began to ask about the monetary situation which had forced her to do this film. "I had over 300,000 dollars when I married Aly Khan," she said, "and I came back broke." I remembered something Virginia had once told me. It seems that Aly had a print of *Gilda* and that he would run it for himself every couple of months. It was Virginia's theory that he had fallen in love with *Gilda*, and when he discovered that Rita wasn't the same, Aly had to sort of implement his idea and be stimulated by the film.

'Anyway, that night was the first time I really talked to her. She's not very articulate, but she had been opening up, un-burdening herself, and I really felt for her. It was about 9 p.m. when I realised that I had to go and join Jimmy to work on the scene, and I told her so. And that beautiful woman looked at me and said, "I'm boring you."

'It hit me how hurt she was and now I felt terrible because I had just wanted to join Jimmy to get her script done. I said, "Oh my God, no—it's just work. I'm not bored." And I wasn't, don't you know. But I wished I hadn't brought it up because she was opening up, which wasn't typical of her. And now it was as if she felt that she hadn't anything to say anyone would care to listen to. It made me feel terribly unhappy that she should feel like this, and that I should have been the cause of it. From that moment my heart broke for her. I tried to be as gentle and loving as I could while we were working together. This beautiful, lovely creature who thought she was boring when she talked.'

'*Sultry Rita Hayworth returns in exciting* Affair in Trinidad*!*'

When at last the script was finished, a copy was sent to Rita by way of the William Morris Agency. The next thing a furious Cohn was phoning Sherman saying, 'The broad doesn't want to do it.'

The whole studio seemed to know that for all of Sherman's *légerdemain* with script and behind camera, the project was going to be a lemon. Sherman thought so. The crew thought so. Jean Louis who designed the 'fifteen breath-taking gowns' thought so. It was terrible. They knew it was going to be a lemon but it would still make money. For Rita it was a very second-rate film that let her feel the studio's total lack of concern for her. She couldn't fail to realise that in the end, it wouldn't be Bert Granet, or the writers or director who would carry the can if the film failed, but herself. She was the one the public was paying to see. If the film bored them, they'd blame her waistline, or the fact that she had aged, or motherhood or something, but her. Until now, Rita hadn't been in a position to say or do much but, with the script before her, the truth of her situation was inescapable. She could ill afford to have her salary cut off, but, like an animal at bay, she balked. On her instructions her agents had no alternative but to inform the studio. Cohn told Sherman to discuss the matter with Abe Lastvogel, the head of the agency. Sherman explained the situation anew, trying to convince Lastvogel that he must make Rita see reason. In the present situation the argument amounted to nothing more than the fact that she couldn't afford a law-suit against the studio, and that the studio had already invested too much money in the film for them to drop it and find something better. Agents are good at that.

Sherman: 'I told him [Lastvogel] that it wasn't a great script. We all knew it, but it was a saleable piece of merchandise, and that, though it wouldn't do her a great deal of good it certainly wouldn't hurt her. And that what she had seen was only the first draft and we were willing to bring somebody else in [Oscar Saul] to hypo the whole thing and goose it up.'

In the end, after more revisions and several weeks off salary, Rita capitulated. In the meantime the studio had leaked indiscreet, highly biased stories of high-hatted and temperamental behaviour on Rita's part.

After the film was over and she was already well into her next one, Rita good-naturedly told Louella Parsons, 'I didn't mind when you called me temperamental when I first started my picture and had trouble. I wasn't trying to be difficult. I realised how terribly important it was to have a good picture as my comeback. When we reported to work and I found that the script was not even completed—I refused to continue. So I was put on suspension. The minute the screenplay was finished, and it was good, well, as good as we could make it, I went back to work.'

Sherman continues: 'I tried to hypo it by surrounding her with new faces and some attractive local colour to give the film an exotic flavour.'

Rita's working relationship with Sherman was as happy as it could be under the circumstances and she sincerely appreciated his help. Nevertheless, she couldn't help feel that she was being crassly exploited.

Bob Coburn had taken her last official studio portraits and now took the first ones since her return:

'The old Hayworth was gone. Like you pulled a screen over her. She was a very lonely gal and it came through. The closest we ever came to an argument was during that period. I had her for three days and she just bowed her neck and wouldn't do what I asked her to. And I said to her, after all, we've gotta get some magazine spread and it's up to you and me to sell this picture because it's a real lemon otherwise. I talked to her for about half an hour and I could see this curtain coming down over her eyes. I asked her whether or not I'd hurt her feelings. And she said, "No." I said, "What then?" And she said, "I'm sick and tired of this cheesy Hayworth." And I said, "Rita, that's what people are buying." She just didn't feel like it—just didn't feel like it.'

Sherman: 'At the start of shooting she was very shy, and very insecure. She hadn't been in front of the camera for three years. When it came to playing dramatic scenes I was very gentle and careful with her because I could sense her insecurity and nervousness. But little by little I saw her get her confidence back, and become more relaxed in front of the camera. To a degree Cohn was right when he said she was great for reactions, because she has a marvellously expressive face, and in films, when you cut to the reaction of someone, it's much stronger than cutting to them talking. Garbo had that. I enjoyed working for her, doing things to get her to open up. I was just sorry that we had nothing better to do when it would have mattered a great deal to her personally just then.'

Sherman was right. Some of her pain seeped into the finished film. What Rita felt while working she mostly kept to herself, but the camera could pry the secrets from her. She played Chris Emery, the wife of a murdered painter whose foolish brother suspects her of complicity in his death because she makes her living working as an entertainer in a nightclub, the crossway station of films like these. It was a role to which technical

Rita in the throes of her 'I Do What I Like' number—with Glenn Ford and choreographer/actress Valerie Bettis looking on, April 1952. (Lippman/Columbia)

competence or theatrical training could bring little, a role which required more than acting skills to bring it to life, it demanded that special brand labelled 'Rita Hayworth—STAR'.

More often than not, the people who hired a star treated them as if their fame was something to do with breathing, or washing their hair once a day, every day. But in front of the camera, it's zero time, and it's the star who must stand there, trying to remember what it was they did before, what it was they're supposed to have that will suddenly start up when the director says 'Action!' With each picture they must start from scratch, with no way of knowing what it is that's missing when they can't turn it on and come up empty, all the while fighting back the feeling that they were never that good and had nothing in particular to begin with.

While a thousand similar emotions and reflections are going

'Don't tell me I'm just one more.' (Lippman/Columbia)

through Rita's mind, the lines spin-out, her make-up is smoothed, strands of disengaged hair are neatly adjusted and the miracle is actually taking place once again. Instead of a callous broad in a dumpy dive fending off insulting remarks with a disdainful shrug, the camera catches the all too real pain. And that undercurrent packed the wallop when we watched her come-back on thousands of screens, in thousands of dark, cavernous temples of hushed loneliness.

She had lost none of her rapport with the camera. The animal magnetism vibrated as strongly as ever, there was no denying the fullness of her physical beauty, and over it all, like a delicate but firm grip, there was that aura of calm that sheltered storms. But the expansive sense of youthful, careless freedom that had lent such a sparkle to her musicals was no longer there. Only in her dancing was it evident, but even there, it trailed an undercurrent of ache. On the screen one saw glamour, romance and exotic locations, but beneath it one felt her ache, felt she ached in her 'fifteen breathtaking Jean Louis gowns', felt she ached while tossing her head and abandoning herself to the sophisticated bump and grind routines on the dance floor. A silent ache haunts the film, and draws one back into the shadows to see it again and again in a hopeless effort to come to terms with its secret tug on the memory. The story is a dog's dinner beneath a Colombe D'Or crust, a blatant throwback to the studio's Poverty Row beginnings. From Goddess of Love to Goddess of the Gutters. But it works. Because she works.

To throw a further smokescreen over the empty proceedings, Glenn Ford was brought back to play the bullish Steve—in the obvious hope of some more of that sexual antagonism that shot through their previous films like a hot poker.

'SHE'S BACK! WITH THAT MAN FROM *GILDA*!' screamed the poster lettering over a shot of Ford slapping Hayworth.

'*Don't tell me I'm just one more!*' Steve says, hauling off at Chris in the best Gilda style.

But Gilda had been a pretty, spoilt child. Misunderstood to be sure but greedy with youth and the power it grants to toss off clichés as samples of wit. But Chris isn't Gilda. This woman aches with memories—experiences a feeling of *déjà vu*. It's not the woman, it's the part. Chris is a loser. Even her name lacks glamour. Tomboys, not sirens are named Chris. And why was this haute coutured woman of the world showing off like a loser in run-down nightclubs for the Diners' Club crowd of 1952? Gilda could have burst out on that dance floor, daring us to think our worst, laughed and left without giving it a second thought. Chris Emery looked as if she knew what she was doing; that time was running out and that the devil was on her heels. This can be the stuff of tragedy or trash. But, the film's defects would yet become its virtues.

The studio's publicity department had their work cut out and proceeded to tackle it with gusto:

> Cynical, disdainful of the undesired attentions lavished on her by the Island's males, Chris becomes involved in international intrigue when police suspect a suave cosmopolitan who specialises in obtaining and selling government secrets, of being responsible for the murder of her late unlamented husband.

On that pretext, the story sends her off into situations where the F.B.I. might fear to tread and where actors go to die.

> The discovery by the dead man's brother [Ford] that he is passionately in love with the 'Trinidad Lady' adds to the suspense and drama of the film.

He slaps her face. 'DON'T TELL ME I'M JUST ONE MORE!'

Glenn Ford, too old to sulk all the time but effective, his puppy dog appeal lurking behind a belligerent façade, walks through the film with a stormcloud on his brow and treats Rita like a life raft. The chemistry still strikes sparks. He recalled for me: 'We were very delighted to be working. Just a film. I didn't think about the similarities with *Gilda*. Later, when we saw it in the projection room I saw how deliberate the comparison was. We both kind of resented it, but didn't say anything. How are you going to argue with the studio? After all, it went out and made a lot of money, so they must have known what they were doing.'

SLAP! 'DON'T TELL ME I'M JUST ONE MORE!'

Affair in Trinidad, promised the announcers' voices on the radio, 'is just about the perfect vehicle for Miss Hayworth's welcome return to the screen, giving her considerable scope for her considerable talents. The impassioned romantic scenes between Rita and Ford are scorching in their impact.'

'DON'T TELL ME I'M JUST ONE MORE!' My eyes water, her head spins to one side from the blow as her hair flies to cover her shame. Steve's fingers grip Chris's arm tightly above the elbow as he attempts to pull her off the dance floor to the shocked looks from the other guests. The dance, to the flaunting lyrics of 'I've been kissed before', really had been something. Good enough to get Ford's dander up. Both numbers, this one and the earlier calypso-based 'Trinidad Lady' by Lester Lee and Bob Russell, gave the film an exciting lift. Like everything else about the film, they were another spin-off on the *Gilda* formula, but they worked.

Sherman: 'The day we came to shoot the first number we were already about three weeks into the film. Something electric happened. The shyness and insecurity she showed in her early dramatic scenes had completely disappeared. It was just as though she had been hooked up with wires and somebody turned the switch on. There was now a sauciness, marvellous, intriguing and provocative. She looked out at the audience with a sexy

"come-on" look and this great authority. It was a complete
reversal—a Jekyll & Hyde transformation.' Most of the
ad-campaign was built around Hayworth's dances.

TWO DANCE ROUTINES IN HAYWORTH RETURN...
HAYWORTH AND SULTRY
DANCING BACK ON SCREEN IN *TRINIDAD!*

The Rita Hayworth fans who love to see their favorite star
dance will get their wish in the exciting new film, and her first
scene shows her doing a wild, uninhibited tropical dance to
calypso music. Later in the picture, at a fashionable party, Rita
suddenly steams things up with a sultry, sophisticated dance
which devotees of hot rhythm call 'real gone'. She moves in an
atmosphere of sophisticated, primitive beauty. Wait till you see
Rita Hayworth! Don't miss Rita Hayworth and Glenn Ford in
her new picture, *Affair in Trinidad*.

SLAP! 'DON'T TELL ME I'M JUST ONE MORE!'

As Steve walks away, leaving her isolated in the middle of the
floor, Chris stands frozen, while eyes from the crowd like search-
lights beam over her. She stands, without expression, without
emotion. Silently, ever so softly, a real ache flows from every pore,
collects around her, and becomes a pedestal beneath her feet.
Memory hell! That's why one went to the movies. That's being a
star. And they don't teach *that* at drama school.

The upshot was that Rita was revealed to be, as never before,
the *auteur* of her film. Her presence, in collusion with the camera,
was capable of creating a poetic dream world. It had been so in
her other films, but never so exactingly as in this one where there
was nothing to detract from her. *Affair in Trinidad* was/is valid
only as a Hayworth film. Take her away and you have a crater.
But she is in it, so it works. Hayworth exists on film like a Beatrice
without a Dante, Eurydice with little hope of finding an Orpheus;
Rita without Orson, without Aly—no longer a princess. Just a
woman, on her own but with her one true and constant
lover—the camera.

Did women like her exist before there were movies?

When the film opened in New York on July 30th, there were lines
around the cinema from early in the morning. The ads had done
their work. Rita would do the rest.

CHAPTER VIII

TILL NOW

*When you write your story ... please don't hurt anyone
I've discussed. I'm not angry and I'm not bitter. I've
made mistakes, but I hope I profit by them.*

Rita Hayworth, 1952

I

Because of problems and delays, *Affair in Trinidad*, a modest black
and white studio-shot feature, came in at a steep $1,200,000. Soon
after its release, despite the lukewarm critics, it had more than
made its money and stood to gross a hefty profit. In case the
stockholders hadn't read about it, Hayworth was well and truly
back, still surefire box-office. Even while the film was on its first
rounds, Rita was already busy at work in a Biblical opus, *Salome*,
while Somerset Maugham's *Miss Sadie Thompson* was being made
ready for her. The latter would give her a chance to be something
more than just a sex symbol or Love Goddess. Both films were to
be shot in colour and at some expense, while projects that would
take her well past the mid-'fifties were being prepared with her in
mind. Her position as one of the surviving giants of an industry
now lunging into a shaky new decade was sure—sure as anything
could be.

Hollywood found little fertile soil for survival in the 'fifties.
That was the decade of hoola hoops and H-bombs, of
ankle-length dresses, Korea, and the sleep-walking peace that
came with President Eisenhower. It was the decade of fall-out
shelters in back yards. When, on November 1st, 1952, the first
H-bomb was detonated there was no record of a pin-up having
been pasted on it. This time, when it exploded, a whole island in
the South Pacific was wiped from the face of the earth. It
launched an era of fear—fear of Communism; fear of subversion;
fear of war; fear of annihilation; fear of fear. Now television came
into its own, changing social habits as people stopped going out to

The way the world wanted her. (Coburn/Columbia)

movies and stayed home to eat a TV dinner, eyes glued to their favourite shows. People were going to baseball, football and Europe, but not to the movies. From its peak position as America's fifth largest industry, Hollywood fell overnight out of the top ten. The movie moguls fought back; there was 3-D—lions in your lap and all that—Rita did one of those; they invoked God in an upsurge of biblical epics—she did one of those too. There was Cinemascope and Cinerama for which you had to have eyes on the side of your head. But the only sort of musicals they were making anymore were pre-sold broadway hits—like *Pal Joey*.

Teenagers had graduated from adolescence to become Rebels Without a Cause. Clad in black leather jackets and tight jeans, we sported removable tattoos and spouted an untranslatable beebop lingo understood only by the tousel-haired girls wearing costumes identical to the boys. We no longer cared for the faces or dreams of our elders, finding new idols to mirror our complexities and our disillusionment with the values for which our parents had fought only a few years earlier. Our heroes were Marlon Brando, James Dean and Elvis Presley—men who ruptured the old models, though linked to the Bogarts and John Garfields of an earlier generation. But we had no equivalent heroine. The staunchest female box-office stars of the 'fifties were the last assembly-line women like Doris Day, Susan Hayward, Jane Wyman—hardly the embodiments of establishment unrest. Women's Lib was almost upon them, but the conventionally packaged image of All-American Womanhood had fallen on hard times. More than the men, the female stars had stood for the great consumer society.

True, for a good part of the 'fifties, the system, though lagging, still steamed on. Even as the monolithic studio operations were winding down, they kept on with their work. They created Debbie Reynolds, Liz Taylor, Kim Novak, Grace Kelly, Doris Day and Jayne Mansfield, stars whose popularity was attributable to familiarity—new faces, in old moulds. The exception was Monroe. But for those stars who could still claim that opprobrium so much of what it meant was now trivial or gone.

In 1957 the Russians launched their 'Sputnik' into the skies and the race for the stars was on as well. The days of Hollywood's supremacy seemed to be lost in another century.

Monroe was now the Love Goddess, but even if the New Era wasn't as rosy as the old for Rita, it wasn't for anybody else either. As the symbol of her generation, she retreated from the pinnacle to make way for Monroe but, still a favourite with the public, she

August 16, 1952—Rita and Aly: There is talk of reconciliation. (Associated Press)

remained on the heights. One regrets the broken contracts and the films she never made—like *Barefoot Contessa*, *From Here to Eternity* and *Joseph and His Brethren*, but not because they would have altered her position significantly. One regrets that she wasn't in *Barefoot Contessa*, which Ava Gardner played—with its original story of the Spanish dancer who became a big star and married a European prince—because it turned out to be a good film. We'll never know what *Joseph and His Brethren* might have been—it could have turned out as another clog-eared *Salome*. One regrets the films she didn't make only because it means there are fewer films with her in them. One not only regrets that her marriage to Dick Haymes ended, but that it was also the cause of another contractual split with the studio, keeping her off the screen for several more years at a peak time in her life when beauty and experience had found such a happy unison—as evidenced by her performance in *Miss Sadie Thompson*, and echoed so fervently in *Fire Down Below* and *Pal Joey*.

Considering her career as a whole, Hayworth continued to work as much as any of her contemporaries and more than most of them in the 'sixties, though not in the leading roles. It wasn't just that she was less in demand or that private problems made her difficult to work with, but that the studio system that had supported the stars had fallen apart. There were fewer films and those there were sought their stars from among the faces on the street. Columnists in the 'sixties wrote regretfully of the Rita who took the mother role and second billing to girls of the moment like Claudia Cardinale, Rosanna Schiaffino, and Elke Sommer. Journalists who had once criticised her for disturbing the morals of their young, sighed longingly for the Hayworth of the headlines, and hoped nostalgically for newsworthy squabbles. But Rita was more philosophical than they were. If the part was good, what did the billing matter. She enjoyed her work. When cub reporters tried to provoke her by asking her how she felt when Monroe, Taylor, Novak, Raquel Welch or some other current face got the headlines, she happily told them, relief in her voice, 'They can have the headlines, I've had enough! The only headlines I want are on my acting.'

They still imply she is a cipher, a violin on whom anyone could play, a woman moulded by her husbands, as they interpret her passiveness for weakness. She has survived too long in this highly competitive business for that charge to hold. Marriage to Orson Welles didn't make her a bigger star, nor espousal to Dick Haymes a lesser.

This chapter is a resumé, not a conclusion of the life of an actress and a woman whose career over the years has provided one of the more romantic chapters in the history of the cinema.

In August, Aly returned to her life to try for the hoped-for reconciliation with work already under way on *Salome*. For a brief time their marriage was again an on-and-off thing. The strain she had been living under might offer one explanation for her subdued performance as the biblical striptease princess sixteen years her junior, with whom Rita shared only one point in common—they were both famous dancers. As the bad girl of the Bible, Salome made a good story. As a good girl in Columbia's Technicolor opus, she made a decidedly bad movie. *Affair in Trinidad* works because it is every inch a Hayworth movie. *Salome* stars Hayworth but the plot is tortuous and her character risible.

Originally, the Judean sex kitten danced for Herod in exchange

for John the Baptist's head on a silver platter, but it wouldn't do
to outrage puritan concern and lose audience sympathy for
Hayworth so Rita danced to *save* him. Even so, you can only
tamper with the Bible so much, and the Baptist's head still had to
come off. Her mother Herodias (Judith Anderson) gets the blame.
When the head comes in, interrupting the only good thing in the
film, Salome, still nowhere near the last of her seven veils, screams
in horror, Herodias cackles demonically and Herod (a finely
cured piece of hamming by Charles Laughton) rushes around like
a lunatic, fearing the instant wrath of God.

William Dieterle's direction has rarely been more Teutonic.
There was little here to remind one of the man who created *The
Hunchback of Notre Dame*, with its marvellous mass crowd scenes,
and later the supernatural romance, *Portrait of Jennie*, far more
spiritual than this present endeavour, even though *Salome* took
him and his crew to the Holy Land for some 18,000 feet of
authentic desert exteriors. The effect could have been achieved
cheaper, easier and probably a damn sight better by going out to
Palm Springs. *Salome* may have been 'The first biblical epic to
have shot all its exteriors in the authentic historical locations' but
the camel that carried Rita in the scenes shot in Palm Desert,
California, an old pro called Ruby who had previously carried
Marlene Dietrich and Eddie Cantor, effortlessly stole the show
from the Holy Land. Perhaps Dieterle, who never made a move
without consulting the stars, should have listened to them, for as
the film's author, Jesse Lasky Jnr recalled, 'Dieterle was tortured
by astrological considerations and had gone against the advice of
his consultant astrologer in making this film. He was directing like
a man who knows he's fighting a losing battle. He'd psyched
himself badly.'

The script, reputedly inspired by twenty-six verses in the New
testament, failed to ignite. While a lot of fun can usually be drawn
out of those awful slabs of dialogue Samsons and their Delilahs are
wont to quote at each other, it needs a saint not to stifle a yawn
with lines like 'You Romans are all alike, hearts of marble
chipped out of the same quarry.' And the idea that Rita should be
thrown out of Rome because she's a bad influence on the morals
of the most degenerate empire in the world needs to be taken with
a granary of salt that is not forthcoming. Rita a barbarian?

It's a shame that the film turned out that way, because it
should have been fun. Sets and costumes were good, the all-star
cast impressive, and Hayworth a natural choice. It was a shame

she had not done it when de Mille had first wanted her for the story back in 1940. But without de Mille, who knew what he wanted and what the public wanted and didn't need the stars to guide him, Rita was as uncertain as the script of the motivation behind her character. She was rarely more subdued, which was fine for the spiritual but death for the one thing that might have saved the film—the barbaric and the sexual. Her love scenes with Stewart Granger were so lacking in excitement that they wouldn't have caused a ripple in a Sunday School.

Jesse Lasky Jnr had been de Mille's scriptwriter for many years but, momentarily at odds with his boss, he had brought the idea to Cohn at Columbia. 'Apparently Cohn, who up till that time hadn't been aware that I was already under contract, had wanted something that he thought I could do well as a possible picture for Rita Hayworth, and had said, "Go out and find Jesse Lasky!" So, they looked around and found I was at the studio under a seven-year contract I should never have signed, and working in utter misery saving the worst pictures they ever had. Ben Kahane said, "The man wants to see you." "Mr Cohn?" I whispered. "Thank God I'm saved." I went to see Mr Cohn who was having a massage, being kneaded while sprawled on a marble slab in his office. He said, "I want you to write a de Mille picture for me." I said that nothing would be a greater pleasure. He said they had a little problem—a Rita Hayworth commitment. He'd given her a script which she hated. It was the old story. Now he wanted me to come up with an original story, get an okay from her, and then do a screenplay. It had to be fast. He needed a story by Monday and this was Friday! He said, "Go get a damn good idea. Your contract with the studio is seven fucking years. You go take your ass off and get an idea." So I went home and tried to remember all the ideas I had while I was with de Mille, and came up with *Salome*. I sat down, read everything I could on her, dug back into Josephus, found nobody had said she was good or bad, which gave me a new angle, and went in with a fifty-page treatment on Monday. What was de Millian in the original was the tremendous conflict in every scene, and a suspended image, a snake under every bed. Not much character but a lot of visual suspense.

'I gave it to Cohn. He told me to go to my office and wait by the telephone. Soon enough, Rita Hayworth was in his office, and two hours later I was called back in. There was a funny little man sitting in one corner with a hat over his eye, while Harry Cohn was enormous behind his desk with a cigar that looked like a deadly weapon. No sight of Rita. For the first time since we met he said very politely, "Sit down, Jesse. I read it and we're going to do it. It's exactly right. Rita liked it," and thank you very much. I was ready to write the screenplay immediately, and told him how excited I was by the greatness of the relationship between father, daughter and wife. He said, "I'm afraid not, Jesse. You see, I not only have a commitment to Rita, I also have a commitment to Harry Kleiner." And, pointing to the man in the corner, he said, "Harry, meet Jesse." I protested that it was my story. He said, "Read your contract."

'I walked out blind with rage, and so miserable. My revenge came when the movie came out. I went to the preview and thought it was a bloody horrible film. Unfortunately my name was on it as original story writer. At the point in the picture when they bring in John the Baptist's head, someone in the balcony shouted, "Dig that crazy dessert." There was a howl and the rest of the film was gone. *Salome* didn't have the spectacle, the dash, the sweep, the highs and lows that you get in a de Mille picture.'

The genuine saving graces were the sets and costumes—especially those Jean Louis created for Rita. Some of these created their own problems, but he overcame them with Gallic finesse. To avoid the need for a bra or lift, the straps of which would have shown, and yet give the illusion of youthfully firm bare flesh beneath the multi-coloured semi-transparent veils, he created a plastic body stocking to give an illusion of nudity, while retaining the shape for which Hayworth was famous.

Soon after, when Marlene Dietrich came to Jean Louis as a private client, the stocking became part of her standard stage wardrobe as audiences marvelled at the way she kept her figure.

The last word on the film belongs to my local radio station announcer who confused the Judean Princess with a delicatessen. After finishing the evening news, he launched into the adverts, and entreated us to 'Go and see Rita Hayworth's SALAMI ... it'll take your breath away!'

After her work was completed, Rita joined Aly in Paris for an attempt at a reconciliation. Their private life had never been out of the news and it returned to the front pages when Aly arrived in the middle of August loaded down with presents for Yasmin and Rebecca. It was important that something be worked out between them, if only because Rita's daughter was also fourth in line to the Aga's wealth and position and thus an object of keen interest to his millions of followers. Aly's cause was inadvertently aided in a dramatic manner when Yasmin swallowed some sleeping pills thinking they were sweets and had to be rushed to the hospital. Their distress as they waited and worried and his concern temporarily brought them closer than they had been for a long time. When he left to return to Paris, Rita agreed to follow as soon as her work was finished. When her boat steamed into Le Havre this time she was met by Aly's car and driven straight to his house on the edge of the Bois de Boulogne. But any hopes of a quiet family life by a fireside were short-lived. Rita's feelings about Aly's friends, many of whom she considered to be hangers-on sponging on his generosity, had been pointed enough for Aly to have realised it would create problems all over again. She said, 'I don't want to live in a house where there are eighty friends of all kinds coming and going, and I don't want to be photographed in the salons of Paris or at dinner in big restaurants.' Other events, including strong rumours of an affair Aly was having with another Hollywood film star, spurred Rita's last decision. She moved to the Hotel Lancaster and announced through her Paris representative: 'I am bored with Aly's entourage.'

Despite the pressure, she kept her true feelings bottled up when questioned at Madrid airport where she had flown for a visit before going back to Hollywood. She smiled as photographers snapped her, denied rumours of a romance with the singer Robert Savage and spurred further speculations as guest of Spain's most eligible bachelor, bullfighter Luis Dominguin. Police took precautions to avert demonstrations by Catholic activists to protest against what they regarded as 'immoral conduct' involved in 'Miss Hayworth's marital affairs with Prince Aly Khan'.

Back in Hollywood she went ahead with her plans for a divorce, while Aly's romance with actress Gene Tierney started to make headlines.

On January 27th, 1953, the Nevada courts granted her a divorce on the grounds of 'mental cruelty'. Rita asked nothing for herself, only for her daughter. The court awarded $48,000 a year against Aly for Yasmin's upkeep, and custody of the daughter to the mother. The court's decision concerning Yasmin became the subject of a long legal discussion.

Back in Hollywood, Rita was determined to show a happy face as she went out on dates with actors Kirk Douglas, Victor

It took all of photographer Bob Coburn's skill and Rita's renown to sell *Salome,* with advance promotion like this. Note area between legs which the Hays office returned and marked, 'Retouch as indicated.' (Coburn/Columbia)

Mature and old friends. Even occasional dates with singer Dick Haymes, who had been working at Columbia while she was making *Salome* and had usually shared a drink with her in producer Jonie Taps's office at the end of a long day's rehearsal, had failed to stir more than a passing comment. The affair, when it started to make headlines, was to come as a surprise to even the most prying Hollywood snoop. Meanwhile, pre-production on *Miss Sadie Thompson* was under way, and with no romantic complications looming, she devoted herself to preparing for the part that had already challenged Gloria Swanson and Joan Crawford. For the first time in her long career she had a role of substance, the kind she had long hoped for. She undertook the challenge with enthusiasm, fully aware of what her success as Sadie, the part that had been a legend on Broadway, could mean to her future as a sex symbol in transition to a new phase.

The role was significant in Rita's career. While fitting her like a glove and satisfying those who looked to Hayworth for sex, it rounded out a new image, eclipsing in the process the former one of youthful conqueror. It played up those qualities already apparent since *Affair in Trinidad* and would cling to the roles she played for the rest of the decade—still the star but off the pedestal. While contemporaries like Ava and Lana and Betty Grable continued to play star parts in which age and experience were not visibly noticeable (even in her mother roles, Lana pursued her star image) Rita was noticeably turning into a character goddess—almost a contradiction in terms. Before, she would have been driven to her death by the hand of Fate; now it was problems with passports, and the sheer weight of life dragging her down. There's no glamour to be found in that. Pathos and sympathy in the audience arose as much from her acting as from deliberate casting to incite memories of what she had been. When all the parts are as good as Sadie Thompson, that can be an advantage, but otherwise it creates the uncomfortable sensation that we are asked to laugh at those we love. True, *Pal Joey* gave us a last look at the musical, omnipotent Hayworth of *Cover Girl*—even if the role was that of the other woman who stands by while hardly juvenile Joey goes off with a younger rival; but she had numbers that showed such *élan* and *ésprit* that Joey's choice was hard to grasp. With that exception, Rita's films from there on featured her as a loser.

Apart from inserting several lively tunes by Lester Lee and Ned Washington and a torrid dance by Rita to one of them, shifting the fanatical reformer from a missionary to an influential church leader, changing the period to post-World War II and watering down the sex-based Freudian connotations, the story, or what remains of it, is the familiar one of the gal with a bad reputation stranded on a tropical island when the ship she is taking to New Caledonia is quarantined. While a happy sight for the Marines stationed there, she immediately arouses the wrath of the reformer (Jose Ferrer), a fanatic who sees evil in people having a good time. Recognising Sadie as an entertainer in an infamous Honolulu clip joint he had forced the authorities to close, he denounces her as a prostitute and orders the local police to deport her. Sadie at first fights back, then succumbs to his zealous bible-thumping influence and repents. Her decision to take her punishment by going back to the States and, ostensibly, prison, is blasted when the reformer rapes her, then commits suicide having

found the evil he sees in others strongest in himself. Sadie returns
to her old ways, and marries the marine sergeant (Aldo Ray) who
loves her.

The studio initially shot the film in 3-D but except for its
première New York engagement they released it in the normal
ratio.

Of the three filmed versions, including Swanson's
gutsy leathery rendition and Crawford's intriguing but ultimately
unappealing stylised playing, Hayworth's comes across as the
warmest, the most human; the Sadie who carries an
emotion-tugging conviction when she pleads with Davidson not to
send her back to 'Frisco. She's real, she has range, she evokes
compassion. They may have toned down the character and the
script—Davidson still calls her a harlot and a prostitute, but you
are meant to think that at heart she is only a blowsy good-time
girl and not the hardened two-bitter of the original,—but you can
see what Davidson feared when she lets rip. They never did know
how to censor Hayworth when she really danced. 'The Heat is
On' is a moment of undiluted eroticism arising out of this period
of repression. She sweats!—prickly beads of perspiration cluster on
her face and bare arms like hot pearls, whipping up the Marines
to a steaming frenzy that finds a sympathetic outlet in the
overflowing foam from their beer bottles—but that said it all.
While the streaming rain shadows outside the hot little room
spread like tattoos across the walls and faces to emphasise the
claustrophobic atmosphere so soon to build up to Davidson's
moral collapse and suicide, Hayworth shakes up a storm. If that's
how she danced when Davidson first saw her in Honolulu, it's
understandable why he should have been so disturbed. This is
Maugham's Sadie, too, the Sadie of his short story, *Rain*, from
which everything sprang.

Hollywood, still recovering from its own witch-hunts and
reminded of them by the spectacle of continued investigations that
made gripping TV viewing, was careful not to offend the
watchdogs of morality; thus it wasn't altogether the screenwriter's
fault that the treatment of Maugham's sex, sin and redemption
story was a bowdlerised and watered-down version of the original.
It didn't help Jose Ferrer much that that religious zealot, the
Reverend Davidson, came out of the wash as an up-tight reformer
whose ire seemed to arise more from being kept awake at nights
by Sadie's noisy gramophone and her beer-swilling companions
than by a divine call to seek out sin wherever he found it. The

Reverend Davidson is one of those parts that tends to bring forth exaggerated playing in actors, but the collar gives him a moral authority and a standing in society that lends rich Freudian overtones to his single-minded pursuance of a good-time girl. Ferrer, who had accepted the role against his own inclinations but on the advice of his agent to offset any damage after he had been hauled up in front of the House of Un-American Activities shortly after winning his Oscar back in 1951, agreed.

'I had been grilled and cross-examined by Ward Bond and other Hollywood "heroes" who decided I was all right. But Hedda Hopper, one of the great "patriots" of her day, was still fighting a rear-guard action against me. So when my agent said Rita is Columbia's hottest star and if Harry Cohn will put you into a picture with her, it would dispel any lingering hesitation anyone else might have about hiring you. I accepted the job, on that crass, opportunistic basis.

'The trouble with the script was that in those days they didn't dare call a spade a spade. All the things in the story thought to give any offence were quietly eliminated. They made the Reverend Davidson, Mr Davidson, so that no religious group would be able to say "How dare you" and create trouble—although it was hardly a new story. So they had to write in lines like "You're no priest or missionary. You try to act like one but the collar won't fit!"'

The critics, while pointing up the incongruities in the script, almost unanimously praised Rita's performance and even Academy Award winner Jose Ferrer freely conceded that her performance carried the film. No less an authority than notorious misogynist, author Somerset Maugham, thought her the best of his Sadies. Yet it failed to ignite at the box-office the way her previous films had. As far as Cohn was concerned it proved his point. He had wrangled with Rita even before filming began about the downbeat appearance she had adopted for the role against his wishes for a glamorous sinner whose past would be implied in her wardrobe but not in her face. He felt that the public wouldn't go for so dramatic a change in their idol. Possibly the new sorry headlines that involved her private life also influenced public opinion to some degree.

The film opened in New York on December 11th. But whatever benefits Rita might have derived from proving herself to the critics' satisfaction—now that they were no longer blinded by the packaging—as a remarkably subtle screen actress, were overshadowed by the new turn in her private life. She had married singer Dick Haymes in a private room at the Sands Hotel in Las Vegas, on September 24th. Her two daughters attended as brides-maids and a battery of newsreel cameras and photographers recorded the event for posterity. The marriage came as the climax to increasingly unfavourable publicity for Haymes (and to Rita for her decision to stick by him).

An in-depth article that appeared in *Photoplay* several years later when Rita's romance with producer Jim Hill was attracting attention, stated an opinion from which few who knew Rita would have dissented: 'If there was one marriage that was pre-destined to failure before the ink was dry, it was the marriage to singer Dick Haymes.' It became apparent soon after three-times married Haymes arrived in Honolulu, ostensibly to give a concert in Waikiki—and told the press, with Rita at his side, 'she is the only woman I have ever loved'—that the auguries were not good. Front office pressure to drop Haymes failed.

In 1948, blond boy-next-door Dick Haymes had been the hottest singer in Hollywood—a box-office draw in musicals like *State Fair*, *Up in Central Park* and others, but as in the case of another crooner his career had soured soon after. When he met Rita he was featured in a Columbia programmer, *Cruising Down The River*. With alimony payments to two ex-wives piling up, and just separated from his current wife, Nora Eddington Flynn, he was almost bankrupt. The same day as his third divorce came through he married Rita. One month later he was arrested for being behind in his alimony payments to his second wife, actress Joanne Dru. A few days later a Deputy Marshal handed him a $1,071.37 bill from a men's clothing store. The Internal Revenue attacked his earnings. A garage got in on the act by suing him for an eighty dollar petrol bill.

On top of everything else, the U.S. Government attempted to deport him because of a waiver he had signed declaring himself an Argentinian citizen (though of American parents). In effect this meant that he had been free from military service during World War II when, with the field clear of leading men, his career had shot forward. It took two years before the Government dropped its case. Until his troubles were settled, Rita, who could not have foreseen the cost to her career or her pocketbook, stuck by him. it may have been that she felt partly responsible for some of his troubles. He had left the U.S. to join her in Hawaii, then not yet a state of the Union, and laid himself open to the U.S. Department of Immigration's decision to make him the subject of a test case of the newly adopted McCarren Act. This decreed that any alien working in the U.S. who left the country without state permission would be deported to their country of origin.

While the case was going to the Supreme Court, Haymes was allowed back on a loophole based on Hawaii's position as a U.S. possession. Even before the case came up, his marriage to Rita, a U.S. citizen, re-entitled him to legal residency even were the court decision to go against him.

Rita was again under increasing censure. She was losing the sympathy that had built up for her when Aly's romance with Gene Tierney, even before the divorce, made it apparent that Rita was the innocent party. It must indeed have been galling to realise that, while her last film had to tone down the Reverend Davidson so that no religious bodies could take offence, there was no such discretion when it came to life. A broad spectrum of religious leaders of all denominations, when asked for their comments on the marriage, rose to the cue with true Old Testament zeal. Under the guise of moral outrage at the effect this marriage would have on filmstruck youth, the criticism keyed itself to the hypocritical mood of an era that was finding itself on a quicksand of changing values. Of course Hayworth wasn't the only one to attract moral censure: Monroe was attacked for daring to paint her lips a bright red and wear low-cut dresses, Brando for wearing leather jackets. Even worse hypocrisy pursued Lana Turner in the tragic death of her lover that climaxed with her as the star of a three-ring courtroom drama. Anyone who waxes nostalgic about the 'fifties must have slept through them.

The couple arrived for a stay in New York that ended up with them besieged in their thirteenth-floor suite of the Madison Hotel, by two Deputy Sheriffs seeking the arrest of Haymes on a civil writ for debt obtained by Haymes's second wife who claimed he owed her more than $50,000 under a property settlement agreed back in 1949.

Haymes spoke to the Sheriffs through the locked door, refusing to come out until he could see his lawyer. The Sheriffs stood guard in the corridor should he change his mind. Also there, in case he could help, was Hayworth's lawyer, Bartley Crum, but the couple were unable to let him in in case the Sheriffs got in first.

They had no food sent in until one of the Sheriffs telephoned Haymes promising him 'immunity' while lunch was delivered.

April 27, 1954: Rita and Dick Haymes carrying her daughter Yasmin, leaving White Plains.

Though Haymes was broke he was unwilling to go into bankruptcy, preferring to pay his debts if and when he could. Thirty-six hours later, after the couple had come to an understanding with Miss Dru by phone, the siege was lifted. Rita was heard to wryly comment, 'It's going to be awfully nice to see a clear, unobstructed corridor.'

Meanwhile, on the strength of the marriage and Rita's agreement to star as Potiphar's wife in another biblical film, *Joseph and His Brethren*, with a script by Clifford Odets, to be produced by Louis B. Mayer as his first independent production for Columbia after leaving M.G.M., Harry Cohn advanced Dick Haymes $50,000 to help him settle some of his bills.

The next débâcle broke in the press in April, soon after Aly had flown into America to settle the situation of Yasmin's upbringing and financial arrangements, at the same time using the opportunity to stay with Gene Tierney, who added to the convolutions

by being in the midst of a movie co-starring her with Rita's one
time fiancé, Victor Mature. Instead of meeting Aly's lawyers in
Bartley Crum's office as agreed, she and Haymes made a badly
timed decision and suddenly left for Key West, Florida on April
7th, without informing even her own lawyers. While this incon-
venienced the lawyers, some of whom had flown over from Paris
for this meeting, their feelings could be soothed by their fees. Far
worse were the repercussions the ill-fated move were to have on
Rita who awoke to find herself smeared across the nations' front
pages accused of child neglect. She had left her daughters, aged
four and eight, in a home she had rented in White Plains with a
housekeeper to look after them. When one of the girls caught a slight
virus infection, the woman, unable to reach Rita, panicked and
phoned the newspapers. The story was too good for the papers to
hold until the facts could be checked with the mother. A vicious
storm broke over Rita's head as they raked over her past and
reported that the children had been left to roam loose, unprotected
and unwashed. She flew into New York to a blaze of flash bulbs
only to find that her daughters had been placed under protective
custody on charges hurriedly filed by the Society for the Prevention
of Cruelty to Children. Rita was visibly shocked and upset. The
charges proved to be unfounded. Both fathers called them utter
nonsense, as anyone who knew Rita's concern about her daughters
would testify, and both of them backed her in court with deposi-
tions stating that she was, on the contrary, a very good mother
indeed. Even so, the emotional battering of the last few months
was wearing her down. Things only got worse. A batch of letters
from a man who turned out to be a crank, threatening to kidnap
or maim Yasmin unless Rita returned to Aly and the Moslem
faith, created new fears and more unwelcome headlines. For Rita,
memories of a near-successful attempt to kidnap Rebecca while
living on the Riviera with Aly and another, terror-filled night in
Paris when she and Aly were furiously chased by would be kid-
nappers in the early morning hours, their cars careering around
the deserted Arc de Triomphe at ninety miles an hour, still strong
in her memory, these were nightmare times. Her paranoid fear of
cars dates from that time. After the man had been tracked down,
she suffered a nervous collapse, requiring hospitalisation.

Haymes's problems, too, were not over. He awaited the outcome of the deportation hearings at Lake Tahoe with Rita and at
the same time his two previous wives were swearing out warrants
for his arrest for non-payment of alimony.

Back in Hollywood to begin work on *Joseph and His Brethren*
Rita and he rented an apartment in Westwood. Haymes now set
about advising Rita on her career, soon dictating not only the
style of her hair, costumes and film roles, but suggesting that he
produce and co-star with her in *Joseph*. This created new problems. He had already persuaded her to dissolve her Beckworth
Corporation through which her films were made under exclusive
contract to Columbia, and to form a new producing company,
Crystal Bay Productions, with himself in charge.

So far the projects had gone little further than a few
pre-production meetings. Clifford Odets was still working on the
screenplay, though the construction of sets and some costumes for
her part were under way.*

Lee J. Cobb had been signed as Potiphar, but there were
difficulties in finding an actor to play Joseph. Rita, who shot tests
with almost every elligible young man in town recalled the endless
days of strange faces scrubbing the marble floor as she entered
saying, 'How hot the Egyptian sun is today.' She cracked up one
day when having said her line, she looked down and found a
highly incongruous Jack Lemmon energetically scrubbing away.

Neither Louis B. Mayer whose first independent project this
was meant to be now that he was no longer at M.G.M., nor Cohn
could stomach Haymes as Joseph, thus further postponing the
stipulated date of shooting. As a result, Rita filed a damage suit,
claiming $214,284 against Columbia for not fulfilling their con-
tractual obligation and won an out-of-court victory. Columbia
counteracted with a suit of their own, claiming the same amount
and releasing details of her contract to the press. They added that,
on the assumption that she would make the picture, the studio
had lent her husband $50,000 and that it was agreed she would
pay the money back at the rate of $14,000 a year.

Cohn, who had been looking for a replacement for Rita should
she again decide to take a leave of absence, and having failed with
several Hayworth look-alikes now thought he had the perfect bet,
a dark-haired Polish girl he had seen modelling refrigerators on
television. Her figure was trimmed to svelte proportions and her

---

*Clifford Odets, one of America's leading playwrights, had a great regard which he
expressed both publicly and privately for Rita, whom he considered one of the most
under-rated actresses in films. Several years later, after she had left Columbia, he wrote a
screenplay for her which he also directed—*The Story on Page One* (1959), a trial drama
concentrating on a wife accused of plotting her husband's murder. To make it she returned
to Twentieth Century Fox, almost twenty-five years to the day after she first began her film
career at that studio, and to one of her finest performances.

hair colour changed to platinum. The public was informed that lavendar was her favourite colour. True, after seeing one of her screen tests, Cohn's publicity manager, when asked for his opinion, told his boss, 'Harry, you've achieved the impossible. You've just discovered a girl who can become the last of the great silent screen stars.' Cohn gave him ten minutes to get his ass off the lot. When the story got back to Rita she said, 'Some people have all the luck.' But Cohn had chosen right. The new girl became Kim Novak.

Joseph was abandoned; so was Haymes. Travelling as Mrs Philsbury, and looking like a woman loaded with cares, Rita boarded the Santa Fe Super-chief with Yasmin and Rebecca, en route to New York. Caught by the press in Chicago, she admitted that she had separated from Haymes. She filed for a Reno divorce and departed for Paris with the children so Yasmin could see her father. She was granted an *in absentia* divorce on December 13th, 1955. As with all her other marriages, Rita has added nothing about Haymes that might denigrate his public image, though it cost her a great deal and left her with a lot of bills to pay—not least the $50,000 Columbia had loaned Haymes on her cognisance. Grounds for divorce were 'extreme cruelty, entirely mental in nature'.

II

So here she was, alone, unemployed, with another failure to try to block out and no one to turn to for understanding. She needed to rest, to gather her strength. For a time she holed up, keeping to herself, living in Europe with a half-formed idea of moving there for good, especially to Spain, where she always felt so much at home. Her dates were few, and quiet, attracting no attention since romance played no part in them. But she still had a contract for two more pictures to be released by Columbia before her commitment to her studio would be finished. So, when director Robert Parrish called to offer her a role in his new film which would be part of her Columbia deal, she listened. She had been off the screen for nearly four years. Her come-back created a stir, but no longer the excitement there had been. Now Marilyn Monroe's arrival in England to make *The Prince and the Showgirl* with Sir Laurence Olivier had the press occupied.

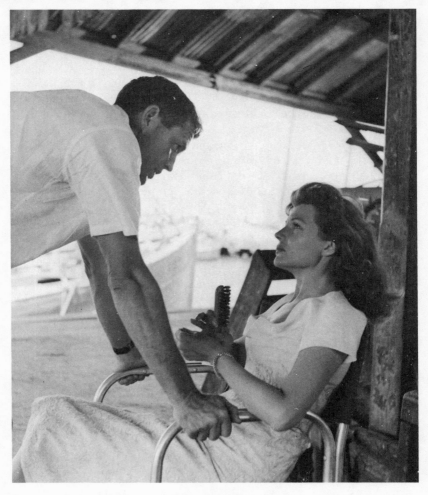

Going over lines with director Robert Parrish on location in Trinidad before it's time to get back on the set of *Fire Down Below* after another lengthy absence from the screen. 1957. (Columbia)

Fire Down Below should have been a good film. It came from a screenplay by novelist Irwin Shaw. It was his idea to book Rita Hayworth after they had failed to get Ava Gardner for the part. Parrish, who had begun his career at Columbia as a very successful editor (*All the King's Men*, etc.), eventually becoming a director, hadn't known Rita then except to pass her in the corridor. 'She had a unique beauty, just the structure of her face alone was exciting to look at.' He had heard the rumour, among others, that Cohn detested Haymes so much that he was trying to get him into a jam so he could break up the marriage. But now that Parrish met her he was as surprised as people always were to realise how little she was like the woman she was meant to be, and both he and his wife took her very much to heart. The prospect of working with her excited him. Except for the leading lady the film was already cast with Bob Mitchum and Jack Lemmon, when Parrish, now living and working in London, went to Paris to see her. They had some trouble contacting her at first. Not even the studio knew where she was, but a mutual friend, humorist Art Buchwald, found her address for him.

Parrish: 'She was staying at the Georges V and agreed to play the part after seeing the script if I could clear it with the studio because she was still under contract to Columbia. I phoned Harry Cohn because he always took an interest in her work, and asked him if we could have Rita. Cohn asked "Would she be any good in it?" I said, "Yes, or I wouldn't ask her."

' "How does she look?"

' "Great."

' "Okay! We'll work out a deal."

'That was it. The girl's role was not a star one in the usual sense. It was a character part, but like the others in the film, Bob Mitchum and Jack Lemmon, she'd liked Irwin Shaw's script and wanted very much to work with a good writer. I think another reason the film appealed to her was that I came to her at a time of personal crisis in her life and the film gave her a chance to work on an island for a couple of months, secluded and away from her personal problems in Paris. They must have weighed pretty heavy upon her. I can recall one time she was sitting on the beach with a bag of mail that had been forwarded to her. She got lots of mail but never opened any. She sat there with all those letters, tearing them all up, unopened, and let them float away. Bob said to her, "Hell, it might be cheques." "I know," she said, "but there's bound to be more trouble than money."

'All three of us, Bob, Jack and myself, adored her. We took care of her, joked with her, understood her. When she got married to Jim Hill she wanted Mitchum, Lemmon and me to be at the wedding.*

'We spent about eight weeks in Trinidad and had a crew of about eighty people working with us. We fell a bit behind

---

*The camaraderie that arose between Hayworth and Mitchum was renewed when they co-starred opposite each other in her last film to date, *The Wrath of God*, a Western shot in Mexico.

schedule out there. Then Cohn sent a man who had been on all of Rita's films and was sort of a spy for Cohn. He reported back to him on what was going on, except everybody knew what he was doing. I was afraid of what Rita might feel, but when she saw him she just said, "I wondered when you were coming on this picture."

'Everything was fine out in Tobago, but when we got back to London for interiors we had some trouble. It wasn't anything to do with us; she absolutely trusted Shaw, and Mitchum and me and literally did anything I asked her to do. But there were others involved, and there wasn't the same sort of rapport with them. We were in London and there was a close-up to do of Rita—she was playing a woman over the hill but still beautiful and I wanted a beautiful close-up. The cameraman was lighting it on her stand-in while we thought Rita was in her dressing room or something, but she was quietly sitting on the set where nobody would notice her. One of the producers came by and saw the set-up, and said, "Why the hell are you taking so long? No matter how long you take, she ain't gonna look any younger." Well, Rita overheard this exchange and walked off in tears. From this moment on she began to act like a star, and I can't say that I blamed her for it.'

Her confidence in Parrish was marked by her performance. Her face was no longer that of a girl or a Love Goddess, but revealed a mature, experienced woman, life mirrored on it with telling grace. It mightn't be what one expected but it was no less attractive for being no longer a packaged, glittering façade. And there was a quiet, adult chemistry that smouldered in her clashes with Mitchum—even while some of the lines, spoken with haunting conviction, collided with all the dreams attached to the image. Even the dance that rekindled the old fires in our memories failed to alter the final impression. It was the last of a purely erotic exploitable nature Rita would ever do and the fire lit and the flames shot high. She joins a carnival crowd during a stop-over in Trinidad and a frenetic limbo suddenly turns into a hedonistic solo with its sweaty eroticism trumped by the spontaneous removal of her high heel slippers—a gesture with all the erotic force of a stripper's last veil.

But something was wrong with the film that was finally released, and it was all the sadder because it needn't have turned out that way. What was, in Shaw's original script, an unusual approach to the familiar situation of three lone outsiders coming

Rita relaxes on the beach with friend and co-star Robert Mitchum between takes for *Fire Down Below*. (Columbia)

to terms with themselves, ends up as the dreariest of trudges through tropical backwaters, a re-hash of those old Hayworth clichés. Originally, it started with the doctor being called to a wrecked and burning ship in the hold of which lies a trapped Jack Lemmon. Lemmon refuses to say who he is or what he's doing there. The doctor examines his possessions and discovers a photograph. One of the other characters tells the story ... cue for flashback. We go through the whole of the Lemmon/Hayworth/Mitchum triangle and come back to the present, when Mitchum rescues Lemmon (now his deadly enemy) but retains the girl. The flashback format meant that suspense was maintained all through the script— Would Lemmon escape? Why was he there? Who'd get the girl? etc. That's the way it should have been.

Parrish cut the film in London then sent it to Columbia where they completely re-cut it. The flashback format was dispensed with, the script was slashed, the film re-edited to take place in chronological order and a special scene inserted wherein one of

It's the photographer's art that brings together the three stars for this still. Coburn shot them separately because Sinatra never had time to pose for posters when the two actresses were available. (Coburn/Columbia)

the minor characters receives a letter from Lemmon and his voice reads it over aloud to explain why Lemmon is on the ship. This scene, shot later, was so badly recorded that the audience couldn't hear the plot point. Rita now appeared almost at once with little dramatic justification as she stands on the dock with a packed suitcase, a cocktail dress, nowhere to go and a look of *déjà-vu*. Naturally, promoted as a Hayworth comeback, the hopes shared by the principals for an adult story suffered as the publicity insisted, yet again, in comparisons with *Gilda*.

In that context, a line like Mitchum's after the first passionless kiss is exchanged, 'I am proud: I don't make love to the dead,' and Hayworth's to Lemmon about herself, 'I am no good to you, no good to anyone, armies have marched over me,' stirred audiences to laughter. And I can still recall the hot anger I felt when I saw the film on its saturation release. Didn't they care? But of course they were right. To carry off a moment like that called for the daring of youth, not the voice of experience.

Columbia was preparing *Pal Joey*, the Rodgers and Hart musical originally bought for Rita when she would have played the young mouse Joey settles for against his better (opportunistic) nature instead of the rich society dame who could afford to keep him in the luxury he so obviously prefers. Gene Kelly, who had created the role and was originally to have played it in films, was no longer considered box-office for a starring role in an expensive production. Cohn wanted Brando, but Sinatra, who

July 17, 1957—Hermes Pan's choreography for Rita's number 'Bewitched, Bothered and Bewildered' was an enchanting swan-song to her spectacular song and dance career. (Cronenweth/Columbia)

had a commitment with the studio and who had previously lost out to Brando for *On The Waterfront*, demanded the part. Kim Novak, the studio's rising Golden Girl, played the mouse.

The studio had originally considered Dietrich and then Mae West for the role of Vera Simpson, who began her rise to the queen of Nob Hill as a burlesque house queen known as 'Vanessa the Undresser'. Because Cohn had had a row with Dietrich over a dress and Mae West refused to play a role in which she'd lose the man to anyone, of any age, the part was still uncast. It came as a surprise to the industry when it was offered to Hayworth. She, after all, was younger than Sinatra and, as the studio's reigning queen, might justifiably have felt insulted to lose the hero to the new girl deliberately groomed to take her place. But people were even more surprised to hear Rita had accepted and they were disappointed to find that the expected fireworks between the stars were never forthcoming. If Rita disapproved of Kim or felt in any way slighted by the preferential treatment given to her younger rival, she never commented on it—her attitude came as no surprise to old friends. Rita was never insecure when it came to competing with another woman. For Hayworth the role was a way out. In the event, she nearly walked off with the film as well.

It was to be her last musical, her last film at her old *alma mater*, her last encounter with Cohn and the last time she played a role which in every way was that of RITA·HAYWORTH—MOVIE STAR. She lost Sinatra but got top billing, even though he was then one of the top box-office stars in the country. When asked why he conceded the billing, Sinatra, who had not always behaved with grace during production, told newsmen, 'To me, Hayworth is Columbia. They may have made her a star, but she gave them class.'

During the shooting of her big solo, 'Bewitched, Bothered and Bewildered', Harry Cohn was seen by Antonia Morales standing silently on the edge of the set from where he looked, she thought, longingly at the woman he had had under contract for twenty years but had never owned. Rita didn't see him.

When she returned to work there several years later, as the only woman in a multi-million-dollar production, *They Came to Cordura*, it was as a freelance artist. Things had changed. Cohn, the last of the moguls, was dead. At his funeral attended by a *Who's Who* of Hollywood notables—some of his friends and many of his foes— Rita was a noticeable exception. But that could have been as much due to her pathological fear of death as from her dislike of the man.

Pal Joey is not the classic film musical it should have been— but it was a smash and a fitting farewell to the place that had been her home for so long.

III

Given the choice, Rita has always preferred to rely on a man—to advise her, to look after her, to love her. Someone older. Someone wiser. Where her heart was involved, she had only grown older. She married soon after *Pal Joey* the man she had met while making it, producer Jim Hill, long one of Hollywood's most eligible bachelors and two years her senior. Hill, a quiet, cultured, social man, was co-producer in the firm Hecht-Hill-Lancaster, for whose thriving company she made her freelance debut heading an all-star cast in *Separate Tables*. The marriage, though filled with new hope, ended in another divorce. She has never remarried. Asked about her marriages she said, 'I didn't want five husbands but that's how it ended up.' When asked how many husbands a career woman should have she demonstrated the dry wit that usually marked her answers to personal questions, 'Six, but then seventeen has always been my lucky number.'

Since her last marriage, there have been other men in her life, some more serious than others like her affair with the actor Gary Merrill with whom she came back into the headlines when their open-air bouts in Rome became public, but no marriages. One of her friends put it, 'When she's in love, she's like a little girl —she makes herself pretty, sits by the phone and waits. Rita is a girl who will always need a man to love her, and she'll always look.'

Her daughters have grown into women with lives of their own. Having been involved in enough headlines as children they do not seem to have sought them out as adults by seeking careers in their mother's profession. While it's naïve, given their parents, to expect them to be left completely alone, they have dealt with their heritage in a dignified, adult manner. Rebecca Welles who in many ways has had the worst of it, has married; her sister Yasmin Khan, who has inherited part of her grandfather's wealth and much of her mother's looks, quietly studies classical singing in New York where she lives. Rita is fiercely proud of both of them. She bristles like an outraged lioness when anyone attempts to gossip about them, as one dignified hostess learnt to her cost, her face drenched in a good chablis from Rita's glass, for suggesting how easy things must be for Yasmin, by being related to the Aga Khan.

In the 'sixties the past first became passé, then camp, then

Rita adjusts her own make-up on the set of *I, Bastardi,* an Italian quickie released in the U.S. as *Sons of Satan* in June, 1969. (Warner Brothers)

fashionable. More recently it has grown harmless and respectable. Colleges now offer courses in film history; books by authors who probe into every aspect of Hollywood, its myths and myth-makers, proliferate. Old idols re-emerge in huge posters and blow-ups, coathangers, T-shirts and pillows, as modern symbols and artefacts. *Gilda* is a cult film. Today's young models and movie stars strive for that 'forties Hayworth look, but the original remains inimitable.

The past years she has lived too much on her own. It's not the way she planned it but that's how things have worked out. Producers still wanted her: There was talk of various stage débuts— Garbo's role in a musical version of *Grand Hotel;* a straight play with actor Gary Merrill; a musical based on *All about Eve,* that would have her taking over the Margo Channing role from Lauren Bacall—but her lack of self confidence was a handicap she could no longer overcome and she got no further than rehearsals. Men still wanted to love the Love Goddess—In that respect she had grown more wary. If most of the films she made in the last years are negligible, almost forgettable, hardly comparable to the pictures of her heyday, Rita continuously brought a touch of distinction to

Rita with her last husband, producer James Hill, on the set of their troubled co-production, *The Happy Thieves,* where their marriage was going through its final crisis in 1961. (United Artists)

her work, belying reports of problems during shooting, for she is one of those the camera loves. Neither age, bouts with the bottle, ill health or the wrong lovers can take that away from her. Her name still kindles that excitement. The English actor Peter McEnery who was to have worked with her on the film which illness and insecurity prevented her from finishing, told me an incident that occurred on her first day before the camera. Word had gotten around and the area was crowded with grips, technicians, electricians and actors from other sets. When she walked on the sound stage they looked, then they applauded. It was a token of respect from her peers who understood as few others can, that when the camera's eye turns to focus on her, it mirrors one who could say without flinching, 'I did it myself.'

Rita on the tennis court of the Beverly Wilshire Hotel. (De Wan Studios)

A happy time with growing daughters: Rita at the graduation of her eldest daughter Rebecca. On the right is her sister, fourteen-year-old Princess Yasmin (June 9, 1964). (Associated Press)

A MEETING

Somewhere between Raymond Chandler, Nathanael West, F. Scott
Fitzgerald and the fan magazines lies the true city of Los Angeles.
It veers between a Chandleresque cluster of little streets with low,
stuccoed, hacienda-style houses in downtown Los Angeles, and the
landmark nightclubs like Ciro's, the Brown Derby, and the Château
Marmont hotel. To most people Los Angeles is a city dominated by
Sunset Boulevard while the homes of the stars in high-priced Brentwood, Bel-Air, and Beverly Hills appear one-dimensional like studio
prop cut-outs on back lots. Within its precincts every conceivable
architectural style, short of a cave dwelling, is represented.

Los Angeles was a sunny one-horse town with narrow tree-lined
streets and orange and date groves when film-makers first discovered it and turned it into the last boom town of this century.
Through distance it was safe from the 'Trust wars' then splitting
the Eastern sea-board film-makers into violent enemy camps, and
because of its climate it was ideal for filming the year round. The
town expanded to keep pace with an enterprise that mushroomed
overnight from a cut-throat squabble among fly-by-night operators into the fifth largest industry in the country, outstripped
only by railroads, textiles, iron and steel, and oil.

Although Hollywood itself is only one of many boroughs, and in
fact most of the major studios one thinks of as part of it are outside
its boundaries, to the millions who flocked there as to Mecca, or
who read about it, Hollywood was, and still is, a state of mind
encompassing them in one great conclave. Today Los Angeles is a
city of over ten million inhabitants, spread across the third largest
geographical area of any city in the world, rambling for more
than sixty miles from the Pacific Ocean across hills and canyons
until it fades out into the desert. Freeways cross-cut, join, congest,
intermingle, and separate as they branch into a hundred different
directions linking this complexity and looking, as your plane flies

in at night, like some crazy spider's strategy stretched across a lunar landscape.

I met her in August, 1973. She lived in Beverly Hills within sight of the Beverly Hills Hotel and next door to her old co-star, Glenn Ford, whose TV antennae probe the sky, marring her view of manicured lawns and the pruned trees which discreetly obscure residences from public view but not from each other. Police patrols guard the streets, keeping them safe from intruders. If you come on foot you run the risk of being arrested or at any rate questioned. It's not Fort Knox but neither is it the easiest place in the world to rob. But anyway, hardly anyone walks much in Beverly Hills except the occasional crank and English wives with their poodles while their husbands are busy at the studios.

To get to Rita's house you wound your way past Loretta Young's, while a little beyond lives Fred Astaire. Frank Sinatra's police-guarded mansion is a brief walk up the hill from which it overlooks the city. Many of the street names seem to have been inspired by the stars: Young, Pickford, Fairbanks, Hayworth. But it's more probable that movie stars took their new names from the streets than vice versa.

A letter stating the reasons for my trip to L.A. and expressing hopes for a meeting was rewarded by a favourable reply, setting a date and suggesting her home. My pleasure was tinged with surprise; I'd been warned that she was very shy, that her moods fluctuated dramatically and that being forced to recall could unleash great depths of bitterness. I comforted myself with the fact that Hollywood friends are notorious for looking at the worst side of things and that being laid low by a common cold could be turned into something as dramatic as attempted suicide. People who knew her said she wouldn't be interested in seeing anyone who came to pry into her life, that anyway she couldn't, or wouldn't, talk. Local journalists from the *Los Angeles Times* and other papers who had met her were smugly sympathetic, but dampened my enthusiasm. They said she looked good but said little that was new or revealing. Thus I had written more out of politeness than with hope.

The morning of our meeting, twenty years after *Affair in Trinidad* had begun it all for me, my feelings were mixed. I was unsure what I'd get; unsure, too, of what I expected and I practised what I would say to her and how to keep my 'cool'. Like most of the Love Goddesses of our era, her private life was public knowledge. Of course it's not her private self at all but only another side of the image. Would she go beyond it? Could she? Yet she knew what I had come for and was willing to see me to discuss her career. I promised myself no illusions. From her movies and publicity I knew of a score of conflicting Rita Hayworths, and though I knew most of them were fabricated, still I half hoped for a miracle in which I would arrive at her home and a perfectly mapped out scenario would take over.

Since Rita hasn't been under a contract since leaving Columbia and wasn't working on a film just then, there were no studio publicity people, agents or lawyers to act as barriers, watching that nothing compromising would pass her lips, or difficult questions mine. It was a sweltering hot California afternoon when I parked my car in the paved driveway that led off the little side road in front of her house. In reply to the bell a plumpish middle-aged maid with an ice-cream face and an orange squash voice opened the door and led me into the cool, high-beamed, single storey Spanish house, dominated by an airy living room. This opened out into the other rooms while the back wall was one large picture window with a door leading into the neatly kept garden. In the middle of the lawn, a deep but empty oval pool looked like a blue egg shell crater waiting for repair men to fix the crack across the bottom.

I unpacked my equipment, then sat back on a comfortable white divan. The furniture was functional and like the predominantly ochre colour scheme, relaxing. What decorations, works of art and paintings there were, obviously belonged to and complemented their owner. As I realised afterwards, it was the first house in her life Rita had bought and decorated by herself. There was nothing of the glorified dressing room about it. In contrast to many sumptuously designed and furnished Hollywood homes, whose style clashed with that of their owners or reflected the taste of an expensive interior decorator, the Hayworth house was spotless but inviting with a feeling of relaxation that made me want to take my shoes off and sit on the floor. Then Rita arrived with the drink her maid had gone to fetch me.

ʻIn low heels and a loose flowing kaftan of autumnal colours complementing her reddish hair and tanned skin, Rita looked (as movie stars inevitably do), smaller than on film. It's the illusion versus the reality. Her handshake was firm, her eyes were brown, friendly, her smile was *Gilda*. In her mid-'fifties Rita Hayworth was still the impressive kind of beautiful woman whose impact isn't

noticeable at first glance but, like an undercurrent, catches you
while you're still shaking hands and exchanging pleasantries.
Others who had worked with her had said that she was not as
glamorous in life as she appears on the screen, but one really
cannot be long with her and miss what the camera reveals, that
subtle combination of what you see, what you feel and what you
remember. When she speaks there's still that haunting sound in
her voice, and her words breathe like water just below the surface
of the ground and make what she says imply more than she might
mean to.

My feelings about her are understandably subjective, but
objectively (though she can giggle like a foolish schoolgirl after too
many highballs), when speaking after a sudden silence (and then
not saying what you'd expect), you feel you could write a book
about what she meant. It was part of a mystery she had on the
screen that belongs to Rita and which the studios could not have
given her. I'm reminded of *The Lady from Shanghai* when Elsa says
to O'Hara, 'I'm not what you think I am. I'm just trying to be
like this,' and he replies, 'Keep trying, you might make it.' This
duality when she was young, was undoubtedly part of what
attracted such diverse men as Cohn, Sheehan, George Cukor,
Charles Vidor and Howard Hawks to work with her, and Judson,
Welles, and Aly Khan to marry her. There's nothing of a cipher
about Hayworth when her eyes bore into you—especially after a
question or remark she resents. It's not always predictable that
what may have been meant as polite chit-chat won't be taken by
her as an intrusion into her private life. In that respect she takes
after her mother. A remark about some member of her family,
that may have been intended as a compliment, can boomerang
and result in her loose-limbed body freezing up, icicles forming
and something more lethal flying in your direction. Her moods
are mercurial; a smile can be guarded, but then she laughs and we
relax again.

No sooner had we settled down to talk in the adjoining den
than the phone rang. A top agent she had been trying to contact
was returning her call. Rita suggested I take the conversation
down, but I could only hear her side. She wanted work. Judging
from her reactions his response was less than lukewarm. Rita tried
to sound him out. She listened, sometimes knitting her brows
intensely, looking at me and pulling faces as if to say 'Get this,'
then suddenly breaking in with 'But I'm not as old as Davis or
Crawford. I want to work. Can you get me any work? You

already have a lot of old stars? Honey, I'm not an OLD star. I'm an actress.'

I wanted to leave the room but it seemed more tactful to stay silent and make notes about things to ask her afterwards. Nothing was resolved on the phone and after she hung up she spoke about a TV talk show she had just taped with Dick Cavett, and the English film she had begun but never finished due to a virus she had caught in London. Suddenly, referring to the earlier telephone conversation, Rita said, 'I don't want anything special. Just to do a job and be paid for it. But they put you into pigeon-holes. They see you as who you were and that's it.' But there was nothing sad in the way she spoke about it, nor did she seem weighed down with regrets or memories of times when agents would have promised the moon to get her name on their books. Her philosophical acceptance was summed up for me by her friend Antonia, who quoted an old Spanish proverb as the cornerstone of Rita's behaviour: 'Take what you want from life—and pay for it.' One has only to look at her life, private and public, to see that she has always paid: That the strength she sought in others; the decisions she relied on for from others, in the end, all had to come from her. It makes all the more remarkable how well and for how long she has held up. As with others of her era, horror movies and TV are about all that is available. What she feels about the situation, should one get close enough to ask, would be hinted at in a shrug and the downward twist of her expressive mouth.

What the conversation on the phone brought home, and I had already realised, was that questions that began with compliments were self-defeating. She has had a lifetime of them and they hold little more than false echoes for her. A job is something you're paid to do, and flattery won't make you do it any better. Tell her she was simply marvellous in something and she says 'Yeah, thanks dear' or 'That was my job, dear'. It bore out what another friend had confided: that a lifetime of being misunderstood or taken for granted by people, of being treated like a workhorse in the studio on the one hand, and the flattery and fawning that comes with success on the other, had turned a naturally hesitant and shy girl into a very wary woman. Perhaps relaxing in the company of old good friends like Hermes Pan, Fred Karger, or Antonia Morales, Rita unburdens more, or even shows anger and bitterness at events. But these are not sides she shows to strangers. Except for this one very personal almost accidental insight into her present state the former Margarita

Cansino showed me Rita Hayworth to the best of her ability.

I searched her face for Gilda, for Cover Girl, for Dona Sol, and found it when she moved, at times only a shoulder, saw it when her head suddenly arched back on her neck as she let forth a loud roll of laughter that scattered her little girl voice and caught her thick copper hair off its guard, sending it tumbling around her face in the familiar manner, and when she pulled at the corner of her mouth with her index finger and thumb, or got up to serve crackers and refill our glasses—then, time and again, the memories of the past brushed on the present. It was apparent that Rita doesn't like to feel she's being watched. She turns aside when you look too long, feigns to toy with her hair, her kaftan, or her drink. But her gaze remained penetrating, suspicious.

We began by looking through piles of faded yellow stills, taken in her early days at Fox when she was still Rita Cansino. She fell about laughing, bursting into bubbly shrieks, especially over a. session that showed her heavily oiled, wearing an Egyptian head-dress for some publicity stunt comparing her heavily re-touched profile to that of Nefertiti, while she was working on *Charlie Chan in Egypt*. It was typical of the hare-brained ideas publicity departments thought up to keep the company's name and product in the public's eye.

Rita: 'They used to do that kind of nonsense when they still had the studio system. Fox, Metro, Warners ... it was their idea of selling a personality. But who'd know that was me if you didn't already know? I wouldn't if my name weren't underneath.'

Rita fights back memories, but has forgotten little: the first steps she took as a dancer, the hours and years of hard work it took to create what the public accepted as Rita Hayworth.

'The way the studio sold me, you'd think I popped out of some package, ready made. My father's family were all dancers. I was trained as a dancer since I was four years old. Honey, they had me dancing as soon as they could get me on my feet. It was a family tradition but the reason I had to do it professionally was that we were broke. Very broke. NOTHING.' She gives a harsh laugh. 'My brothers became businessmen; they didn't have to rely on a precarious career like dancing or acting. Because it doesn't last long—it's very short-lived money-wise. Forgive me for saying money.

'I was eight when we moved to Los Angeles. My father had a studio on Vine Street and Sunset Boulevard. After my classes were over I had to take care of my two brothers because my family was working. So we used to go to the movies. We'd go to the Iris Theatre where they had all the silent movies, because it cost so little—ten cents for kids—and I used to take them and we'd sit there for hours. I liked Jeanne Eagels and Ruth Chatterton, and all of those people. I always wanted to stay longer but Vernon and Eddie got angry because they wanted to leave when they got tired of that stuff. I wasn't movie-struck but I liked the movies. I never thought at that time that I'd want to go into movies when I grew up, because I was so busy between school and dancing. It must have given me some thought in the back of my mind, like "that would be interesting" but I never thought of it seriously. We just went to the movies.'

You must have been an adorable kid.

Rita (shrieking with laughter): 'I don't think I was very adorable.'

Were you ever serious about becoming a professional dancer?

'No, never,' she says adamantly, her brow knits and the smile vanishes. 'I loved to dance but not making a profession out of it. I wanted to be an actress. I guess that's what I wanted to be because I didn't want to be a dancer for the rest of my life—though it came in very useful, when I did musicals with Fred Astaire and later on Gene Kelly. I didn't have a choice about what I wanted to be. I'd much rather have gone to school like everybody else. I never stopped. I got through with the dancing class; I was still dancing on the way to school, and then back at it again afterwards. Really ... wow! It took quite a lot of energy, but I guess I was born and raised to it. So!' She shrugs philosophically. 'When I was dancing with my father in Agua Caliente, I'd have a tutor between shows. I did four shows a day; at noon and at 2 p.m. After that I went back to school for three hours in Santa Monica. Then I'd drive back to the club, which was about three hours away and do the ten o'clock and half eleven shows. By the time that was over it was 12.30, we'd get home around 3 a.m. and then I'd have to get up and rehearse. That was the routine. I'd also be having to take lessons with my father between rehearsals in the morning and the next show. It was quite a heavy schedule.' She laughs to wipe away the moment and refills our glasses.

'Maybe I had a talent for dancing. But they didn't use me much as a dancer in those early films. They put me under one of those stock contracts. It wasn't very much money. I just thought I was learning a trade. A different trade from the one I knew. That's how I saw it at the time. I wasn't thinking of doing films in

terms of becoming a star. That wasn't the way I thought. I
thought, "I'll have to learn French, learn this, learn that. And I
must go there every day, and have teachers ... work ..." It didn't
happen over night. It took a long, long time. When I was doing
Blood and Sand, and before that *Only Angels Have Wings*, I was
prepared for them because I'd been working the whole time.
Then somebody wrote a critique in *Time* magazine, or somewhere, and they noticed you. So others noticed you. But I
didn't care much about it because I wasn't bothering with reading
them. There was no time to read about yourself, honey, they kept
you working the whole time.

'We played in gambling casinos to people who came down from
Los Angeles and San Diego to gamble. The places we danced in
were like nightclubs, with dinner being served and a floor show in
which my father and I did all sorts of Spanish dances, and then
they went off and gambled. I was always busy and when I wasn't
busy I was sitting in my dressing room. Growing up takes a lot of
time, a lot of care. Discipline from the age of five. People think
you just come on and that's all there is to it. It's all work.'

Were you upset when you read stories about being the product
of a studio?

Rita: 'I couldn't let it bother me. What do people care?
Because people really DON'T care. Just like this dope on the
telephone. They *really* don't care.

'I had to make up my mind what I was going to do. I thought
they—the studios—were going to help me at the time. I would
certainly work for a goal. I did that for myself. They didn't have
to pick me up and hit me over the head and say, "You're going to
do this." I did a lot of movies before I made it, bits and small
parts. I just kept on doing them because it was an experience
doing all these things. Whether it was "Yes" or "No", or
"Hello"—"Yes, Mr Charlie Chan". "No, Mr Charlie Chan"—or
whatever, I did it. Like being in the theatre where you start doing
all kind of bits, entrances and exits and that sort of stuff. I did all
those things. I rode on horseback, though I was terrified of them.
That was when I was doing westerns. They were something else
again. And I did them because that was work, that was my job.
So I don't start from the top.'

If your father hadn't needed you as his partner, and you had
not been seen by Sheehan, do you still think you might have
ended up in movies on your own?

Rita: 'Oh yes. Because of Spanish dancing, ballet training and all other kinds of dancing I was filled with the kind of music and I suppose the kind of feeling I had—I was full of expression. Movies, or some sort of acting would have been a natural, logical outlet for it. One thing just naturally leads to another.'

We spoke of different films she made, some co-stars, some directors. After a little prompting she brought out her own collection of photos of herself in films. She had no private ones, except portraits of her daughters and only a few desultory shots of herself in the film *The Happy Thieves* with Rex Harrison, and that was it. She had collected nothing nor was she overly interested in the mementos of her career though it amused her to look through some of the material I had brought with me. Whatever she did collect or treasure in her career it was apparently not something that needed to be bound in books or stashed away in cupboards. Only a few days earlier one of her fans had left outside her door an enormous collage made up of pictures from her films and had then disappeared without seeing her. She had been touched by the thought, but the collage was stashed in the garage. The things she valued most were very private and include the marble sculpture of the two hands from the time of her marriage to Aly; it goes where she goes and stands discreetly on a sideboard. She sometimes emphasised her words with her hand and my eye was caught by a plain gold band on her finger. Later I learned that though she had been presented with, and perhaps still does possess, quite a fine collection of jewellery, except for a plain gold bracelet Aly had given her, she wears almost none.

And so the afternoon slipped by. The less we spoke about her career, the more she opened up, white wine flowing freely, till at last, talking about theatre, listening to records, Rita was laughing, dancing across the room, and, every so often, humming a few bars from songs written for *Cover Girl*, and *Gilda*. By then I refrained from commenting or complimenting, but her voice is gentle, romantic and musical, like her speaking voice. As part of a then current wave of nostalgia an English pop group, The New Vaudeville Band, had recorded a larky thumpy fan letter called 'Dear Rita Hayworth'. Yasmin had found it in London and sent it to her mother, and we sat and played it while Rita laughed, and loved it and said, 'Wasn't it sweet,' and how she'd like to write and tell them but didn't know how to go about it. The interview was over but Rita Hayworth was on!

While we'd been talking it had been possible to forget that I was with her. Now, released from the constraint of remembering

the past, her face uncreased, the thought lines cleared, the eyes
and lips opened wide to laugh. When I took my leave she agreed
to see me again. I felt the barriers were down. I was wrong—for
though we spoke a great deal after that it was always on the
phone. I might tell her whom I was going to interview, sometimes
she'd comment about someone she'd worked with, but mostly it
was chit-chat. We never met again during that trip. A wariness
had returned. Maybe she'd spoken to advisors and was warned
off giving too much of herself away for free when her life story
could be worth a great deal of money to her. Yet she'd been
adamant when she told me she was not interested in a book about
herself, that she really didn't care, and that she would never write
a book about her life because it was *her* life *not* somebody else's and
nobody else's business. 'I've had enough of that, honey,' she had
concluded one of our talks. And one believes her. I hoped mine
would be a book she could be proud of. 'Honey, I just hope it
makes some money,' she had replied, not unkindly. Then she
apologised shyly for mentioning money.

Inevitably, the more I listened, the more I arrived at the same
conclusion as a lot of her friends and co-workers: Rita is an
intensely shy, self-deprecating and exceedingly private being. Had
she been a star in the 'thirties they'd have described her as
'mysterious'. There was no room for mystery in the 'forties. They
wanted extroverts—creatures of fun and spontaneity whom audiences could take as they found them. They demanded physical
not spiritual gods and goddesses and the studio propelled Rita
into that mould. But her real fascination rested in her silence. The
camera understood that, and so did some of the men behind it,
sometimes. Her silence puzzled some and brought others back.
What really went on behind that mask? Maybe, as Rouben
Mamoulian had said, Rita's mystery is like that of the Sphinx.
The secret may be that there is no secret. Or perhaps a clue lies
buried in the present she got from one husband, *The Lady from Shanghai*. Whatever the answer, the camera has been her true lover.

It was late in the afternoon and the hot August sun was shining
in her garden and through the glass, creating a blinding wall of
light with Rita in the centre as she waved goodbye from her
doorstep. Because of the trick played by the light she looked like a
figure carved in fire; the copper hair and the orange kaftan melted
into a fiery gold and her face was masked in shadows. But her
cheeks glistened because she was smiling and caught the reflection
of light on the top. If I'd willed it as a parting shot, it couldn't

have been improved on. Or maybe it only looked like a scene from a film because that's what the small Canadian boy wanted it to be. Maybe both.

Driving back down the canyon roads, feeling pleased to have gotten through to Rita and patting my little cassette recorder as if it could respond with a shared satisfaction, I thought about Rita now, and then as she was in *Gilda*. It's a curious feeling. Rita Hayworth had been someone I had known all my life but only just met. I remembered something she'd said speaking about her 'image':

'Yes, the image was very strong. It's like a.... [*but she didn't finish the sentence*] They forget the humanity of a person. They think of you as a thing. It's all so overblown. It's very difficult. I've been married. I've had two girls. But everything is so overblown.... [*and again the sentence loses itself in a tense, unhappy silence*] I was certainly a well trained dancer. I'm a good actress. I have depth. I have feeling. But *they don't* care. All they want is the image.'

Several years after we met, I was back home struggling to start writing this book and avoiding the inevitable by thinking of a title. For personal reasons I didn't want to use just her name, though anybody reading her name on a dust jacket would, even without a picture, know who was meant. There had been suggestions. Some I discarded because in the cold light on a clean sheet they seemed mercenary or cruel or too simple or not simple enough. So—*Cover Girl, Human Cargo, You Were Never Lovelier*, and similar titles were discarded. Others became chapter headings. Then I remembered the article that had resulted in the commission for this book called *The Time, The Place and The Girl*—the title of a popular 'forties song and film. I felt it summed up what I wanted this Rita Hayworth biography to be about. I was so enthusiastic about my choice that I put off starting to write for another day and, instead, made a transatlantic call to tell Rita. Her answering service was still asking me to spell my name and I was counting the pennies when Rita broke in with a happy 'Hi!' It was ten thirty a.m. in California, and she had just finished her daily exercises when she heard the 'phone and came from the garden to answer. We exchanged pleasantries and spoke about my discovery of her family crest, a copy of which I'd sent her; she sounded happy, very friendly and interested, and then I told her the reason for my call. What did she think of *Rita Hayworth: The Time, The Place and The Girl?* 'Oh, yeah. . . .' she said, 'Yes, that sounds all right John.' Through the fog that accompanies long-distance calls I thought I detected a hesitation. 'You sure you like it?' I prompted, then quickly told her why I did and she said, 'Yeah, that's fine, John, just ... how about ... if it's all right with you, changing it to The Woman? You know, *The Time, The Place and The Woman.*' In my head was the lilt of a lyric that was now the title of my book. 'Okay, that's fine with me, Rita. If you like that better that's fine.' 'It's just,' said Rita, with a half apologetic little laugh as she said it, 'I was never a girl.'

(United Artists)

INDEX

Action in the North Atlantic, 127
Adoree, Renee, 37
Affair in Trinidad, 107, 204, 219, 287, 291, 297; script problems, 273, 275–7; shooting of, 278–86
Affectionately Yours, 113–4
Aherne, Brian, 106
Air Force, 127
Alba, Duke of, 244
All About Eve, 314
All the King's Men, 306
Alwyn, Astrid, 59n
Anders, Glenn, 214
Anderson, Judith, 227, 292
Anderson, Maxwell, 227
Andree, Princess, 257
Andrews, Dana, 127
Angels Over Broadway, 106, 109–11
Arden, Eve, 155
Armida, 37
Arno, Max, 50
Arnold, Edward, 78
Around the World in 80 Days, 210
Arthur, Jean, 77, 88–91, 96, 97, 102, 155–6, 223
Asphalt Jungle, 14, 97
Assens, Rafael Cansino, 20
Astaire, Adele, 24
Astaire, Fred, 24, 37, 127; and Ginger Rogers, 50, 74, 120, 133, 137, 152; films with Rita, 170, 131–138, 142, 147–152
Astor, Mary, 202

Back Street, 42, 43
Bacall, Lauren, 174, 314
Back to Bataan, 127
Bader, Douglas, 222
Ball, Lucille, 15
Bandwagon, 147, 151, 207
Bankhead, Tallulah, 120
Banton, Travis, 123, 159
Bara, Theda, 71
Barefoot Contessa, The, 290
Bari, Lynn, 115

Barrie, Mona, 59n
Barthelmess, Richard, 97
Bataan, 127
Bauer, Harold, 34
Baxter, Warner, 61, 62
Beatles, the, 230
Behrman, S. N., 52
Belcher, Ernest, 74
Bellamy, Ralph, 114
Benchley, Robert, 86, 131
Bennett, Tony, 184
Bergman, Ingrid, 174, 190–1, 227–8, 256
Berkeley, Busby, 50
Berle, Milton, 15
Berlin, Irving, 85
Bessy, M., 119
Betty a Widow, 54n
Bettina, 261
Bettis, Valerie, 278
Biggers, Earl Derr, 62
Black Magic, 221
Black Orpheus, 218
Blair, Janet, 172, 178
Blondie films, 63
Blondie on a Budget, 104
Blood and Sand, 74, 111, 113–24, 144, 147, 159, 217
Bogart, Humphrey, 127, 174, 203, 289
Bond, Ward, 299
Booth, John W., 26
Borden, Olive, 68
Born Yesterday, 222, 227
Bourbon, Princess of, 261
Bow, Clara, 36, 88
Bowie, David, 230
Bowman, Lee, 157, 159, 172, 173, 188
Boyer, Charles, 140
Brando, Marlon, 289, 301, 310, 311
Brent, George, 63
Briskin, Irving, 91, 94
British Film Institute, 154
Buchwald, Art, 307
Buisine, Paul A., 263

Cagney, James, 37, 111, 113
Cahn, Sammy, 175–6, 181, 184
Cain, James M., 190, 202
Call of the Flesh, 37
Cameron, Kate, 197
Cansino, Angel, 21, 29, 41
Cansino, Antonio, Rita's grandfather, ('Padre') 19–20, 21, 74, 123, 244, 245
Cansino, Antonio, Rita's uncle, 21, 25 and n
Cansino, Carmellia, 20
Cansino, Eduardo, Rita's father, dances in Spain, 21–22; goes to New York, 22–4; marriage to Volga, 25–7; touring, 27–8, 31–4; move to Hollywood, 24, 35–6; attitude to Rita in school, 37–8, 40; and the Depression, 41–2; dances with Rita, 43–9; and Rita's film career, 50, 51, 53, 134, 224, 226; teaching, 74; and Edward Judson, 75, 79–80; war work, 152; death of Volga and his remarriage, 185–7; and Rita's marriage to Aly, 264–5
Cansino, Eduardo Jnr, 'Sonny', 27, 31, 39, 40, 152, 154, 170n, 187
Cansino, Elisa, 20, 21–3, 24, 27, 30, 31–2, 33–4, 35, 42
Cansino, Francisco, 21
Cansino, Gracia, 20
Cansino, Isaac, 19
Cansino, Joaquim, 21
Cansino, Jose, 31
Cansino, Margarita Carmen Dolores, *see* Hayworth, Rita
Cansino, Pat, 187, 265
Cansino, Susan, 185
Cansino, Vernon, 27, 30, 32, 37, 39, 40–1, 64, 77, 79, 187; and World War II, 152, 153–4, 168–70
Cansino, Volga, Rita's mother, 18, 43, 44; marriage to Eduardo Cansino, 25–7, 31, 33; encouragement of Rita, 38–9; temperament, 25, 27, 47, 153; attitude to Edward Judson, 75, 79, 139; death of, 185–8
Cansino family, history of, 18–20
Cantor, Eddie, 37, 292
Capra, Frank, 88, 96, 109, 147
Cardinale, Claudia, 291
Carmen, 119
Carradine, John, 117

Carson, Jack, 111
Casablanca, 192
Case, Anna, 34
Caspary, Vera, 171
Castelnuovo-Tedesco, Mario, 207
Castle, Irene, 23–4
Castle, Mary, 177n
Castle, Vernon, 23–4
Catroux, General and Mrs, 261
C.B.C. Film Sales Co., 86
Chandler, Raymond, 190, 194, 202
Chaplin, Charlie, 29, 35, 72
Charisse, Cyd, 120, 151
Charlie Chan in Egypt, 50, 62–3
Charlot Revue, 135, 236
Cinémonde, 263
Citizen Kane, 145, 211, 220
Cobb, Lee J., 304
Coburn, Bob, Snr, 166, 281
Cohn, Harry, 15, 17, 59, 137, 299; and Rita, 76–7, 78, 84, 102, 134, 136, 143, 144, 145–6, 147, 164, 175–6, 177, 194, 201–2, 308; background and character, 85–7; as head of Columbia, 86, 87–9, 95, 96, 106, 113, 115, 133, 170–71; attitude to his stars, 89–90, 107–9, 192, 194, 203–204, 221–2; and *Cover Girl,* 154, 155–6, 160, 163, 166; and *Tonight and Every Night,* 173, 175–6, 177, 179, 184; and *Down to Earth,* 205–6, 208–9; and *The Lady From Shanghai,* 210, 211, 212, 213, 219; attitude to Rita and Aly, 246, 247–8, 249, 258; and Rita's return to work in *Affair in Trinidad,* 272, 273, 274–8, 279–80, 281, 293–4; and Rita's marriage to Haymes, 302, 304–5, 306–7; and *Pal Joey,* 310, 312
Cohn, Jack, 85, 86
Colbert, Claudette, 88
Cole, Jack, 136, 159, 172–4, 175, 176, 177–80, 181–4, 194, 198–9, 200, 203–4, 205, 207, 208, 224, 278
Columbia Pictures, 15, 17, 18, 51, 63, 74, 76–7, 78, 109, 221, 312; and Rita's contract, 80, 82, 102–4, 204n; studio style, 87–8; and *You'll Never Get Rich,* 131–3; and *Cover Girl,* 159, 160, 166; *and see* Cohn, Harry
Convicted, 93
Cooper, Gary, 55, 59, 105, 127

Costello, Frank, 85
Cotten, Joseph, 145
Cover Girl, 135, 154, 155–68, 170, 171, 174, 201, 227, 297
Crawford, Joan, 59, 104, 164, 274, 196, 298
Criminals of the Air, 76, 91
Cromwell, John, 203
Crosby, Bing, 127, 138
Crother, Rachel, 104
Crowther, Bosley, 197
Cruising Down the River, 300
Cruz Diable, 49
Cugat, Xavier, 148, 152
Cukor, George, 95, 102, 104–5
Culver, Roland, 205
Curtis, Tony, 272–3

Daily Express, 258
Daily News, 197
Daily Variety, 93–4
Dancing Pirate, The, 74
Dante's Inferno, 49, 52–4, 61
Darnell, Linda, 68, 118, 121–3
Darvi, Bella, 71
Davies, Marion, 25
Davis, Bette, 59, 174, 192, 274
Day, Doris, 289
Day, Richard, 123
de Havilland, Olivia, 111, 113
de Mille, Cecil B., 248n, 293, 294
De Moraes, Vinicius, 218
de Sica, Vittorio, 227
Dean, James, 289
Del Rio, Dolores, 49, 65
Dead Reckoning, 202–3
Delta Rhythm Boys, 138
Depression, the, 41–2, 45, 59, 125, 141
Derigon, Paul, 259, 260, 261–3
Destination Tokyo, 127
Deutsch, Helen, 223–4
Dieterle, William, 292
Dietrich, Marlene, 59, 292, 294, 311, 312
Dietz, Howard, 167–8
Dominguin, Luis, 195
Donlevy, Brian, 68n, 127
Double Indemnity, 194, 202
Douglas, Kirk, 295
Down to Earth, 136, 201, 203–9, 218, 221–2, 223

Draper, Paul, 36n, 41
Dreiser, Theodore, 141
Dresser, Paul, 141–2
Dreyer, Carl, 159
Dru, Joanne, 300
Duclos, Jacques, 257
Duncan, Isadora, 110n
Dunne, Irene, 37
Duvivier, Julien, 140
Dwan, Allan, 57, 68–71

Easter Parade, 147
Eden, Anthony, 222
Edwards and Ruby, 85
Eisenhower, President, 288
Elliot, Sally, 141
Ellis, Anita, 135, 198, 200
Ellroy, Lee, 258, 259
Elman, Mischa, 34
Escape Me Never, 187
Esquire, 129
Evergreen, 157

Fairbanks, Douglas, Jnr, 109–10
fan clubs, 57–8
Farewell My Lovely, 202
Farouk, King, 234, 268
Fath, Jacques, 257, 260–1, 265
Fath, Mme, 261
Faye, Alice, 120, 127, 142
Ferrer, Jose, 297, 298–9
Fields, Gracie, 157
Fields, W. C., 140n
Fier, Jack, 211
Film Weekly, 222
Fire Down Below, 219, 290, 306–10
Fisher, Doris, 197, 199–200, 202, 205, 207–8, 213
Flynn, Errol, 127, 139, 217
Flynn, Nora Eddington, 300
Fonda, Henry, 140
42nd Street, 30, 72
Forbes, Hazel, 82
Ford, Glenn, 87, 104, 106, 175; film partnership with Rita, 107–9, 192–197, 201, 208, 223, 284–6
Ford, John, 88
Foster, Norman, 217–8
Fox Film Corporation, 36, 50–1, 62, 72, 89; *and see* Twentieth Century Fox
Foy, Eddie, & the Seven Little Foys, 32

Freed, Arthur, 147
From Here to Eternity, 271, 275, 290

Gable, Clark, 59, 88, 107, 165
Gabriel, son of Elisa Cansino, 42–3
Gallian, Ketti, 62
Game That Kills, The, 93
Gang's All Here, The, 127–8
Gangster's Moll, The, 54n
Garbo, Greta, 34, 59, 107, 120, 129, 281, 314
Gardner, Ava, 14, 290, 297, 306
Garfield, John, 127, 289
Garland, Judy, 135
Garmes, Lee, 109, 110
Gay Illiterate, The, 51
Gay Senorita, The, 147
Gelsey, Erwin, 160
Geray, Steven, 197
Gershwin, Ira, 161
Gilbert, 88, 107
Gilda, 54n, 76, 107, 159, 190–202, 203, 205, 207, 223, 239, 248, 269, 277, 279, 285, 310, 314
Giles, 258
Giles, Genevieve, 71
Girls Can Play, 93
Gish, Lilian, 36
Gleason, James, 205
Gloucester, Duchess of, 222
Gobel, George, 15
Goddard, Paulette, 106, 129
Golden Dawn, 37
Goldwyn, Sam, 166, 176
Gomez, Vincent, 123
Grable, Betty, 14, 37, 56, 120, 125, 127, 129, 130, 135, 142, 297
Grand Hotel, 314
Grand National Studios, 79
Granet, Bert, 295–6
Granger, Stewart, 293
Grant, Cary, 77, 96, 97, 99–100, 101, 127
Greco, Juliette, 71
Greer, Howard, 81
Greer, Jo Ann, 136
Gribouille, 106
Griffith, D. W., 35
Gunn, James, 277, 278–9
Gussow, Mel, 72

Hall, Alexander, 203, 205
Hall, Jon, 63
Hammett, Dashiel, 190, 202
Haney, Carol, 173, 207
Haran, Miss, 248, 250
Hard Way, The, 274
Harlow, Jean, 76, 97, 107, 230
Harriet Craig, 274
Hart, L., 310
Hartman, Don, 207–8
Hawks, Howard, 95, 96, 97, 99–101, 102, 111, 121
Haworth, Frances, 16, 169–70, 221
Haworth, Joe, 26
Haworth, Jean, 16, 26–7, 33–4, 169–170, 247
Haworth, Vinton, 16, 28, 93
Haworth, Volga, 18; *and see*, Cansino, Volga
Haymes, Dick, 290, 291, 296; marriage to Rita, 300–5, 306–7
Hays Office, 194, 197, 202, 225
Hayward, Susan, 289
Hayworth, Rita, returns to U.S. after breakdown of marriage to Aly, 13–8; relationship with her mother, 18, 38–9, 183–8; 'intensity' of, 30–31; childhood, 27–33; at her father's dancing school, 37–40; first professional dancing, 42–3; as her father's partner, 43–9; earliest film work, 49–50; signed by Sheehan, 51–2; in *Dante's Inferno*, 52–4; and fan clubs, 57, 58; grooming by Fox, 59–64; first lead, 64–7; and Zanuck's take-over at Fox, 68, 71, 73–4; Allan Dwan and *Human Cargo*, 68–71; goes free-lance and promotion by Judson, 74–5; her hair, 75–7, 211, 212–3; marriage to Judson, 78–82, 120, 121, 138–9, 142–4; as 'Love Goddess', 76, 121, 129–30, 209, 210; put under contract to Columbia, 80, 82; and Harry Cohn, 84, 89–90, 175–6, 177; changes name, 91–93; Columbia 'B' films, 102–4; and *Only Angels Have Wings*, 95–102; and Columbia publicity, 102–4; and *The Lady in Question*, 106–9; Cuckor on, 104–5; and *Angels Over Broadway*, 109–11; and *The Strawberry Blonde*, 111–3; as Dona Sol in *Blood and Sand*, 114, 118–24; and

World War II, 127, 129–30, 139; musicals with Astaire, 131–8; voice dubbing, 147–52, 135–136; *Tales of Manhattan*, 138, 139–41; *My Gal Sal* and Victor Mature, 138, 141–2, 144–5; marriage to Welles, 145–7, 152, 155, 162–3, 167, 168, 170, 177, 192, 194, 201, 209, 210, 220–1, 226; in *Cover Girl*, 154, 155–167; and *Pal Joey*, 170–1, 289, 290, 310–2; making *Tonight and Every Night*, 172–85; and *Gilda*, 190, 192–202; and *Down to Earth*, 201, 203–9,221–2; and *The Lady From Shanghai*, 203, 209, 210–20; and *The Loves of Carmen*, 223–8; falls in love with Aly, 229, 230, 231, 232–55; marriage to Aly, 256–65; breakdown of marriage with Aly, 266–71, 272, 294–5; returns to work and *Affair in Trinidad*, 271, 272–3, 277–86; and *Salome*, 288, 289, 291–4; and eclipse of old Hollywood stars, 288–291; and *Miss Sadie Thompson*, 296–9; marriage to Dick Haymes, 300–5; and *Fire Down Below*, 306–10; life in recent years, 313–5; interview with author, 319–28

Hearst, William Randolph, 220
Heart of A City, 172
Heart of Paris, The, 106
Hecht, Ben, 106, 109, 110, 111, 140
Heiress, The, 227
Held, Anna, 18
Hell's Angels, 97
Hepburn, Katharine, 95, 120
Here Come The Waves, 127
Here Comes Mr Jordan, 205
High Button Shoes, 227
Hill, Jim, 300, 307, 313
Hiller, Wendy, 227
Hirschhorn, Clive, 157
Hit The Saddle, 78
Hitchcock, Alfred, 190
Hitler, Adolf, 125, 127
Holden, William, 107, 108, 109, 223
Holiday, 95
Holiday Inn, 138
Hollywood, T.V. challenge to, 15; growth of the movies in, 35–6; and the Depression, 41–2; and studio system, 55–9; and World War II, 127–30, 139;

Cold War mood in, 190, 228; and morality, 227–8; *and see* Hays Office; in the 'fifties, 288–9
Hollywood Reporter, 53, 252
Homicide Bureau, 94
Hopper, Hedda, 177, 247, 299
Hornblow, Arthur, Jnr, 106
Horton, Edward Everett, 205
Howe, James Wong, 111
Hudson, Rock, 55
Human Cargo, 50, 67, 68–71
Hunchback of Notre Dame, The, 292
Hunt, Helen, 76–7, 99, 212–3, 278
Hunt, Howard, 139
Hutton, Betty, 129

I Wanted Wings, 106
Ibanez, Vincente Blasco, 115
In Caliente, 49n
In Old Arizona, 61
It Happened One Night, 88
It's All True, 218

Jackson, Helen Hunt, 73
Jaggers, The, 230
Jazz Singer, The, 35, 72
Jergens, Adele, 178n, 205
Johnson Office, The, 166
Jolson, Al, 35, 205, 209
Jolson Sings Again, 209
Jolson Story, The, 205, 208
Joplin, Janis, 230
Joseph and His Brethren, 290, 302, 304–5
Judson, Edward C., 74; promotes Rita, 75–8, 91; marriage to Rita, 79–82, 84, 134, 138–9, 142–4

Kalloch, Robert, 94
Kanin, Garson, 222
Karger, Fred, 77–8, 135–6, 159, 163–4, 167, 170, 173, 177, 179, 184, 200, 207
Keene, Tom, 78
Keep Your Powder Dry, 127
Keith, Rosalind, 93
Kelly, Gene, 155–9, 160–1, 163, 166, 167, 170–1, 173, 184, 310
Kelly, Grace, 58, 289
Kern, Jerome, 147, 148, 151, 152, 155, 157, 159, 161–2, 208
Kerr, Deborah, 271
Keyes, Evelyn, 106

Khan, Aga, 234, 250–1, 255, 256, 257, 258, 261, 263, 264

Khan, Aly Solomen, 229, 230, 231, 234, 235, 301; break up of marriage to Rita, 13, 16, 17, 266–71, 272, 279, 291, 294–5, 302, 303; falls in love with Rita, 124, 237–55; marriage to Rita, 124, 237–55

Khan, the Begum (Yvette), 255, 256, 257, 261

Khan, Joan (wife of Aly), 241, 252

Khan, Prince Sadri, 261

Khan, Princess Yasim, 13, 16, 30, 265, 270, 272, 294, 295, 300, 303, 305, 313

Kid From Spain, 37

King, Henry, 73

King, Muriel, 159

King Cohn, 211

Kleiner, Harry, 294

Knight, Patricia, 177n

Koch, Epstein, 191–2

Koch, Howard, 191–2

Kruger, Otto, 156

Ladd, Alan, 129

Lady In Question, The, 106–9, 192, 193, 201

Lady From Shanghai, The, 170, 194

Laemmle, Carl, Jnr, 50

Laemmle, Carl, Snr, 85

Lake, Veronica, 55, 56, 76, 106, 129

Lamarr, Hedy, 106, 125

Lamour, Dorothy, 56, 76, 115, 129

Landis, Carole, 115, 121, 142

Landry, Bob, 129

Lane, Evelyn, 221, 227

Lanfield, Sidney, 138

Lassie, 190

Lasky, Jesse, Jnr, 292, 293–4

Lastvogel, Abe, 280

Laughton, Charles, 140, 292

Laura, 171

Lawton, Charles, Jnr, 212

Lecuona, Ernesto, 53

Lee, Lester, 285, 297

Leigh, Fred, 157

Leighter, Jackson, 268, 269, 270

Leighter, Leigh, 227, 268, 269, 270

Lemmon, Jack, 307, 309, 310

Leon, Gary, 53

Levene, Nat, 78

Life, 129, 136, 145–7, 210, 230

Life That Late He Led, The, 137

Lisi, Virna, 54n

Little Caesar, 72

Lombard, Carole, 68, 102

Lone Star, 275

Lone Wolf Spy Hunt, The, 94

Loren, Sophia, 54 and n

Lorna Hansen, 218, 223, 228

Los Angeles Examiner, 211

Los Angeles Times, 142

Louis, Jean, 159, 172, 174–5, 198, 200, 202, 205, 223, 226, 278, 280, 284, 294

Loves of Carmen, The, 170, 201–2, 223–7, 228, 247, 252, 260

Lupino, Ida, 94, 274

Lynn, Bambi, 173

McDaniels, Hattie, 114

McEnery, Peter, 315

McQueen, Butterfly, 114

Macready, George, 195, 196, 197, 205

Magnani, Anna, 54

Magnificent Ambersons, The, 210

Maltese Falcon, The, 202

Mamoulian, Rouben, 115–8, 120, 121, 123, 147

Mansfield, Jayne, 289

Margo, 37

Martin, Tony, 104, 139

Martinelli, Giovanni, 34

Mastroianni, Marcello, 54

Maté, Rudy, 51, 159, 172, 181, 185, 201, 205, 212, 298

Matthews, Jessie, 180

Mature, Victor, 129, 141, 142, 144–5, 152, 218, 295–6, 203

Maugham, Somerset, 288, 298, 299

Maxwell, Elsa, 234, 235–7, 238, 241, 258

Mayer, Louis B., 59, 91, 105–6, 170–1, 175, 176, 302

Mears, Martha, 161

Medea, 227

Meet Me In St. Louis, 154

Meet Nero Wolfe, 78

Melville, Herman, 220

Menjou, Adolphe, 148, 149, 151–2

Mercer, Johnny, 148, 151

Merimee, Prosper, 119, 223, 225, 226

Merrill, Gary, 313, 314

Mert & Marge, 93

Mesquiteers, the Three, 78
Message to Garcia, 68n
Metro-Goldwyn-Mayer, 14, 36, 37, 102, 104, 135, 147, 156, 164, 173, 184
Milford Haven, Marquess of, 236
Milland, Ray, 63
Miller, Arthur, 145
Minnelli, Vincente, 147, 207
Miss Sadie Thompson, 202, 204, 219, 288, 220, 296–9
Mr. Skeffington, 274
Mitchell, Thomas, 97, 111, 140
Mitchum, Robert, 307, 308, 309, 310
Mojeska, Madame, 26
Moby Dick, 220
Molnar, Ferenc, 140
Monroe, Marilyn, 14, 71, 97, 145, 179, 182, 294, 203, 230–1, 289, 291, 301, 305
Montand, Yves, 263
Montez, Maria, 114, 121
Moore, Grace, 131
Morales, Antonia, 39, 226–7, 312
More To Be Pitied Than Scorned, 86
Moreau, Jeanne, 54
Morgan, Dennis, 113–4
Morgan, Michele, 106
Morrison, Patricia, 56n
Murray, Arthur, 37
Music In My Heart, 104
Mussolini, Benito, 86–7
Mussolini Speaks, 87
My Brother Paul, 141
My Gal Sal, 120, 138, 141–2, 147, 157

Naldi, Nita, 115
New York Daily News, 142
New York Herald Tribune, 13
New York Herald, 71
New York Times, 13, 142, 197
Newman, Alfred, 123
Niarchos, Stavros, 139, 234
Nijinsky, 34
Niven, David, 139, 221, 223
Noah's Ark, 57
Nora Prentiss, 274
North-West Mounted Police, The, 106
Notorious, 190, 277
Novak, Kim, 91, 177, 204, 289, 291, 305, 311, 312
Novarro, Ramon, 37

Oberon, Merle, 113, 114
O'Brien, George, 93
Odets, Clifford, 302, 304 and n
O'Hara, John, 170
Oklahoma, 147, 161, 173
Olivier, Laurence, 305
On The Waterfront, 311
Onassis, Aristotle, 234
Onassis, Jacqueline, 230
One Million Years B.C., 144
Only Angels Have Wings, 77, 91, 95–102
Open City, 227
Operation Burma, 127
Orfeu da Conceicao, 218
Orleans and Bragance, Prince of, 261, 263
Othello, 220

Paddy O'Day, 64–5, 67
Padovani, Lea, 209
Paid To Dance, 93
Pal Joey, 170–1, 202, 289, 290, 297, 310–2, 313
Palmer, Ernest, 123
Pan, Hermes, 120, 121–3, 134, 142
Pandora and the Flying Dutchman, 14
Paramount, 160
Parks, Larry, 205, 206, 208–9
Parrish, Robert, 305, 306–8, 309
Parsonnet, Marion, 194
Parsons, Louella, 51, 145, 220–1, 258, 261, 264, 277, 280
Passion of Jeanne D'Arc, 159
Peg O'My Heart, 64
People, The, 251
Perry, Joan, 78n
Persia, Shah of, 234, 240
Photoplay, 95, 101–2, 144, 300
Pickford, Mary, 35, 247
Platt, Marc, 172, 173, 184, 207, 208
Poggi, Grace, 37, 48
Porter, Cole, 131, 137, 210, 234
Portrait of Jennie, 292
Postman Always Rings Twice, The, 202
Power, Tyrone, 58, 118, 121, 123
Power of the Press, The, 109
Presley, Elvis, 289
Pride of the Marines, 127
Prince and the Showgirl, The, 305

Quigley, Charles, 93

Racine, 226
Raimu, 106
Rain, 298
Rains, Claude, 205
Ramona, 50, 65, 73, 74
Ray, Aldo, 298
Reisz, Karel, 154–5
Renegade Ranger, The, 93
Rennahan, Ray, 123
Reynolds, Debbie, 189
Rich, Irene, 106
Rin Tin Tin, 72
Ritter, Tex, 79
R.K.O., 37, 93, 207
Roberta, 147
Roberts, Allan, 197, 199, 202, 205, 207–208
Robeson, Paul, 140
Robinson, Edward, G., 140
Rodgers, Richard, 161, 310
Rogers, Ginger, 27 and n, 93, 125, 140; and partnership with Astaire, 50, 74, 120, 133, 137, 152, 170
Rogers, Will, 41
Roland, Gilbert, 73
Romberg, Sigmund, 162
Romero, Cesar, 63
Roosevelt, Franklin D., 190
Rosenberg, Frank, 139
Rossellini, Roberto, 227
Russell, Bob, 285
Russell, Jane, 129
Russet, Val, 142
Ruth, Babe, 108–9

Salome, 288, 291–4, 296
Samson and Delilah, 248n
Samuels, Lesser, 170, 172
Sanders, George, 140
Sanford, Erskin, 211
Sargeant, Winthrop, 209–10
Sargent, John Singer, 198
Saul, Oscar, 280
Savage, Robert, 295
Saville, Victor, 157, 170, 172–3, 177, 178, 179, 180, 181–2, 184–5
Schafer, A. L. 'Whitey', 104
Schenck, Joseph M., 48, 50, 72
Schiaffino, Rosanna, 291

Schilling, Gus, 211
Schwartz, Arthur, 155–6, 160–2, 163, 167, 168–9
Scott, Lizabeth, 203
Scott, Randolph, 223
Scudda Hoo, Scudda Hay, 228
Segal, Vivien, 170
Seiter, William, 147
Sennett, Mack, 72
Separate Tables, 213
Sergeant York, 127
Shadow, The, 93
Shannon, Harry, 211
Shaw, Irwin, 306, 307, 308
Shearer, Norma, 129, 164
Sheehan, Winfield, 50–1, 53, 59, 63, 64, 68, 71, 72–3, 74
Sherman, Vincent, 273–80, 281, 285–6
Sheridan, Ann, 55, 102–4, 113, 274
Silk Stockings, 147
Silvers, Phil, 155, 156, 159, 227
Simon, Simone, 71
Sinatra, Frank, 14, 171, 310–1, 312
Sky's the Limit, The, 127
Sloane, Everett, 211, 234
Smith, Lou, 89, 102–4
So Proudly We Hail, 127
Sommer, Elke, 291
Song of Flame, 37
South Pacific, 178
Spanish Civil War, 74
Special Inspector, 93
Stanwyck, Barbara, 68 and n, 88, 202, 221
Star Is Born, A, 55
Starr, Kay, 206
State Fair, 300
Stolen Life, 201
Stoloff, Maurice, 161
Stoneburn, Catherine, 25n
Storm, Leslie, 172
Story on Page One, The, 304n
Stout, Rex, 78
Strawberry Blonde, The, 104, 111–3, 142, 157
Stromberg, Hunt, 50
Stuyvesant-Fish, Mrs, 22
Styne, Jule, 181, 184
Sunday Pictorial, 252
Susan and God, 104–5
Swanson, Gloria, 36, 296, 298

Tales of Manhattan, 138, 139–41, 144
Talley, Marion, 34
Taplinger, Robert, 154
Taps, Jonie, 208, 296
Taylor, Elizabeth, 230, 289, 291
Taylor, Laurette, 64
Taylor, Robert, 127
Technicolor, 73, 74, 106, 128, 155, 202, 223; and *Blood and Sand*, 111, 115–8
Temple, Shirley, 59
Terry, Don, 93
Thalberg, Irving, 72
They Came To Cordura, 312
This Is The Army, 127
Thomas, Bob, 85, 87, 211
Thompson, Kay, 135
Tierney, Gene, 71, 114, 171, 295, 301, 302
Time, 136, 204, 230, 259
Todd, Mike, 210
Tomlin, Pinky, 64, 65–7
Tonight and Every Night, 128, 172–85, 190, 195
Touch of Evil, 220
Tracy, Spencer, 52, 53
Trevor, Claire, 52, 57, 68n, 202
Trouble in Texas, 79
Truman, Harry S., 190
Turner, Lana, 14, 55, 78, 129, 202, 297, 301
Twentieth Century, 72; *and see* Twentieth Century Fox
Twentieth Century Fox, 14, 67, 102, 135, 159; and Darryl Zanuck, 68, 71–4, 171; and *Blood and Sand*, 111, 114, 115, 117–8, 123; and *My Gal Sal*, 138

Umberto, Ex-King of Italy, 234
Un Carnet de Bal, 140
Under the Pampas Moon, 50, 61–2
Under a Texas Moon, 37
Unfaithful, The, 274
United Artists, 72
Universal International, 42, 85–6
Up In Central Park, 300
Utrillo, Maurice, 258–9

Valdespino, Dorothy, 35, 37–9, 41, 43, 44–7, 48, 139, 265
Valentino, Rudolph, 36, 115, 119

Van Upp, Virginia, 159–60, 167, 191–192, 194, 199, 211, 224, 268, 272, 275–7, 278, 279
Van Wyck, Carolyn, 101–2
Variety, 71
Vaudeville News, 32
Verdon, Gwen, 173
Vidor, Charles, 106, 157, 159, 164; and *Gilda*, 192, 193, 194, 199, 200–1; and *Loves of Carmen*, 223, 225, 226
Visconti, Luchino, 227
Vogler, Gertrude, 102

Wake Island, 127
Wakeling, Gwen, 142, 157, 159
Walsh, Raoul, 111, 113, 121
Walters, Charles, 147
Warner, Jack, 59, 72, 113, 156, 176
Warner Brothers, 34–5, 36, 37, 50, 59, 72, 102, 111, 154, 156, 191–2, 273–4
Washington, Ned, 297
Waterbury, Ruth, 81n, 144, 145
Wayne, John, 127
Welch, Raquel, 291
Welles, Orson, 120, 129, 258, 266; marriage to Rita, 145–7, 152, 155, 162–3, 167, 168, 170, 177, 185, 192, 194, 201, 209, 210, 220–1, 225, 291; and *The Lady From Shanghai*, 203, 209, 210–21
Welles, Rebecca, 13, 16, 185, 210, 221, 247, 249–50, 252, 253, 264, 270, 294, 300, 303, 305, 313
West, Mae, 311–2
Westmore, Bud, 111
Who Killed Gail Preston?, 93
Whole Town's Talking, The, 88–9
William, Warren, 94
William Morris Agency, 204, 279, 280
Williams, Emrys, 238–9, 240–1, 243, 244–5, 251–2, 253–5, 263
Wilson, Richard, 211
Winchel, Walter, 168
Windsor, Duke and Duchess of, 234
Winters, Shelley, 173
Withers, Jane, 64
Wood, Helen, 59n
World War I, 24
World War II, 125–30, 185, 190

Wrath of God, The, 307n
Wright, Joseph C., 123
Wurtzel, Sol, 50, 54, 73
Wyman, Jane, 289
Wynn, Nan, 142, 199–200

Yank in the R.A.F., A, 127
You'll Never Get Rich, 131–8

You Were Never Lovelier, 147–52
Young, Loretta, 71, 72, 73

Zanuck, Darryl F., 68, 71–4, 75, 115,
    118, 171, 203
Ziegfeld, Flo, 18, 26
Ziegfeld Follies, 18, 25, 26
Zimbalist, Efrem, 34